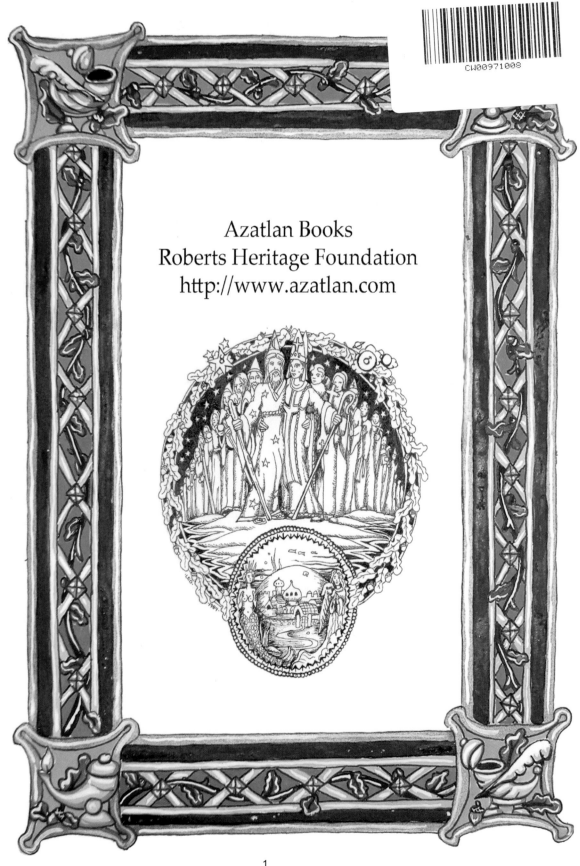

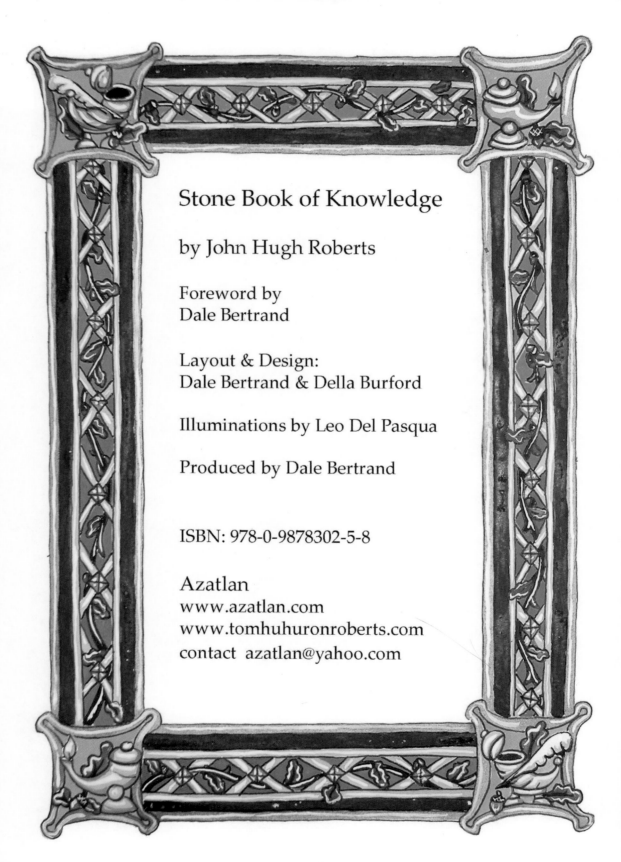

Stone Book of Knowledge

by John Hugh Roberts

Foreword by
Dale Bertrand

Layout & Design:
Dale Bertrand & Della Burford

Illuminations by Leo Del Pasqua

Produced by Dale Bertrand

ISBN: 978-0-9878302-5-8

Azatlan
www.azatlan.com
www.tomhuhuronroberts.com
contact azatlan@yahoo.com

John Hugh Roberts was one of Vancouver's early settlers. In 1882, after leaving his life in Toronto, he moved his family across Canada through Winnipeg where they spent some time helping establish the Welsh community. They then travelled down to San Francisco and arrived by ship in Vancouver in 1884.He purchased land at 10th and Quebec as well as 640 acres near Lillooet. He knew the railway was going through there and he proceeded to clear the land around Quebec Street building the family's first home there. His wife Anne, daughters Sarah and Mississippi and son Tomhu established themselves in the then named Mount Pleasant area.

Mississippi subsequently gave birth to Charles Steele who was the first boy recorded to be born in Vancouver; she also had two daughters, Winnie and Flossie. John Hugh's son, Tomhu, became a noted landscape and portrait painter and began art classes in the later part of the 1880's in Vancouver while his sisters remained home with their mother establish-ing a fine home life of the time.

John Hugh continued to speculate on land and was one of the quiet land developers of the time, never really stepping into the limelight but keeping a "behind the scenes" attitude. Researching his personal diaries from the 1846-47, 1855-1879, 1887-1889, and 1889-1912 gives an impression of a man who was well educated, interested in world affairs and who kept accurate records of his land investments. In his early years he made monies from tailoring, but always maintained a behind the scenes sort of fellow. This could well have been due to his other persona, 'The Last Recorder of the Druids.'

In his early life, John Hugh had three women educate him. He referred to them as 'The Three Mermaids'; one was from Cornwall, Mary Temanmaur; another from Bretagne, Mary

De St John, and his maternal grandmother, Mary Evan Hughes from Llaniestyn, North Wales. These women taught him from the earliest age ancient writings and languages, Phoenician, Ancient Hebrew, Modern Hebrew, ancient Greek and Modern Greek, and the mystical magical writings of the Runes, and Ogama. He was taken to stone circles and to beaches of both Cornwall and Wales in his youth and was given chief parts to play in these ancient ceremonies.

In 1838 he was taken to a cave in Cornwall where he was shown thousands of slate tablets, some in Greek letters, Cuneiform Hieroglyphics and others with pictures, emblems and scrolls. Over a period of some months, he held and examined the writings and etchings in ancient languages on these 'stone books' and became very familiar with them. Later years in his life he transcribed these writings as he recalled them and he referred to them as a 7400-year history of knowledge.

He also mentioned in the writings that he received a charm - and "enclosed in the charm was a key to the hieroglyphics. This book is the culmination of many years of the writing and recording what he called "The Stone Book of Knowledge" ..... which he claims was written by learned men and the interpretation of the Ancient Lords of Teman (Hereditary Druids) these wonderful records which 'contain arts, science, and secrets of the earth and aspects of the Heavens with the veils of inspirations and Revelation". John Hugh claims that he was a hereditary druid appointed to translate the writing by what he called his "guardians". We have to guess who the guardians were but it seems the best guess is the three people who taught him the ancient ceremonies in the first place; his grandmother and her two friends. All of their names had something to do with the word sea and were known as the "three mermaids." The writings culminated in the form of 130 handwritten pages and a 256 page hand-written book he called 'The Stone Book of Knowledge'.

These were left to his son Tomhu when he died in 1917. Tomhu, who had them until his death in 1938, left them to his nephew Charles Steele the son of Mississippi. Mr. Steele passed on in 1978 and my mother received these from his estate by purchasing and being gifted them as most of his possessions were being given away to charity. My mother had previously lived in one of Mr. Steele's houses when she moved to Vancouver in 1964 and kept up a friendship with him until his death.

The papers were given to me in Feb 1979 on a visit from California. I was inspired to study the Druids because of a mystical experience in Los Angeles in 1979 when I saw an ancient being channelled thru a healer. I was told "I would be involved in a path of healing." My intuitive reaction right after this happened and after meeting Dr. David Davies was "I have to study the Druids". A few days later these papers where given to me by my mother on a visit from California. She surprised me and pulled out from under the couch a stack of writings on parchment paper. Examination of the papers revealed that the one on the top was "Chief Festival of the Druids" and the next one The Galecerth of Halloween – which happens to be my birthday.

Over the next 7 years Della, my wife and I tried to understand these writings, but discovered many of the papers were missing and the gaps were just too large to fully understand the writings. In 1986 our friends Tom and Sal Williams returned from a vacation on Salt spring Island B.C. and handed me a book which our mutual friend Doug Atkins had found in the Saltspring Recycling Depot. To my great surprise and shock I immediately realized it was written by John Hugh Roberts. This book of 254 hand written pages was the key to understanding his writings.   Doug found it weeks before and immediately recognized the handwriting as Roberts. This all happened seven years after I received the manuscripts from my mother. Roberts called it the "Stone Book of Knowledge" and he clearly says that when the time is right – 60 years after 1893 when a covenant ended - these records were to be made public.

In the early 80's we commissioned the artist Leo del Pasqua to represent 4 of the manuscripts resulting in 130 illuminations. These illuminations have now been published in 4 books – "The Three Mermaids", "Gaelcerth of Halloween", "Chief Festival of the Druids" and "Nennius".

There are many examples of very strange synchronistic events that occurred over the last 35 years of intuitive research and travels and these have now been put into a book called "Druidical Quest published in 2008
By the writing near the end of his book one can see that he did intend that these be published but for reasons unknown were never put to print. So after all these years we are publishing them to share with those meant to see them.

Here is a copy of the two pages:
"To the Students and those who wish to Learn. What is written on these ancient stones of knowledge very naturally you would like to be told how I became acquainted with them, more particularly since our teachers tell us the Druids left no record of any kind, as far as they know , this may be quite true, but it is not in good taste, to proclaim this No-Knowledge of theirs as a matter of fact. I am one of the witnesses, ,
'That came and saw and conquered, the one at the beginning and the other at the end and the one that came between was also of the same order – called the Hereditary Druids (Lords of Teman). 'That came and saw and conquered,the one at the beginning and the other at the end and the one that

came between was also of the same order – called the Hereditary Druids (Lords of Teman). We inherit a certain right or privilege under the covenant, provided we conform to certain ordinances. Among these rights, are the privileges of reading these wonderful records of nearly 73 hundred years!

As a part of these stones is written in what is commonly called the Greek Alphabet, this alphabet was the first I learned, and as soon as I was able to read, my guardian took me to see these "wise stones", there were many written in these Greek letters, and others in cuneiform hieroglyphics, and others with pictures, and emblems and scrolls---So that I became familiar with them by sight, but was ignorant of their contents, and when by accident I discovered a similar stone in another part of the country, and not wishing to take the stone away at the time, I made a facsimile of the characters and noted the dimensions of the several parts of the stone, this was in the year 1842 AD, six years after this in 1848, I discovered another stone in the ruins of an old church undermined, by the sea, of which I also took a copy, which I have since discovered to be the "Oghama", once common enough in the British Isles.

Again in the year 1887, I made a third discovery in the heart of very large fir tree, which was at least 7 r 8 hundred years old, this time the characters were in a sheet of gum at the 180th ring! It so happened that in the year 1846 I joined two gentlemen for the purpose of exploring in North America, more particularly in Mexico. Before starting my guardian presented me with a small charm under a promise not to look into it, while the giver lived, unless under certain circumstances and if I did see the, I must destroy the original, as soon as I translated the secret.

This I readily promised from regard to the giver rather than any benefit that I expected from it. It turned out however that there was enclosed in the charm, 'a Key' to these hiero-glyphics!!! And for the last nine years, I devoted all my time to the study and translation of these ancient Secret Inspiration, and Revelations.****

He then writes out on the next two pages the lessons:

A table of the Dominical Day and Leap years
Table of the Epacts of centuries
Table the Eclipses of Sun and Moon
The Perpetual Horoscope
Rules of Inspiration and Revelations
The Tetragrammaton
The Migrating Tribe
The Figurative man
The Secret Alphabet
The Seals of the Covenant of the Der-Krisdian
Plus Auxiliary lessons

The opening is a speech by the Oracle of Azatlan which goes as such:

'Azatlan City first Cradle of the Gods,
Home of the Angels, before the great flood,
Hope of the Righteous, Faith of the Her-Der,
Resting at last in,
resting at last in,
resting at last in (the) City of Ner."

In the book he tells of a fascinating history of the travels of the Nergals – Toltecs- the Druidian. He says in the first flood the Druidians escaped in a ship and boats under the Her-Der, and sheltered in Asia and entered into a covenant with six tribes. "About 1000 years before A.S. the Ancient Covenant of the Nergal and Druids was renewed. He explains how they settled in the British Isles and built many remark-

remarkable temples and he says some are still in existence. He also states that "In 5401 at this time the Druids were the most learned men in Europe John Hugh Roberts has a map in the "Book of Knowledge" that is of the land of Teman and said it was submerged in 56 B.C. He speaks of different ancient tones called Manhir and many Alphabets including Numnrt, Nergal, Hieroglyphics, Scroll writing, Picture Writing, Oghama, Runes and the Original Alphabet. He drew a "Giant of the Stones' holding the sun, moon and star which was giving light to the world and being a guide to mankind. In lessons called the Auxiliary Lesson he has the "Talisferies" or "Druid Money" which is a protective mandala – one which represents the sun and the other which represents the moon. Both filled with special hieroglyphics to tell the time of Spring Equinox which was one of the four great Feasts of the Druids. This fascinating record of symbolic drawings and tirelessly recordings are an inspiration for anyone in our day and age to read. Reading the scrolls over a thirty three year period parts are still mystifying to us but has meant we have travelled to many stone circles and powers spots in the world exploring and researching. I have visited the house of John Hugh Roberts grandmother in Wales, and both myself and my wife visited the location of Teman in Wales on the island that sunk, visited the location where Prince Madoc went to sail to America, and travelled to many places in Cornwall where the "Three Mermaids" ceremonies took place and in the process we were enveloped in the magic of the Celtic and Kymrick ways.

Where the writing came from we do not know but we feel the passion for the writing by the man John Hugh who called himself "the last recorder of the Druids". We know he was being mentored by his grandmother and two friends, we do not know if the writings were channelled and part of the

Akashic records or transcribed from something he was given as a child or saw in a cave that he mentions seeing in the manuscripts. He says some are allegory or "Inspired", "to preserve the truth from its enemies as they can-not be translated". Our intuition tells us these records are important to certain people, maybe to understand their past history, maybe for the future. We do not know but in making them public we have to trust they will be found by the right people are they fiction or non-fiction. This is the mystery still unsolved today.

Copies of the remaining 140 pages of original writings will be made available at www.azatlan.com in the near future and will be posted on the FaceBook page 'Druidical Quest'.

Dale Bertrand Dec 10, 2014

An example of the original writings by John Hugh Roberts

Royal S S Belgian Ships Log
Record May 1866 in JHR's dairy
of their 2nd trip to Canada

Various dairies of JHR

Examples of some
of Leo de Pasqua
wonderful
Illuminations

Stone Book of Knowledge
 In progress as written by John Hugh Roberts (1828-1917)
In respect for the author we have kept the original and not edited.

Index

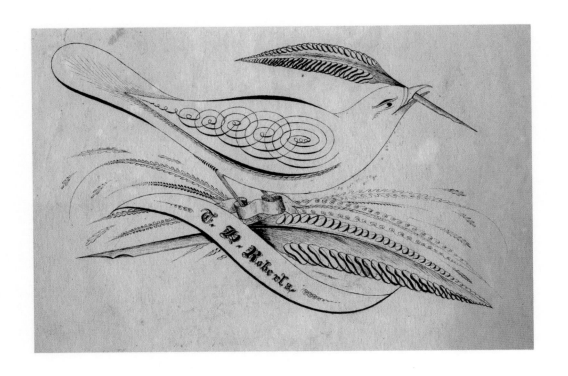

The Inspired Bird, John Hugh Roberts Totem

as done by

Tomhu Huron Roberts.

These Lessons will be sent through the Post
on receipt of Address and $ — separate or together
except the privat Lessons, these can only be
given oraly, or by means of the rule of Inspiration
which must be first Learned, by the Student.
There will be issued also, at certain intervals a
Report of the Lectures, with answers to any
Query in Conection with the Lessons or the
Subject of which, they treat. but under no
Circumstance, will political, or Religious
Questions be answered, or space given to any one
to air their Theories, or beliefs, Fads or Hobbies
unless the same is founded on indisputable facts
in the first place then the fact or Truth must be
Stated plainly, and the theory then may follow
if an investigation "this fact does Not Contra-
dict," "Facts or truths allready Established.
then any theory founded on Such facts, will be
in order, as a Subject worthy of investigation
The privat Lessons, Can be only given, Subject
to Certain obligation, and secrecy untill
"Facsimile" of these wonderfull records are
made public, or in the hands of the Student
the translation intended for the public may
unlimited, for correction, if necessary
and Marked "Corect" by the Proper authoron
the Student Class is formed, and registred. the
may be interchanged with each other

Notes and Quotations:
Intended to be used as references, in conection with the Lessons on "Inspiration"
and "Revelation" or Interpretation, of
Ancient Lords of Zeman (Hereditary. I had
wonderfull records, Called "the Stones.
Knowledge, on which may be read, all the
arts, and Sciences, and Secrets of the earth
and the aspects of the Heavens." those who
wish to become Students, must be able to
read and write in some language, and also
understand these rules of number $+, \times, \div, -$
and have made some progress in the "Lessons"
before been registered, and be entitled to receive
a Copy, or Facsimile of these ancient records.
The principal Lessons which are in pairs
are, "the unit of Multiplication & the three Genders"
" The fractional unit, or Column of Nine, & the Primes"
" The Lesser triads or Rule of Possession, and Great triads"
" The Dominical days & the Epacts" (and the Tables
" The Horoscope, or time place of the Stars. & ☉ ☽ ⊕
"and the Eclipses of the Sun and moon"
" and the common, and Secret Alphabets
A privat Lesson or Lessons will be given
which Cannot be given in writing — the
are tables, which will greatly help the
which he can prove the rules, or other

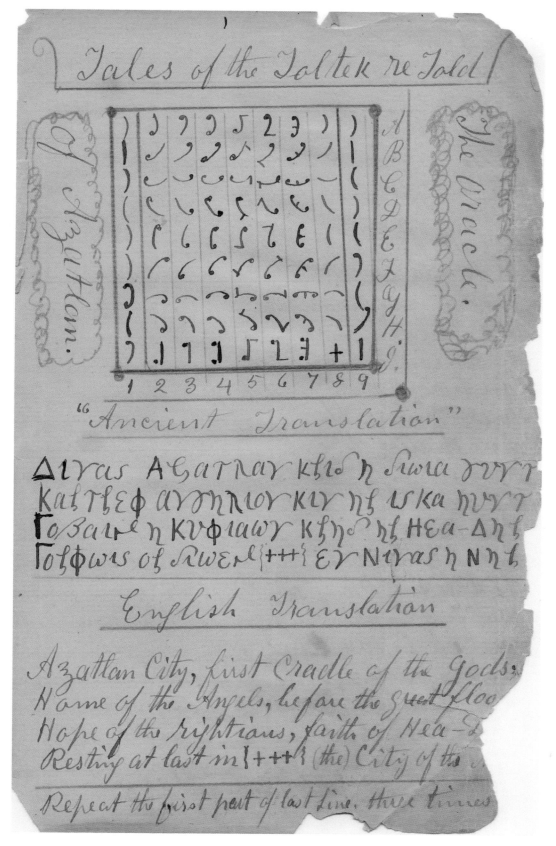

Tales of the Toltek re Told

of Azatlan.

The Oracle.

A B C D E F G H 9

1 2 3 4 5 6 7 8 9

"Ancient Translation"

English Translation

Azatlan City, first Cradle of the Gods;
Name of the Angels, before the great floo[d]
Hope of the rightians, faith of Nea-
Resting at last in {+++} (the) City of the

Repeat the first part of last line, three times

Toltek, or Toxuré Tho. Fair family. Fairies.
According to the traditions, Came originaly
from "Azatlan" this word means the Land
of the Stationary Star, (Supposed to be the Polar Star
all the different tribes of Azatlan originated
in the Secret Chambers within the Earth ⊕
the first Pair were black both. Male and female
the Second was red or Copper Color. the third
pale or yellow, the forth, White. — Azatlan
was Surounded by very high mountains
in the Center was a Conical elevation
in teraces with the top flat, on which a
very remarcable Cairn of great Stones stood
here dwelled the white tribe, the other three tribes
ocupying three Sides of the mountain down to
the Sea which Surounded this Central land.
these tribes lived in peace, each in their respective
Locality, trading with each other, or exchanging
the different Products, the lower regions prod-
used food in abundans, while the upper region
was rich in every kind of Minerals, gold & Silver.
in the Course of time the people increased So much
[t]hat it became difficult to procure food enough
[on]ce they entered into an agreement to gather
[est]ablish indiscriminet marriages, that future
[fam]ilies must settle on the other side of the Sea.

20

at the base of the high and wild outer mountains
many colonies of the Toltecs or the white people
Settled here as their land was not so fertail.
and after a time a new race of Mixed blood
arose. and they entered into a covenant with
with the other four races. this is called the
"Everlasting Covenant" or the very long lasting covenant
by this time the Toltecs had became efficient
in many arts and in particular in boat building
and fishing, — Three brothers one day out
fishing. discovered a Shole of small fish.
which they followed into a great cave. which
was made light by the fish. there was a strong
current outward, the boat was carried along.
emerging at last into an open sea, on the
right of this sea they found a beautiful, and
fertail land, after exploring the country
for a year, they followed a Shole of the same
fish, Setting current. then ruing towards Azatlan
where they safly arrived — and informed the
different tribes of their wanderful discoverys
the result was a new covenant, in which
it is Stipulated, that the three brothers
who discovered the golden land or New world
and the Secret to and from Ancient Azatlan
they and they clane and their decendents. are
apointed to conduct Passengers to or from Azatlan

also, that the land between the sea and the mountain up to the top of the mountains shall be exclusively reserved to the Toltecs and the other Tribes shall settle beand to the westward, in the same order as in Azatlan. a new covenant was entered into, in the new country, that Branch of the Toltec family — decendants of the three discaverers, were called "Nergal" (Heavens founder or discaverers— in the cours of time, the Nergals became aware that the sea was gaining on the land, or els the land was sinking. they sent meseryers to warn the other settlements, advising them to build ships, and place their efect in them when the flood came, the Nergals were sep-parated, because of the mountain barier between the settlements west of the Mountains found refuge in the islands and eastern Asia. here to their great surprise they found other tribes or Nations of whame they had no previous knowledge, these were superstitious, offering human sacrifices, to their many gods, they were also Canibals, and ignarant of arts & sciences. as there were three different complection among the new comers they were called "Druidian" means "the three first" the Druidian entered into a covenant, with the tribes they found in Asia &c.

22

Because of the superior knowledge of the Druidians
they were to act as ministers of state and religion
and teachers of the young, — &c to attend the
sacrifices both public and private &cc
they were to be free from paying taxes, or serving
in war, and to be royal in all things—
these Druidians and the different people of the
Covenant Continued to follow the Sun to the
west. untill they arrived at the shores of the Mediteranean Sea, here they discovered their long
lost friends the Nergals, of the golden land,
who related to them their perigrinations since
the flood, — "When the flood came, most of the
people entered their Ships, but many were
caught in the Mountains, the tops of which became islands. the Ships Sailed Eastward
towards the rising Sun, they landed at the
first land (now Called America) they came to.
here they Settled on the table land mostly,
and built many cities, decending to the
Sea towards the east (Gulph of Mexico now)
they built Ships and sailed eastward on the
Ocean river (Gulph stream) to BEfirlTap,
which they named "ΓΝας ΗΕξιλιν," meaning
"the Blue-Sea-men" men of gigantic Stature
and whose hair was blue! and the Beards.
these people were only found in one island about
the center of the group (now called British Isles.)

23

Here they entered into a Covenant with the Giants and Settled among them, on the river "Sachas." and around the "Temple of Teman" from time to time the Nergals Send out Colonies as far as the Mediteranean Sea, among other Ancient Rome (prior to the Present Rome) & Egypt here they met their friends the Drudiians — and now the Drudiian having told also their tales. they dis covered that they had travelled the whole the full circle of the earth, the Covenant was renewed

"The old Covenant remodeled"

So as not to interfear, with the Covenants — entered into Seperatly by the Drudiian and the different tribes in Asia. &c, and the Nergals and the Giants, in Europe, before this was don the Consent of all the Parties to this Covenant was nescessary, the Drudi — Nergals — Giant an the 6 tribes Objection to the Sacrifices on the part of the Nergals and the Giants, and on the other side objection to halding more land than the person could use ultimetly these differences were adjudged thus. the Giants and Nergals Could hold as much land as a hundred individuals (about 2500 Acres) of any unocupied land, on condition that out of this amount the "Sacret ground" Should be free to all, with highways to and from, the same to be

24

mantained by the Nergals, who also were to
guard the relics, and maintain order, and justice.
they were also to find suitable Canditats for Captains
and Generals of the Army. and the Head Arch Druid
these were to be chaasen by balat, of all the people
it was also pravided, that in the event of certain
disputes taking place, the Canditats may appeal
to the swords of destiny, — one of which was
in the Charge of the Druidian, and the other in
the Temple of Zeman under the protection of the Nergals.
whatever land or praperty the Griants were in
passessian af, were to remain in their passessian
and their decendants after them, or those who
held under a Leas from them forever —
The Nergals as under the ancient Cavenant
Clane, had the right, of free entry to Azetlan.
or to conduct or guide all visitors, to or from
the first Cradle of the gods &c. the Nergals, were
free to atend the Sacrifices, but nat bound, as the
Druidian were; yet the were bound, to keep the
four great festivals, at the praper time of the year.
and in all other respects to keep the Cavenant
of the tribes, and the Druidian. or Druids.
this Cavenant was ratified at the Temple of Zeman.
After this the Druids and the Six tribes came
and settled in Britain and the adjesent Cauntries
Three tribes of the Kimrik and three of the Galik.

These tribes wer warlike. Sacrificing human-beings on their alters, at first only such as had been sentenced to death by the law of the land by degrees, they came to consider human Sacrifice the most acceptable to the Gods, hence they passed a law "that it was lawful for any one to <u>volunteer</u> when there was not enough of Evildoers to be had and if there was not enough Volenteers, they should draw by balat, this was the law in the 54 00 Century (Century before Anno Domini) against this law there was a mijerause protest by the Druids, many of the officiating Priest (Druids) refusing to atend. at these unhuman and revalting Sacrifices. It happened that one of the Druids was drawn and Sacrificed, at this the Priests in great numbers refused to atend — they were charged with a breach of the Covenant, which declared they were to atend all Sacrifice both Public and Privat. ————

A great Council was Called
(to Settle this dispute) of all parties to the Covenant, which declared, that the deserting Druids, had "a moral right to refuse atending any sacrifice except such as had been found guilty by the Law of Such offence the penalty for which was death. but as Such refusal was a breach of the Letter — of the Covenant, it was decreed by the Council.

26

"That henceforth, such Decentes must wear black garments when attending the sacrifices! hence they were called "Krisdion" (black garments) this word afterwards was Corrupted to "Kristian" this happened early in the Century 5400, old style.

"The Culminating Cycle of time"

This Century produced four remarkable persons. In the 1st year thereof was born HΛΛV (Helen) the Holy one of Mount Paran, one of the Hereditary Order, and virgin of the ☉ & ☽ in the 2nd year was born IWᴙ KᴙsᴈƑ (Caesar) the most famous of all the Romans — both direct decendants of the Toltecs — In the 43d year of the Century, or 57 years before A.D. (one of the most famous) died the Arch Druid, and when another was balated for, a dispute arose, as to the right of the Krisdion to vate. in the end an appeal was made to the Swords of destiny. one was called "KᴙΛVꞙΛᴧᴧ" or "Cracea mors" — The great Sword, this was kept in its Stone Sheath at Carnac in Gaul. the other Sword was kept in the Temple of Teman it was called KΛᴧᴈ—ΦWᴧX (Kaledvwlch, Caliburn — Excalibar, it was belived generaly that these Swords Could not be drawn out of their sheaths unless they were favoured by the gods.

27

All the Competitors made a solemn promish
if successful, to cary out the purpose which
should befound written on the Sword —
"Julius Caesar" drew the Crocea mors!
and "Nynian" became the beaver of Caliburn.
and having met on the Share near Zeman
on Crocea mors was written," Consult the
oracle of Zeman, and abide by its Counsel
Nynian declared that he was the guardian of
and he would not allow any one to enter with
arms, if he would give up his Sward he was at
libety to go and Consult the oracle of the Starre
this Julius Caesar refused to do (to give his sward)
but instead Struck Nynian such powerfull
Stroke that the sward became fast in the shield
at the same time wounding Nynian in the head.
Caesar would not let go his hold on the Sward
in this way they marched to the Temple of Zeman
The oracle, demanded of each to give up his Sward
to two virgins, of the Sun and moan, as it was un-
lawfull to be armed in the Temple, Helen the
Holy are received Caesars sword, and by Comand
of the oracle they were married secretly!
after this Caesar returned to his own Country
and in due time a Son was born. to the virgin
he was named "HΛΦΟ᷄ΟᴕΛᴎᴉe" Elva of the sward
but he was afterward called HΛı or Heli —

"The land of the Lords of Zeman"
is overflowed by the Sea, and disapears the
Same day that Heli was born, the mother was
in the Temple, in Travail, all the inhabitants
having left except the giant ΓΛͳ (Guer)
whose duty it was to close the last gate of the
wall around the Temple. at the top of the dambe
Taking the virgin in his arms, he fled with her
along the Casway (ΣαδΓ) untill the water
rose to his shoulders,— a large tree floating by
on this he reached the shore,— placing his burden
down gently in a sheltered place, she gave
birth to a son,— the last of the Lords of Zeman
on the following day being Monday, he named
the place "ΓͳΓ"(·Zhenn) the land was not
inhabited, hence he staked the young lord's
inheritance Starting with "Karak is' imbili"
next he staked, the same amount for the mother
in which Stead a remarcable hill or mountein
on top of which was a well of pure water the
highest Source of the river Sachas that flowed
by the Temple of Zeman,, to the west of this
he staked his own portion in this was "NͳΦͳΓ"
or heaven,, after this many other of the fugitives
of Zeman settled in this part of the country.
and some went fare away to the north. and
other places where they found inocupied lands to settle;

The Scatering of the Nergals

At first was a misfortune to the Kristians or Desenters, among the Druids, the orthodox Druids holding with the tribes to the literal — meaning of the words of the Covenant, mantaining that if a different meaning was given to the words in respect to the Sacrifices, the Same could be ap- plyed to the Stakes of the Nergals! who claimed 100st (about 25,000 acrs) under the Covenant, thus it happend that the greatest number of the Nergals or Toltecs. settled in the North which was then uninhabited before going from Britain they made a Strong- pratest, against the Tribes and orthadox Druids. who thus deprived them of their inalinable rights and declared that when the time Should come they would return, to claim their own, —————

"A Deputation to Caesar"

Composed of Nergals — Kristians, and Some from each of the Tribes, that were opposed to the Sacrifices. visited Caesar, and claimed his aid, arguing that he was in duty bound to pratect the rights of his own San, (becatter of the Sword) they entered into a Covenant, that they would aid him to Conquer the County, pravided he should not in any way interfear with any lands West or North- west of the Sea that now overwhelms the Temple of Teman. — the following year 55 befor A.D. Caesar came }

The Romans conquer the County
__and kept__ Passsian of it for centuries, yet they never atempted to subgect, the lands reserved by the Covenant, not because they were unable to do so, or that, they were not worth the trouble, but the "Caesars" Could not break the Neryal Coven.[t] at this time the Druids were the most learned in Ewrope, and on the whole a Noble order. they were hamperd by their Covenant, which they could not break, all though the other side failed to carry out their part of the agreement. and untill the Stipulated time Came they either Suffered in Silence, or retired from the scene, this to us at the present day, may, appear a weak paint, in their System. yet in the final reckoning may yet prove the best.

✝ ✗ Heli organizes the Kristians ✝

Things had now Came to a crises, the great order of the Druids was Crumbling and splitting the Superstitian of the tribes was appalling and the Sarifice of jnacent peaple, harible. the Neryals had been Scatered, the Romans were opressing, Morality, was unknown to many, the records and the oracle of Ziman Could no langer be Consulted, men took the law into their awn hand, in this maral chaos.

"ΦΕϹΙ ΦΕϹΙ ΦϒϹΙ"

"J Came, J Saw, J Conquered" No Sooner
had the great Caesar pronounced these words
than he was assassinated on the floor of the Senate
in Rome, by Brutus, his supposed friend
Heli his Son at this time was about 14 or 15 years
of age, and his mother yet alive in Britain
the great oracle of Teman had fore told that
"a Son of the gods would offer himself as a
final Sacrifice, after that no imperior sacrifice
Cand be offered, for ever. — Heli, was recognized
as Such an his mother side the Holy Helen.
and having reached the years of maturity. he
offered himself as a final sacrifice. here
a dispute arose, by the law of the land he had
a right to offer himself, but this would do away
with any further sacrifice, this did not meet
the view of the most superstitious of the people.
the day came when a great multitudes Con-
gregated on the Secred ground of Stonhenge.
and as was the custom they came unarmed,
as the victim stood by the alter, ready to be
sacrificed, — as by a Shake of magic, the alter
was Surounded by a band of armed giants
wearing Shiny helmets. and the three plumes
and drawing their Swords, the Captain mounted
the alter, and waving his Sword, Comanded
Silence

The address to the multitude

Here is a victim, a Son of the gods who has offered himself as a final Sacrifice, to Save you from your Superstition and cruelty. No one will dare to offer an inferior victim, he has Suffered all that a man Can Suffer this offering is accepted, the gods do not require his blood, and we are here to save him you Cannot tell who we are, or how we came, nor how we came by these sharp trusty sword and these shining helmets and the Plumes! but by these you know we have authority. which man of you will dispute — we have the power, to Save the victim, we shall use it if any of you have the temerity, to disput it. you have Spillt enough innocent blood if you must have more it will be your own. then addressing his Campanians. Said, Comrads, and Peers of Azatlan, from this Sacred ground leads a highway to the Sea, No one has a right to bar that road against us, our mission is to Conduct the victim to the Sea! an this they formed to march with the victim in the center on one side of him his baner (Helirs) was unfurled, an the other side a man Carried a long wand, by which he could create a wind that the Strangest Could not withstand.

33

A Cry of sacrilage was raised
and an atempt was made to regain the Victim
this asult Cast them dear 350 were slain!
the man with the wand leveled it, and soon
the road was cleared, and they march to the sea
where a Ship was in waiting, and as soon
as they came on board, She Sailed away —
that is a brief accaunt of the Taltecs up
to near the end of the 54th century old style.

From this time Heli devoted his time to the
organizing first of the British Kristians
and the Sign was **X** (St andrews cross) multiplied
the Secand was the Raman arder. sign **+** or
the great sward, the third was the Eastern. the
sign was **+** (Sign of addisian) in Palastine
these orders were established about six years
before A.D or 5394 of the old, JP 4707.
The **X** arder entered into a Cavenant with
the arder of the Neyals, or the Fairies —
be it remembered the Fairies then were not
the mythical biengs, as they are Suppased to
be at the present day, they were real enough.
Heli, Maried a virgin in Palastine in
accardance with the mariage laws of the Druids
faunded on the Sutability of the Cantracting party
he named this Son before he was bain, after one of

34

the most famous god of the Britans "HESVS
Heli left the ✝ order in charge of John the Baptist
and afterwards to his son who was crucified. by the Jews in their blind zeal for the
faith of their fathers, they did not however
break his bones, and he recovered from his trance
through the Elexsir of life used by the Druids
after his resurrection he went to his father
and his father now being an old man, made
his patrimony over to his son, as well as that
of his mother (Helen) and that of the Giant ꝏ.
which he had inherited from them, henceforth
the name of "jesu" became the distinguishing
word of this part of Britain (continue to this day)
for many centuries this order of Kristians.
of Saint Andrew (Druidical christians)
(until the Romish order gained the ascendacy)
flourished. and observed their Covenant —

we are now nearing the mystic dimland.
we find three mystic names of one blood.
ꝟ IΩΛ. HΛI. IHΣ. bound together by HΛAN
= $\dot{9}\dot{6}\dot{2}$ $\dot{4}\dot{2}\dot{9}$ $\dot{9}\dot{7}\dot{9}$. bound or x plied by $\dot{4}\dot{2}\dot{1}\dot{4}$
= $A\frac{8}{6}$ $\Theta\frac{9}{0}$ $A\frac{7}{8}$ fractional units. $\Theta\frac{5}{1}$
from these we come to inspiration that
requires the rules of Revelation to read
from these to allegory without its Key!
and here we are, are totaly in the dark, grauping

The Taltecs disapear from Britain only to be rerremembered in the traditions, but they now reapear in the pleasent land between the Seas (America) in their first home after the flood, and after some centuries of Peace and prosperety, they were over taken by another flood more dreedful than the first, the sea that overwhelmed them now was a <u>môr</u> of Scarlet that overwhelmed their souls. a terible nightmare that gives them no rest at night, nor plesure in life during the day time

Chronological dates, of some of the faregoing, event. ☉ ☾ ✳ = the great triad = the Julian period when the golden continent Sank below the Sea the Taltecs took refuge an the highest mountain now island of the Pacific, on the island now Called Easter island, about 2300 miles west of the coast of South America. near the tropic of Capricorn, 2500 found Shelter — here the perpetual fire of the Covenant still burned. hence the place was called "Ti-tan"-de-Dance" the island was too small to support Such number of peaple, — after a great Storm they found Several dead wheals thrown on the Shore which they made into boats, in which they Sent out a Select crew, to sea if they could find Some other land, or assist, others in distress

36

Having cruised "about for many weeks,
they landed on the Cast (of South America) which
they named "Lan-ti-tan" (Zera del fuego)
three years after the Deluge. or O⊃* 2365.
on the high table land they built a city
which they named "Ti-ti-Ka-Ka" here they
dwelled intill 2700. here they were joined
by many more from the Island, moving
northward to Kusko and the head waters
of the great river (Amazon) some went
still further north, and others followed the
great river to the ocean "Atlanti"
here they dwelled intill 3000. when they
again moved northward, and again met
on the Plains of Anahuac (now mexico)
here they built many cities, when the country
was visited by a terrible plague 3111.
and many people left the country. Some sailed
on the great river of the ocean (the Gulph stream)
and some fled to ancient Azatlan in the North.
and others to the north east, here having built ships
Some Sailed Eastward, and in the year 3714.
reached the islands of "glas merdin" this
name was given because of the great giants
they found in the central Island. (Britain)
with these "Blue-sea-men" or giants they
entered into a Covenant, dwelling together in peace

37

"They named this island "Teman ti'tlan" during the next thousand years, nine or ten more ships arrived, from the west, up to 4714 or the 5400 Century of the old Style (Century before A.D.) these different arrivals settled around the Central Sea (Mediterranean) one of these in Italy, and founded "Ti'mor tani" (ancient Rome of the Catacombs And now came the rearenging of the ancient Covenant and the settlement of the Druids, and the Tribes of the Covenant in the west of Europe, henceforth the Period used will be Anno Domini = A.D. and — A.D will mean before or less than Ano dani.

Building the the 3 famous Temples before A.D. — Temple of the ☉ 997. — A.D. (Solomon's) the Temple of the ☽. — A.D. 979. Temple of the ✳ 799 – A.D that of the moon, is the Temple of Teman; that of the ✳ is called the Great Temple of the north — or the Beth-Kimri. Temple of the Covenant. about 771 — A.D. Assyrians, invade Israel. and the De danans Ireland, — destruction of the kingd'm of Israel. in 721 — the Babylanish Capt'd 606 — the Skuthik, Cav't 666 – A.D. (= 4047) the Century 600 before A.D. or 4800 of old style is one of these important cycles of time. we find the Scuthic Empire terminats. in Asia and the rise of the Babylanish & Persian Empires in the west "Kochaidh," was elected King of all Ireland.

He married the Princes, "Tea-Tephi" of the Royal branch (Nergal-Toltek) the Kimbri and the Skitai (Scyths) migrade north westward 400 before A.D. the Kimbri, under Brennus. invaded Italy, exterminate the Etruscans. on the Plains of the Po. and in 390 before A.D. marched on Rome, which they burned in 331 before A.D. the Kimbri and the Skitai under Dromichaetes defeat and slay Ptolemy. and in 279 A.D. they cross the Helespant, into Asia, ocupied galetia, in 250 before A.D. the Kimbri & Skitai entered into a new covenant. and also with the Belgae, Kimbri. in 100 before A.D. the Belgae settled in Britain, and the Skitai (or Scots) in Ireland, and Teman titlan disapeared; the Roman general Marius defeats the Kimbri. in 101 before A.D. the Kimbri and their allies the Tutons. settled in Denmark. the Century 100 $\frac{B}{-}$ AD = (5400 old style and 4613 of the triad) in this Century also began the Christian orders. we must remember the odd years. of the Century old style is "of the Century" that is the Century comes after the odd years but in the new Style the Centry is before the odd years. the odd years are the same in both Styles, and also the unit of the Century, — having shown how the Toltecs came to Europ— I shall now shew the reason they left it, — and their expectation of returning.

Teman and its wonderful Temple

When the Nergals (Toltecs - Fairies) first arrived
at the Islands which they named ΓΓαsΗεξξιγ.
they found one island about the center of the group.
occupied by a race of giants, of which they had
no knowledge, this island was low and fertile
near the Sea, with a high Stone wall surrounding
the whole island. to keep out the sea from overflowing
the center of the island was more elevated, and near
the center a Circular hill, on top of the hill a great
boulder or rock. very smooth and polished. it
had many rooms or compartments, lighted by
day as if dimly through a frosted glass or horne
but in the night it was brilliant beond discription.
within were many of the dead giants, one of these
in a Siting posture, supposed to be yet alive as
it would answer any question put to it, this
was called the great oracle of Teman. like all
the others its color was blue, whatever this color
was it preserved the flesh just as in life, yet
it never eat or drank, allthough food and drink were
offered, nor yet spake unless spoken to first —
and moreover, there were times that it did not speak in words, but answered in writing (Hieoglphics
when also the questions had to be put in writing.
there were priests or interpeters. in atendance to do this
There were one hundred Stone houses in the island
from this it was called Καγγξε — or Hundred.

There was not a female among these giants
their tradition was that each had emerged from
the inner chambers of the earth, into the Rock Temple
when they were very young, they could not remember
they live to an old age, they are not all of the same
Color untill they dye themselfs in the Blue river!
they were of a peaceful disposition but would
not permit any of the Nergals to visit the Temple
they ultimatly entered into a Covenant, because
they wished to have wives, as the Nergals had.

In this covenant.
it was Stupilated, that the "Gods" (Giants) could
select a wife from the unmaried wemen
provided she gave her concent, and also the parents
gave their concent, but only one could be selected
and She must Share evry thing in comman with
her husband, and be allowd evry liberty that
her husband Claimed, and the children if any to
be taught the Language and Science of the Nergals.
that She and her children should be at liberty
to visit her People aniece evry year. as he visited
by them. if unable to do so, or send, or recive,
a written Communication, — The Nergals could
not enter, or dwell, within the Sea wall, unless the unanimous Consent of the Gods (Giants)
was first had, — The laws of the Gods Could not
be altered, nor their language, or Teretorial rights.

41

be modified as long as one of the gods lived,
or any other god or Godes that may come into
the garden from the inner chambers of the earth
to take up their abode within the sea walls.

The language of the gods
was remarcable, all names (names) contained
one of the following consanants, g. Ng, C or K, & Kh
or the gutteral consanants. they had nine vowels.
prior to taking to themselfs _wives_, they lived to
a very _old age_, but after mariage but _few_, more
than one hundred and 20 years. the last of the
ancient gods was a female, from whome the
Holy one of mount Paran (Helen) was a direct decendant.
The last god that died in Teman was "gog magog"
the children of these gods were also called gods of
Teman, as distinguished from the gods of Azatlan,
but mostly the Lord-Gods, and the nergals
were called Lords. — The ancient gods were
all dead when the sea overflowed the land,
at the time of the Covenant. there were one hundred
Stone houses in Teman, one for each god—
but there is nothing to show whether, the one hundred
were all living then, or whither the dead were counted
when the Nergals came into passesion of the Temple
only Nine males and one female mummies were
found. of the great giant, including the Oracle
these giants guarded the secret Passage from the Temple
to the chambers of the earth with great jelausy—

42

The Earth is a living thing

the same law or rule governs it, as governs all
living things, the highest order of all living things
on the earth is man, conceived in the womb
of the earth in the Spiritual Chamber, born in
"Azatlan" having a given time to dwell on the
face of the earth, that he may gather wisdom by
experience under the Sun, and preserve that
which is good, that he may enjoy a happy future.

observation

The Tolteks at first thought that all the different
nations or races were born as they were, in Azatlan, afterwards they found the Giants were
born in "Zeman" and the races in Asia
met by the Indian, had not come from either
Azatlan or Zeman, (perhaps from the Garden of eden)

The reader if he or she will have the oppertunity
to study these ancient records, must not juge
them by the present day theories, not even in a
Scientific Sense, for even in this we are very
wide of the fact in many things, and as to
Thealogy, it is as much a matter of guess as
ever it was among the Tolteks, perhaps more!
The Tolteks belived in many gods (high order of men)
their ideas seems to be that the Gods were the highest
development of amalgamate Creation: from the
eternal elements, (not that one god erected the elements
as well as other things from nothing !!!

The Taltec Moral Cade;

Was founded on certain Postulates, & Axioms
1st "That Certain things Called "mater" exists.
this mater ocupies a certain amount of space.
it has dementian, Lengh, Bredth & Thickness
2nd Mater consists of Primary atoms, of which
there are many farms or figures, which are
unchangable, in their form and force, this
force or power, while the atam is free in space
causes it (the atam) to revolve on its center.
3rd The Primary elements, are of atams of one
farm, whether Primary (single) or Companent, (plural)
ten were known at first of the Primary elements
4th Nine out of the ten Primary element. will
Combine to form a body, while the tenth
which is of circular or globular atoms, acts
as the mative power, when atached to the Body —
5th That which exists, must of nescerrity —
existed allways in Some farm, because it is
not pasible to produce something from Nothing,
Nither is it pasible to reduce into nothing any thing
that exist, (the primary elements are eternal ++++++)
6th The seeds of all things Plants and animals
were first produced within the earth, by a certain
praparthan of the Primary elements, these were
under favarablee Canditian, develaped or
created, and this Creatian in trun repraduce seed.

44

7th The earth (Θ) is a creation of the elements and ultimatly must return to the elements. because it is not possible for any bodily form to hold together for ever, the form must change. this change is produced by the force or power inherent in the atoms composing the body— when two or more atoms are combined by reason of their forces, pressing one against the other. a new Center is created around which the body revolve the time this will last can be mesured by the units of its several atoms and their position. &c c

8th Man stands at the head of the animal creation, there are three stages or order of man kind, known by the numbers 3, 6 & 9. 3 represent, Men in common, 6 a man of understanding a wise man, & 9 the highest order of men Lords or gods, the mighty men, and the Judges.

9th this No represents the Key of knowledge— and the state or condition of Man after death. and by it, Revelation of inspired words are made plain, to those that have understanding

10th Inspiration is the act of transfiguring words, in such a way that a person of understanding, can resolve them back to the original or reveal their true meanings, (Revelation)

It is quite evident that a Moral code founded on such Axioms, must differ from one founded on the Axiom "That three persons in one made all things out of nothing!

Synchronological Tables.

or travels of the Nergal-Toltek and the Drudian
were gathered together and placed side by side in
the Stone records after the renual of the Continent.
We'll start with the Devisan that travelled eastward, from the South east of the golden Continent.
now the Island of Rapa-nui (jun-ap-ar)
now called Easter Island, near the tropic of Capricorn
about twenty three hundred miles west of Chili
at the time of the sinking of the Continent, 25000
people saved themselves by climbing up
the high mountain of the three Volcanoes —
the waters of the ocean put out the fire but
did not enter the great Templ of the Giants.
on "Matu-kab-kao" (ōk-ōk-ut-am)
where a great store of food had been deposited
1st Crater. Rano-kai three miles in diameter, the
monument Crater is also large having more
than 150 Stone Images and Colasal mon-
alitho, Tablets &c : Lat 27° 6 South, and Longitude
109° 17 west of Greenwich. this was the Souther
settlement of the Nergals (the most south easterly
Island of Polynesia.) 9 miles long by 6m broad
by the native it is called Rapa-Nui: it means
"Big-Rapa" the Images is called "Moai" the
Island from which the native came they call
Rapa-iti (Little-Rapa) their religion was the
"Tabu" to 1862, they became Roman Catholics.

46

The traditions say that "Hesus" was chief of the Neigals. (also called gods of the Mountains, when the deluge came he saved his People by leading them through a subteranean way to the Temple on the top of the burning mountains. these People were in the habit of holding once every year a great Congres (sunod) or listed Rod, at different Settlements along the coast (east) when the flood came they were Congregeted, in sight of the three Volcanoes now known as the three Craters of Easter island or the Rock of Resurection, or Cornes stone of the golden Continent. (Polynesia) in all these island Water is called "Wai" (in fact there are very few Consonants used.)

$\Omega au = 24, 1, 9 = 16 = 7$, or $\natural$ the god of time.

here then we will start the Chronology, with the first year of the old Style (now nearly 7300 y) and the first Tablets ever writen, doubtless these tablets are yet in existance !!! $* * * * * *$ The first Seven hundred years old Style, were Counted after the flood, Then in conjunction with the Great Triad or $\odot D *. 1 = 687 \underline{\Omega au}$ or the first or Greater flood, happened 3069 y before Noah's flood, vis 2362 $\odot D *.$ the 1st year A.D or new style = 4714 of the $\odot D *.$ I shall use the great Triad period (Julian Period) years after the flood of Ω

1, "HΣΥΣ" was elected king of the Tallek. or the gods of the mountain of the 3 fires. and crowned on the Rock of Resurection

3ʳ the 1ˢᵗ ship sailed eastward from the Rock and after an apsence of one year returned loded with food, and relived them from famine giving a good account of the land they had found at this time there was 25000 people on the Rock and the stores of food placed there before the flood had now been exhausted. it was decided to build ships and migrate to the mainland. leaving 1000 people on the island. ———

5ᵗʰ 24000 left the Rock of resurection & settled in "Titannia" (Teradelfuego) (now called South America) Maving Northward along the Table lands they built the city of "Titikaka", afterward, they spread North- ward building many cities as far as the Sun goes, that is as far as the Tropics (of Cancer) at the beginning of the 1ˢᵗ Century after the flood —

100ʸ. Many islands were discovered, over crowded with people, great number of these joind their country men an the mainland during the next hundred years, and many also from Azoltan for the Nigals continued to visit that country the people had now advanced in arts and sciences and had discovered a new ocean (Atlantic)

48

200ʸ the Neyals discovered the great River of the ocean (Eridanus) or Gulph stream, following it fast to the North, making many settlements on the mainland & the islands. 300ʸ to 686—7 ʸ after the great flood a succession of periodical plagues and great mortality troubled the different settlements, a ship crossed the ocean along the river of the sea and discovered another Continent (Europe) adgaining which were a Group of islands — here they found another race of men of great statute, they entered into Covenant with these people, (the Covenant of Glasmerdin) or the Blue men, these people had been in the habit of observing a certain seremony when the ☉ & ☽ & one of the planets were found to be in a certain possission &c. it so happened that the three luminaries were all in line or equal when the Covenant was signed therfore the date is placed thus $\overset{\odot}{i}\overset{D}{i}\overset{*}{i}$) 6 8 7. (if we add to unit these two different periods they are both = 3 Sepparatly and 6 united. 111 devided into 687. = 6 $\frac{21}{111}$ or $\frac{7}{37}$ now 687 is the period of the planet mars ♂ the gᵈ of war during the next thousand years the Neyals or Talteks and the giants Spread over Europe and the northern part of Africa, 1700 ☉ ☽ *

1700 to 2362. eight great floods happened
the last (the 9th including the first.) Noah's flood
as the Ninth flood; this is = to 2362 ⊙D ⁂
in this flood the great valley of Depranbani
with its hundred cities was overwhelmed
and a great Sea now covers them (Mediteranean)
~~~~~~~ Noah's flood 2362 ⊙D⁂ ~~~~~~~
Thus between the 1st great flood and the last there
was a space of ~~3014~~ years let us now see
what had became, of the Dridian, who At
the 1st flood escaped in Ships as boats under
Hee-Dêr, and found Shelter in Asia.
and the island to the South & east.- here
they also found other races of men, Wild
Namadic tribes turbulend and savage
with Six of these tribes they entered into a
Covenant, and Succeeeded in founding many
Cities, in different parts of Asia, and also
establishing Dynasties, as those of Assyrian
monarchy by Nimrod (Narmin) ~~2962 ⊙D⁂~~
Kingdom of Abraam in Arocan. 2714 ‥‥
Kingdom of Argas, by Inachus (Israel) 2854 ‥‥
Kingdom of Athens, by Cecrops ("peed) 3154 ‥‥
The first Tyrian dynasty Ali-Baal. 3663 ‥‥
Destruction of Tray by the Greeks — 3530 ‥‥
The Genist High priesthood — 3300 "
Destruction of Ancient Rame — 3333 "
Building of the present Rame — 3938 "

1. Egyptain Dynasty, Pyramid, Ghizeh 2213 '''
2. " " 3rd & 4th end of pyramid building. 2613 '''
9th Dynasty, Sesostris & Ramesses II.
the Temple building period, — Exodus of the
Israelites. (1280 before A.D.) or 3433 oo+
Babylonian Dynasty (Kandis) 3145 '''
1st Assyrian Dynasty (Asshur &c) 3263 '''
1st Dynasty 10 Kings. 2d. 6 King. 3d 10.k 4th 2 kings
the 1st of the 4th Dynasty was "Tiglathi-pal-esar.
or Tiglath-pileser, of the Hebrews 4238 oo*
this King extended his power over Babylon.
in the time of Ukin-zira, 1st King of 9th Dynasty
he also defeated Rezin, King of Damascus.
he also defeated Ahaz, King of Judah.
and Pekah, King of Israel; Phoenicia.
Moab, Amman, and Edom, made sub-
mision (Tiglath reigned from 745 to 727 BC)
Phoenicia. had seven principal cities
Tyre—Sidon—Berytus—Akko (Acre)
Byblus—Tripolis.th Arodus. the 1st Dynasty
of Tyre, had 12 Kings. 1st Abi-baal. 2nd
Hiram, 3rd Baal-uzur. 4th Abed-ashtoreth.
5th — 6th Ashtoreth. 7th — 8th — 9th Eth-
baal. the 12th Pygmalion. the most important
monarchs were 2nd Hiram (Ciramus)
9th Eth-baal. 12th Pygmalion. 2d was
contemporary with David & Solomon. (Kings)
and aided in building King Solomon's Temple.

Eth-baal, was Contemporary with Ahab, King of Israel. his daughter "Jezebel" he gave in marriage to Ahab (and the worship of Baal, among the Israelites) Pygmalian was the father of Dido. under him occurred the Colonisation of Carthage. 3833 ⊙☽* or 850 BC. The Building of the Present Rame 3962 " 751

"The famous order of the Druids" "⊙☽"
About 1000 years before A.D. or ⊙☽* 3713. or 4400 the Ancient Covenant of the Neyals & the Dridian or Druids was renewed, with some modification under this Covenant multitudes of the Tribes, settled in Europ. More particular in the British isles. among the Neyal – Talteks, "the Kimri" were and "the Tutons" (Cimbri & the De-danans. Teutons) and the Keltik. (Celts) Tribes were numerous the Teutons, were the same as the "Tuath de danan" in Ireland, about 470 BC or about 3943 ⊙☽* The Skythians (Scots) Settled in Ireland 3983 730 BC about the Same time, the 1st Captivity of Israel. happened about 700 BC. the fam Kingdoms of Ireland began 4013 ⊙☽*
During the 7th 6th and 5th Century before Newstyle or 5000 – old style. or 4200 ⊙☽* the Gaul, or Kelts, settled in western Europe, Covenant of the Beth-Kimri, and the building of three remarkable Temples, by the Neyal "Talteks. 1st Temple of Solomon 3716 ⊙☽* or 997 before A.D.

2d Temple of Juno (the auter walls) 3734. a 979. OD*

3d the Great Temple of the Triad +++, 3914 a 799. BC

these wanderfull Temples are yet in existance
but their exeact location is yet a mystery.
the old style respectivly are, 4403 – 4421 – 4601
for the next three hundred years the Druids
may be saide to have reached the Zenith of fame
and the arts and Sciences were highly Cultivated.
we have now reach the last century. old style
5400 (the hundred years preceeding Anno Domni)
or the new Style. or from 4613. to 4713 OD*
Many remarcable persan were born in this
Century 4613 OD* was born HREV. the
haly ane of mount Paran, in 4614. was
born Kaius Julius Kaesar (of Rome)
their mariage in 4656. or 57 yr before A.D.
their anly San (HM) born in 4657 (56 BC)
and the anly San of HRi and Mabi. 4709.
we have now arrived at the begining of the new
Style the 1st year of which = 5401 OS = 4714 OD*
at this time the Druids were the most Learned
men in Europe, More particular the Nergals, (or Hereditary order,) Taltek or Fairies.
at this time there was Six of the tribes which
had entered into Cavenant with the Druids.
and anather tribe (Giants) in Cavenant with the
Nergals, those Seven tribes had an allated

53

District or Country, but the two orders
Neisal & Druids) had a common inheritance
among all the Tribes, three of these tribes —
belonged to the Kimrik nation, and three,
to the Keltik. nation, and the giants.
Kymrik. tribes 1st in Armorica or gaul
2d in South Britain, 3d in Central Britain.
from the Thems to the Humber. and Wales. westward
4th (gaelic) North England and lawland of scotland
to the Friths of the Farth and Clyde, & isle of Man.
5th North Britain or the Highland of scotland.
6th in ireland, 7th (giants) occupied a county
centraly between these tribes now covered by
irish sea and St George chanell but at
the time of Julius Caesar, was an island
at high water, but connected with Wales by a
Caseway (Sarn) at law water. here was
the famaus Temple of Teman (gods land)
each of these tribes spoke a different tongue.
and what is rather remarcable is, the same
speech is used to this day "in the extreem western part of each of those devision of the
tribial boundy, except the 7th now submerged
and the 2d may be said to be a dead language
allthough there were plenty of old people that
spoke this language allmost exclusivly 60 or 70
years ago. — Britany — Cornwal — Wales. isle of Man
Highland of scattland & Conacht in ireland.

54

The Submertian of the land of Zernan.
took place in the year of the ☉* 4657 (563 BC)
or old style 5344. and the Scatering of the
Giants (Gods of Zernan) or the Zeutans,
About this time the Moral revolt, of certain
Priests of the Druids became very Common
in valuing a serious dispute with the tribes.
who at this time had became very Superstitians
in respect to the sacrifices, having changed
the law to Suit their own peculiar ideas,
at first only Such men as had committed
Such Crimes, that were Sentenced to death by
the law of the land. were sacrificed on the Alters
but now the law was that any one may vol-
-enteer, if there were not enough of evil doers.
and in the event of not enough Volentees,
they may be chawen by lot, it happened
the lot fell an one of the Druids and he
was Sacrificed, ! the Druids Priests had
pratested against this kind of sacrifices.
and now a great numbers refused to atend.
Claiming that this was Contrary to the Covenant
and that the law that permited Such. was
an unrightrous law. — the tribes however
held that Since they were in the magarity.
the law was legal, unless declared void
by the high Council, of Nine! at last such
Council was called, and its decree was —

55

The High Council of Nine.

were selected, one from each tribe, and
one from the Order of the Druids. and two
from the Nergals as they represented the Giants.
the result of their deliberation was that,
the desenting Druids had a moral right
to refuse atendance at such sacrifices
as were not mentioned in the Covenant. and
therefore they could not be deprived of any
right under the Covenant, — yet as they had
brake the letter of the Covenant "which declared
they were bound to atend all Sacrifices private
and public." the decree of the Council of 9 was
"; that henceforth when atending public sacrifice
they were to were Black garments, at all public
sacrifices." the name of such garments then was
"Kris dian" or Black gown, this name
is now corrupted into "Christian" as this
word is found on the Stones of knowledge
Long before Christ was born. and as there
were thousands of Christians before his day.
is it not reasonable to believe that the Name
Christ, came from Krisdian, or christians,
of which order he was a member, than that
the order derived its name from Christ —
which as a matter of fact was not his name!
there were Christians before his Father was born

(H 2)

56

"Covenant of the Dei-Krisdion"

This covenant was signed in 4666. 47 years os* B.C.
or 5353 old style. and was to last 1940 years.
with about 60 years. Called the day of Judgment.
as the Nerpals and the Giants, did not sacrify any
Living thing on their alters, they naturaly helped
the Christians all they could to destroy the horid
human sacrifices practiced by the Tribes, and some
of the Druids, alisted, because of this Covenant.
at the time of this Covenant, Heli (the Father)
was about Nine years of age, and his name is
found in this Covenant, as the last of the gods that
were conceived in Zeman, and born in the wilderness.
Now this Covenant was signed in Zeman, not—
withstanding that it lays under the sea many—
fathoms, as a mater of fact it is posible to reach
the ancient Temple of Zeman to this day through a
supteranean passage, provided you are in the secret.
as the early Christians of Britain were in 5400
(th Century preceeding Anno Damini, and long
after that as their names are found on the rocks.
but Such Christians were in Covenant with the
Nerpals (Jolteks) the guardian of the relics.
who at first protected them in Zeman, and after
the County was over whelemed by the Sea, they still
befrinded them on their many reservation in
many parts of the County (Reserves were 25000 acres)

"The New style Record"

In the Tales of the Tolteks, we have given a brief Synopsis of the old Style Traditions for fifty four hundred years, each of the hundred years has a character (Alphabet) which may be seen at the begining, observe the reading of these Characters in order, is to start on top of Left hand column to the bottom then begin again on top of 2ᴰ Column (not Counting the margin,) or from ⟩ to Ⅎ =54% or the Column numbered 2 to 4 at the foot of square the 8ᵗʰ Col. begins the New Style or Anno Domini that is from ⟩ to ⎟ or first to ninth century a Column is Called a Cycle, and the new style begins with the 7ᵗʰ Cycle, hence forward we Shall use this style in conjunction with the ☉ ☽ ✳ about the middle of the last Century of the old style Julius Caesar became the Governor of Gaul) here he found the Druids, as ministers of State & religion, these Druids, learned in arts, & Sciences. and well advanced in Astronomy & Geology — and possessing a most wonderful records. the Callender of Rome at this time was very defictive. which Julius Caesar corrected in $\underline{4669}$ ($45 \frac{BC}{-}$) making it to correspond with the Druidical Callender very near, he made every 4ᵗʰ year a Biscextile or Leap year, including the Centuries, whereas only one in every four Century is a Leap Century !

Before this he had discovered, that the Julii to which family he belonged, were a branch of the Hereditary order of the Druid (Neys als or Tallets) who built ancient Rome, (Rome of the Catacombs) this he discovered by the Druidical records — thus he became entitled to certain privelages in this order, pranided he undertook on himself the obligations belongin to such privelages this he did, — qualifying, as a Competittor, to draw the "Cracea Mars" (Red death) this event may be considered the first act in the drama of Christianity. — in the year 57. $\underline{BC}$ or $\odot D * 4656$. died "the head Druid" and several candidates at first sought to be elected, politics ran high then, because of the great split in the order of the Druids, Concerning human sacrifices. the six tribes or nation, who insisted on it and "the letter of the Covenant Druids" holdin with them. while "the moral decenters;" the Neyals and the Giants, opassed the sacifice "of innocent men" under any circumstance, (or law to the contrary) so evenly balanced were these great parties, that it was agreed to appeal to the swords of destiny, the "great sword," or Klay-more. † was kept in a stone seath at Carnac, Gaul. and the "hard edge sword" or Calibum—Excalibar was kept in the Temple of Teman in Britain.

The great sword was drawn by Julius Caesar.
and on it was written, "Place me in the hand
of the virgin of the sun, and moon, in Teman"
Numian, drew the other sword, and on it was
written, the Temple of Teman is sacred to the
gods, he that comes to the Temple armed, shall lose
his life, unless he is redeemed by a virgin"

The swords are crossed

Julius Caesar, landed on the shore. not far from
the Temple, here he was met by Numian, who
demanded to know how and for what purpose
he came to this sacred land thus armed, as
if for battle, Caesar answered, that he carried
the sword of destiny, that he was going to place it
in the Temple, and to consult the great Oracle.
and I said Numian, as the Guardian of this
land, will not permit any armed man to pass
me, without trial at armes, this sword which
I carry is also a sword of destiny, and a battle
with these must end in death of one or both of us.
but if it is your wish to consult the oracle, it
must be done unarmed, give up the sword or fight
Caesar, knowing, that if he fought with such
heavy weapon as the Cracea mors was, he must
do so by main force, using both hands, hence
after a few thrusts, he swung his sword around
and struck with all his might — Numian received
the blow on his Shield, which was nearly cut in

two, at the same time Martatz wounding Numian in the head. Caesar failed to withdraw his sword from the shield, yet would not loose his hold on the sword, allthough at the mercy of his opponent. and thus they walked together to the great Temple. Two virgins of the Sun and moon came out and received the Swords, which they placed at the back of the oracle, with the shield, and to this day these Swords and the shield have not been Seperated or removed —

The great oracle Speaks.

Saying to Numian, thou wast entrusted with the Sword of destiny, and commanded to prevent, "an armed man to proceed to the Temple, or a bloody sword to the place of — (mystery) or any maner of metal into the — sacred chambers,! hast thou complied? by this time Numian had fainted from the efect of his wound, and was carried away —

To Caesar the oracle, Spoke, thou art a man of great valor, and also of great violence clever, and learned, in many things. honorable and charitable. yet thou art lacking, in the "rules of revelation," "ΦΕΝΙ-ΦΕΔΙ-ΦΙΝΙ" (veni - vedi - vici) J Came J saw J conquered these words are written by inspiration, Speak them not, unless Sure of their true meaning,!

"The Prediction"

Every action is followed by a result, and
when the kind of act and its time is known,
the result and the time of its culmination
can be foretold, by those that are learned in the
Science, provided always that no counter act
or unforeseen circumstances shall interfere.
The wise man will endeavour to take into
account all possible contingences, and time
while the rash man acts, trusting to chance!
The probable result of the act of this day,
which was a rash act, by the Bearers of the ✗
(Swords of destiny) is that the one shall die of a
lingering death from the wound he received
because he did not strike in time, but
instead trusted to his shield, which proved
unequal to the violence of the great Claymore
and thus, honor is tarnished, and the Sacred-
place, has been insulted by violence, in
future the host of the Sea shall be its Guardian
and this will take place before another god (Lord)
is born in Teman. !!! or the ☉ makes a revolution,
as these Swords represent the Sun (☉) & Moon (☽),
their coming together was a conjunction (☌ ☉ ☽)
from the conjunction to the full is 15 days = ☺
and a year with the Lords is as one day =
in fifteen years from this day thou art likely
to suffer a violent death; the cycle of indiction.

in future Seeks wisdom, and make all the amends possible for the violence offered to the great oracle of the Temple of Teman, which in future will cover itself with the ocean, to the fullness of time. Consult the Holy one of mount Paran (HꓘEV) She may favour, and redeem thee. She is a godes. and as such must be respected and obeyed. when She Comands, — study the times. and faithfully Cary out your Covenant ✳✳✳✳ "The words thou hast heard," if used with knowledge and discration, may help you to pass the Critical point of your life, but if used without a full knowledge, will precipitate the Crises.

The marriage.

of julius, and Elen, took place ☉)✳ 4656. (or 57 BC) after one month, Caeser went to Rome. with the understanding that he should return in two years. Should there be an issue from the marriage, Should he be denied a peaceful entry into the Country, he my do so by force of arms any where South or East of the land of Teman but the land of Teman and the Countries North and west of it were to be forever free from the arms of Rome. and the Negal hundreds be respected.

"HꓘꝖOꙄ-O-ꙄNꞒe" or HꝚe, was the only issue of the marriage in ☉)✳ 4657. or (56 BC) in ☉)✳ 4658. (55 BC) julius Caesar came with an army = and landed notwithstanding all opposition.

The chief object of this second visit of Caesar. was to see that the Nergals or Lords of Teman who had been deprived of their ancient inheritance (Teman) by the overflow of the Sea the previous year Should be permitted to preempt any vacant land as Stipulated by the ancient Covenant (25000. acres) or dwell within such reserve allready passed. by members of the order, — At this time there was a great Comotion among the Druids and the Tribes in respect to the Sacrifices, and the Tribes had began to pass laws, which were ultra virus, to their ancient Covenant, and the rights of humanity Claiming, that because they had a magarity, they Could under the Covenant pass such laws. So long as all were subject to the said law, and the only appeal, posible was to the Swords of destiny and as these Swords are now under the Sea. the magarity must rule! Such decleration. Seemed to indicate, a resolve to prevent the Privilage of the Nergals, to take up any more land than the Tribes themselps and the Druids were allowed namly Such amount as they could make use of — on receiving assurance, that these right should be respected, Caesar returned to his own Country, and with the assistance of the Nergals (Toltecs) Corected the Callender, in 4669 (45 BC) he was assassinated in the Senet at Rome. ☉* 4671 (42 BC) The most famous of all the Romans !!!

"Inspiration & Revelation"

The Covenants of the Druids, demanded that every Member of the order, should as far as circumstances permitted, Cultivate the arts and Sciences, and Peace and good will among men, — every new discovery was to be registered on the records of the order, for which purpose Men were appointed. At the same time, these records were to be kept secret from all outside of the order. For this double purpose, the art or science of Inspiration was made use of to keep in disguise such Secrets, and Revelation is the art of unvailing these hidden things these two rules are the opposite of each other as × and ÷, or + & —, as these rules are founded on the rules of Numbers, it will be an easy matter to teach all these rules to such as are versed in the Common rules of numbers.

"Square Root"

The inspired part of this rule, is to ×ply any No by it self, but no more than three figures (Root) the higest No then is $999 \times 999 = 998001$, (the three periods of twos) is the first part of Revelation as the Sum results from ×tiplication, we must reclaim the original by devision ÷, 99. period ($9 \times 9 = 81$.) find highest figure × by it self Contained in 99 2d find whither $\rightarrow$ = 1 or 9 (81 is so more than $\underset{\rightarrow}{\&} 1$)

"The rule of Revelation"

Devide the Sum given into periods of two from → the right

$$\left(\begin{array}{ccccc} 1 & 4 & 9 & 6 & 5 \end{array}\right) = \text{the right hand figure of Sum}$$

$$\left(\frac{1}{9}\; \frac{2}{8}\; \frac{3}{7}\; \frac{4}{6}\; =\frac{5}{5}\right) \overset{=}{\text{or}} (\text{the root of}) = \text{right figure}$$

take the figure corespondy to Sum

when there are but two periods there will be two
figures, in the root, the left hand period. is the
higest figure ×plyed by it self that will go into period
and the right hand period will have the figure
Corespanding as 1 or 9, 4 or 6. but 5 is always 5
and a cypher is always a cypher (0 are forever 00)
2nd When there are three periods. the will be three figures
in the root, as 4·66·56 (216) 2×2 = 4
that will go into 4. without a remainder. then
take the left hand figure of the Second period
= 6. double the 1st root 2 = 4 Subtract it from the 6.
= 1, there remains 2 (discarded when only three periods
for the right hand period the unit of which is 6 =
either 4, or 6. for a trial say 6 $\left(\begin{array}{c}3\;6\\3\;6\end{array}\right)$ 16× $\left\{\begin{array}{c}9\;6\\6\;6\end{array}\right\}$
$\frac{1}{1}\;\frac{4}{4}\;4 = \frac{5}{4}\;6$ there we know the root of this Sum is 216.
observe in this trial we know the 1st & 2nd are 21.
an the right place either 4 or 6 as a trial figure if
when ×plyed it Corespands to the Sum it is the right figure
but if not it will be the other figure, without a trial
there are Some variations, as 60·37·29 (777)
$\overset{\div}{14}\left(\begin{array}{ccc}\frac{49}{11} & \frac{20}{1} & \frac{49}{20}\end{array}\right.$ Difference
here the left hand figure of 2d period
is reduced by the difference of the square of the period.
the following examples will make the rule Clear —

66

Root	Square	Root	Square	Root	Square	Example
100	1.00.00	10	1.00	1	1	Root. 999
200	400.00	20	4.00	2	4	× 999
300	9.00.00	30	9.00	3	9	8991
400	16.0000	40	16.00	4	16	8991
500	250000	50	2500	5	25	8991
600	36.00.00	60	3600	6	36	99.80.01
700	49.00.00	70	4900	7	49	Square Root
800	640000	80	6400	8	64	there are 3 periods
900	810000	90	8100	9	81	hence 3 figures in the root

This square root is the highest used on the records
in inspired writing, called thii-Krist.
thus $9\,9\,8\,0\,0\,1$ apply the signs of possession
to the greek alphabet, "Κ ϛ ϒ Τ Θ Ι Ι" It is
to be observed that the word Krist, begins
and ends on the right I = K and ! = J. and
the three figures $9\,9\,8$ = thii (reading from the right)
the root of this Sum is $9\,9\,9$ = $I\Sigma I$ (J=si)
observe if the Sum is devided in half 998—001
the unit of 998 = 8 and 001 = 1, or the equivalents
of Oxegen and Hydrogen that form Water!
allegoricaly this Sum is the foundation of
the Christian order, and the substance of its
theories seems to me visible through the Mist.
after the Christian Covenant. another form of
inspiration came into use. which J shall try.
and explain as briefly as possible ——

"Primes & Fractions"

In the Lessons an Inspiration, there are
about one thousand words given. with the
index number corresponding, as Example
Rule — Write any word in any language.
then number each letter as it stands in the alphabet, if the Sum has no more figures than five
seek the Sum in the index, but if there are more
than five figures devide the word into Syllables.
and give the Syllables in their order as if so many
words. if such a Sum is found in the primes
write the word apposite. if not found take
the nearest Sum that is less. write the word
apposite, then add up your own Sum (not index)
up to one figure, write this figure as numerator
of the fraction, Subtract the right hand figure
of the Sum, from this unit numerator, place
as the denominator, write this fraction on the right
of the word. — this is inspired writing ——
Suposing the (the sign of Possession is used) word
to be "IOHN" = 9 6 7 4, the nearest index is
9631. = Kh, $\frac{8}{4}$, this fraction may be written "44
or Kh-44, that is Kh-NN. — before or beginning.
observe the nearest index 9631 = JOVa ! god
".in the beginning was the word" is this Coincidence?
Again find the word I∑I. (as shown in the □ root)
the number of this word is 8991." cut off the left figure
we have one of the factors in 998001 = Krist !

"The Revelation of Inspiration"

The different kind of Inspiration have a particular kind of sign, where by we can at a glance tell by what Rule it was written. in this case we'll supose the sign to be ☩, this is a true sign an angle of 90° appling this to the word, and th frac-tian if any. we have the original sum —

Same time all the words in a sentance is thus treated, but usualy only one or two words, about which the sentance is made, — and the rest of the sentance is left unchanged. Translatars, have offten made a most lamen-tahle mistakes, by omiting these signs. theaugh ignorance. of their great impartance and Same time Translating the inspired word itself, and thereby destraying "th key" alltogether. It is to be observed, all the keys. are found by the greek alphabet! So called, as a mater of fact this alphahet was barrawed by the greeks. — it was invented by the Druids!

"The unit of Multiplication"

This is anather farm of inspired writing, here any Sum whatever is added up to one figure find this unit figure and opperate as shawn.

1	2	3	4	5	6	7	8	9	9	= unit of Sum
.	:	.-.	××	∷	+·	.	.	+.	-.	= Opperation
×	×	×	×	×	×	×	×	×	×	
•	?	?	?	?	(	(	••	••	••	= Sign to be Shawn

The Gender sign.

Explaination of the table – ×̣ Means Xply once
–̣ Subtract one from the Sum then xply once, +̣
× add one to the Sum, then Multiply once,
×̣
×̣ Means Xply twice, first by the Complement, then
xply the product by by any single figure (from 2 to 9)
observe 5 is the Complement of 4. and 4 the Comp't of 5.
To the Sum Multiplyed add the "Gender sign"
the sign index of this kind of jnspiration
we may Supose to be X or some word or
Letter equivalent. Such as "Amen" (unit 4)
or □, we may naturaly Conclude that the New
Testament jnspiration are Mostly "on the square"
according to uclid all right angles are = to one another

      The Revelation of X. unit X
Can be made by reversing each operation
devide what has been multiplied. add what has
been subtracted, or subtract what we added.
Supasing 9,674 = added up ÷ 2 = 8/ we will
xply by 7   67718: this Sum or gender being shown
first j'look at the gender which is femenine. then
j'find the unit of the Sum to be 2, j ÷ accordingly
and find that the Sum 67718: means IOHN.
or John! if the translator had omited the gender
sign or placed one dot in sted of two, j'should
thereby be misled. and devide by 2 = 33859,
There are several other rules of jnspiration
which are but (Comparitively) seldom used,
the □ the +̣ or the ×̣, might be called general.

Examples in the three different rules.
First the word H.ΛI. (Heli, English version)
the No of the word = 7 2 9. = □ root 5 3 · 1 4 · 4 1 [amen, 11, en]
there are three periods = 7 × 7 = 49   49 ÷   81   9×9
41   + 6 0
here the figure 1 on the right must have either 1 or 9
for its root, will try 9 = 81 from 41 = 6 + to subtract
7 is the 1st root = 49 from 49 = 41 or left figure of 2d
6 from 41 = 35. from this double the 1st root 7
= 14) 35. (= 2 · the number of times 14 in 35 (729)
this is one of the exceptionly hard sum.
Analysis 5 3 1 — 4 4 1 having divided the
word in two equal parts we find the unit
of each part = 9. also the two parts together 9
by subtracting one part for the other difference is 90.
the right hand section 4 4 1 begins & end on the →
= A d d a. or Adam. the male root. the
5 3 1. or Female root reads from the left E v a
the original meaning of the words is Father. !
and Mother ! but read thus 5 3 1 4 — 4 1 =
" The good place " or rather the place-good.
or thus 5 3 · 1 4 · 4 1 reading from the right
A x S a Φ E. — ach-da-ve, Him of good Linage.
hence it was said Heli was of the Gods, or one
of the Lords of Teman, or the good place
which was overwhelmed by the Sea about 56 years
before anno Domini — when Heli was born.
So that he was about 50 years old when his Son
Jesi. was born, he that was crucified !

71

2nd Example. we found by the first example,
that the number of H Λ ι (Heli) was 53144(1
we cut off the right hand figure, = 53144?
we now find the nearest prime viz, 53101 =
E·S? we now add up the number 53144? = 8/4
now if we convert 8/4 into plain figures = 44.
or D'N. here we have two abbriviated words
E·S? — D'N (j'esu — d=n) The Man Jesus)
it is said he was named before he was born.
and as the name is the product of the number
of Heli, that is the square root of H Λ ι = 729.
now if the "E·S? 8/4 be considered inspired. the
Revelation. will be by converting "It to the sum
And it is thus done "E·S? = 590. X ÷ = 53100;
9/4 = 44 added, this is the No of H Λ ι → 53144
                                          + 44
3rd Example by the unit of xtiplication —
5 3 1 4 4 added to unit = 8/x of the Fem gender : (×9)
4ˊ.7̣.8̣.2ˋ.9̣.6̣. = "Dêr—u s i w" Heirs of the Druids
from this it appears that this H Λ ι was a god
or Lord of Teman the Sacred land of the Neyrals.

          The Sign of Possession.
has a regular rule. which will be explained
when the rules are properly understood, but as
far as applied to the alphabet it is simply this
the alphabet is devided into three parts from A to I
= ˊ from K to S = ˊ from J to the end = ˋ or /I\ this
is the ancient Bardic sign; used yet in Wales —

By the sign of possession we reduce the figures nearly one half, that is each letter has but one figure, whereas in the alphabet the majority have two figures, that is not all, an important gain will be found in dealing with words written by inspiration, or made to take a different form, or meaning, from the original.

"The perpetual triads"

This is another form of inspiration, the Name or Number is reduced to 3 figures. and every successive product will be three figures or places. the word Es? would be = 590.–555–615–384–627–694.

these triads are called generation. to the right Generations to follow, and to the left gen'' Back 694, = Oin.— Lamb, or 694 = Dia – god. the triad 627. begining & ending on the → = "HΛΩΛ" or Elai, one of the form of the Name of H.U. the three triads 555–615–384. added up =

(6 hundred. 3 score 60)   6 · · ·   6 (≠6)   6   and 6 —

the 1st is added to the left = 600. the 2d = 60 and the third is added to the right = 6 thus 6606. this is = the year of the great triad ⊙ ☽ * or better known to day as the Julian period. observe. there are 6 twice in 6 · 15/6, the last 6 from 15 is called the Judgment day from 1893 to 1953 AD the ancient Covenant ended in the first (6 6 6 6.0)* by that time a new order of things will be established.

"The Tetragramaton"

Is another form form of Inspiration. vis.
The word John. Alphabetical $9\,15\,7\,13$ - $9\,6\,7\,4$.

The Squares are 1 less
than figures in word
the answer (revelation)
is found from either
the triangle or Squares

observe the word is written
at the top & added up to unit
which place at the top of ◇
then cut off the right hand figure
of sum. place in the Square ◇
Subtract ﹥ from ⌃ place
at the bottom of square ◇
on the ﹤ of the Square place
a figure when added to the ﹥
shall be = in unit to the ⌃
that is a Tetragramatan.

```
9 15 7 1(3
   = 5
9 15 6 (6
   = 3
9 15 (3
   = 6
9 0 (9
  - 9
8 (1
- 8
0      1 9 3 6 5
       8 9 6 3 5 3
```

```
. 9 6 7 (4
    - 4
9 6 (3
  - 6
9 (0
-9      0 3 4
0       9 6 4
```

From the first Tetragrammatan cut off the left fig ﹤
Subtract from the remainder of word, for a new word
out of this 2d word form the 2d square same way
continue untill there is nothing left. you have the
from either of which the original word can be told
from the ◇ by writing the left and right figures in two
lines then adding the two lines up (begin at the bottom)
from the ▽ by writing the Subtracted figure on right hand fig

The ancient Stones " called Manhir (maenhîr)
or Long Stone, were generaly written after this Maner.
in Britain for the most part in Neigal Hieroglyphics.
Fac Simile of two Stones found in Kerri, Ireland.

1   2

Some body pretended
to read these hieroglyphics
to this efect 1.

{ Nocati magi
magi ret (ti) }
(The Stone) of Nocati,
the son of Macraith.

2d = Magi magi
Uddami, }
(The Stone) of Uddam
Mucai.

Supposed to be read
from the botom upwards
by the OGham
Alphabet !!!

No doubt the Translator was misled by magi
but magi magi, makes too many Macs
even for Ireland, the fact is, he drew on
his Imagination, entirely, entirely! —
The Translation is beautifuly green! but,

a boomerang Nevertheless of little use to us
unless to play a tune on the "Ogham" Alphabet
which you may do up as down as the whim takes you
I shall give here a translation of another stone
which I found in the ruins of an ancient Church
that had been partly undermined by the sea (about
1848-9) of which I took a copy of at that time
and which is evidently the same kind of writing
as the Kerri Stones, but a little more elaborate —
Many years after I accidently discovered a
"Key" to this Ogham, Stone, after a while
I was able to read it as well as if written
in Common figures or letters, and I am
prepared to prove, to the satisfaction of any
unprejudiced person, that it is a Self evident
requiring no further proof than it Contains
There are three Columns, at the top of the first Column
is shown the full Moon (☺) and near the bottom
in the Middle of the Six Crosses is the (☺) Sun
this Column is the Common Cycle of the Epacts.
the Middle Column Contains the Centuries from the
Century 5400 old style or century before Anno Domini
to the end of the 22 Century of A.D. the purpose of
it is to discover the age of the Moon at any time
during these Centuries, this it will do, by the average
of time and will never be more than one day out.
which is owing to certain irregularity in it Motion.

The Alphabet,

1	2	3	4	5	6	7	8	9	10
I	II	III	IIII	IIIII	—	=	≡	≣	⚏

11	12	13	14	15	16	17	18	19	20
(	((	(((	((((	(((((	⌒	=	≂		

> = one ten ⟩⟩ = two tens.
these were notches on the edge.
⟩⟩ = 30 or nothing in Epacts)
The right hand Column
is the Rule to find the Century
Start with the Middle Cross
at the foot, Count five ≡↓
twice, and Six ＼↑ once.
when the foot is reached Start
again at the top, or vis versa
the months on the left margin
as shown here was not on the
original Stone. neither the
alphabet, as given here.
Observe, the Cyphers are
not given for 1800 = 18 = ≡.
Opposite this in first Column
Stands IIII or ¹/₄ Epact.
of that Century. & the 5 = years.
Count downward one Epact for each year in excess
the Epact thus found will be the Epact of the year
to which add the number of the Epact opposite but
not Counting the tens > = Age of the ☽ in the first.

Maen hir. Stone

Observe, on the Epact Colum are Six crosses +
as sign plus. and three minus — signs
the + makes the Epact of the century one more,
and the — makes it one Less. and the Cycle
must be changed accordingly (advancing by 11)
I Submit that this is a perfect rule, Capable of
of proof, leaving no room to doubt the facts.
Should the Kerri Stones Interpreter see this
he may Consider a new version advisable.
In the locality where this remarcable Stone
was found Some old people there related to
me Some Curious traditian Concerning this
Stone and also a prophesy, like all Such it
was well mixed with Superstitian, Some —
famous Prophet they told me of the name
of "Robin Ddū" had once lived there at the
time when the Sea was a good mile from the
old church in which this Stone was placed
in the wall behind the Alter, where it was hid
from view by a Coat of plaster, Fairies appear
to be rather troublsom at times in that locality
when they came to visit this old Church in which
they held a high Carnival at Certain time of the year
the old Parson, on Such ocations Cleaned the
Plaster from the Stone. and left the door unlocked
the Fairies on leaving the place in the morning
left a good Sum of mony on the Alter —
and the Stone was plastered up again for another year.

In the course of time a new minister arrived who knew nothing about this "Fairies" Stane. this time the Fairies found the doors locked and the Stane hiden, then these Feries who hitherto-fore had ever been kind to the poor, Generous to the minister. and a great blessing to Mothers! this night they committed a great offence, a sacri-ledge, they bracke all the windowes, carring away every thing movable in the church and left on the Alter in place of the money, they left a piece of Parchment, Covered with hieroglyphics and Greek letters, threetning the minister with dire vengeance for breaking the ancient Covenant. the minister sent this parchment to the Pope. and he in the name of God and the holy-Saints, Excommunicated the Fairies for ever! after this the before mentioned Prophet. declared that because the Stane belonged to the Fairies who had left it there as a blessing, on Condition that it should be free to all wo wished to con-sult it. on a certain day in the year (full moon) because it was a "Magi" Stane (Stane of destiny) if this was refused then the hast of the sea would destroy the church, and the land, Ships should anchor over its ruins. and the monsters of the deep (Môr) palute its alter! and all this they declared had litteray Came to passs.

79

"The Runes of Scandinavia"
And the Tree Runes (Caelbren-y-Beirdd) in Wales,
are so called because found more plentifull there
than in other countries in Europe, these alphabets
seem to have a common origin and a common
object, in conection with the order of the Druids
which was composed of three semy independant
orders "The Ovits. or Mechanics. The Bards
and the Druids," after the dispersion of the Neirgals
when their country was overwhelmed by the Sea.
in about 56 years before A.D. who had untill then
kept the records. these people were some time called
the Gods, or Lords of Teman, Giants. or Fairies.
the word Ovid, (Ο Φ ι ν ε) means a Natural —
philosopher; a teacher of Science; an Artist.
the order of the ovites adapted the "Futhar"
(Mute) the Bards adapted the "Tree Runes"
(Kaebren-Beirth) as declared by the poet Taliesin.

Mywi wir Taliesin	Myself am Taliesis
Pen barth y gorllewin	The head bard of the West
A wn bôb Gorsin	That knows evy sprig
Gogow Garthewin	In Deviner's Cave.

It is evident, that the purpose of these kind of
writing was to keep some secrets in the order
which they did not wish to be made public.
for this purpose they made use of several rules.

ᚠ ᚢ ᚦ ᚩ ᚱ ᚳ ᚺ ᚾ ᛁ ᛁ ᛏ ᛡ ᛒ ᛗ ᛃ ᚤ ᛟ ᛏᚤ

observe all are formed on the upright Stroke |
or the Secret number of the Druids, = to 9.
which is the only letter without a Sprig or branch.
equal to the letter I (ee, a preposition = to, towards
and also in the nominative case = "Me". if we
count the 9th letter from the Left it = g. and must = 9.
the 9th from the right = S. and the must = 9 (Ng'ᴧS)
the unit of the word "Sain," (Sound, a tone,
an accent.) is **23** = 5. and five is the highest No
of Straight Strokes in any letter. Like the "Ogham"

"The Tree Runes"

I had the opportunity once to take a Coppy
off a Stone, under rather peculiar circumstances
the letters are formed in a Similar manner. but
the Same form do not Stand for the Same Sound
it would appear,— The finding of the Stone.
about the year 1849. I paid a visit to Some old
Druidical Stones, because I had heard that
there was a Stone the inscription (that no one
could read) on this was unlike any ever seen.
having failed to discover Such a Stone. I made
enquiries, an old man told, me he had heard
his grand father Saying that Such Stone had
been standing on "the Morva" grassing lands.
which was pointed out to me. but Said he —

No one living to day has seen the Stone.
but many have seen the "Fairies' dances
and hunting for the Stone, and some people
belive, and declare that whenever any one tries
to find this Stone, the Devil will appear in the
form of a bull, and chase them away, then
turning himself into the form of a pious minister
will ask the frightened man to kneel down
and thank the Saints, and the virgin for his
deliverence from the Bull, (he will not mention God!)
having thanked the old man I went my way
and notwithstanding the hint about the Devil.
I found myself hunting the lost Stone. coming to
a wide drain with water in it, I could have
jumped it but for the parsel I had. which was
too fragile to use roughly. a little way off there
was a foot bridge to cross. I started towards it.
at that instant I heard the bellowing of a bull.
behind me, turning round. also saw his majesty
pawing the ground, then starting to interview me.
I took to my heels, that is to say in polite English
I took my two heels with me, as far as the bridge
then turning round, discovered the bull all but.
on my heels, I dropt it that time, my 'ells
found themselfs in the water, and I in a
stooping position under the single Stone bridge
placing my parsel on the ground, I waited to

82

see the next performance of the D—l, — Presently
j heard him bellow and pawing the ground, clutching
my stout walking stick in my right hand, stepped
out, there was his tail conveniently to my left hand
taking a firm hold, and planting one foot against
the bank, I introduced my friend, the walking stick
to his rumpus! the next thing j knew was that
I was flying through the air! at least j was
not walking on my heels, nor yet on my head
between my "Han" and myself there is a kind of free-
mesonary, we understand the grip, my staff
acting on the grip, lamed the bull badly —
then we began to go round the circle, the Bull's
intention was to give us a rise in the world,
which we were too modest to accept, well at
last the Bull laid down to rest, and myself and
stick, went to recover my grip bag, and to rest
under the stone, to give the Bull or D—l chance
to turn into a better state — as j was thus sitting
down on the edge of the bank, I could see
the under side of the stone, it was covered with
Hieroglyphics! but where they began or ended j
could not tell, j took a copy of them, as well
as j could, marking the points of the compass
At present, it would answer no purpose to
give this, — and j shall leave it to you to decide
whither the D—lish Bull, or my friend's staff, had
the stakes!

83

A B Γ Δ E Z H Θ I K Λ M N
1 2 3 4 5 6 7 8 9 10 11 12 13

Ξ O B P Σ T Υ Φ X Ψ B.
14 15 16 17 18 19 20 21 22 23 24

The Capital Letters of the greek Alphabet is a
Coppy of this alphabet. using Stright lines insted
of the Semy circle, inas much as this alphabet
as Shown by the Stone records, is older than
the Greek Nation, and it is known that the
Greeks used another alphabet before adopting this
if it is evident that each of these letters are wards
and in some at least they adopted the word
as the name of the letter. without translating it.
it must be borne in mind, that this alphabet
is represented by one single character in the
in the Nergal alphabet, or by a single figure
and the sign of Possession, I shall give a
facsimile. of this Kind which I found in a
Cave over the Stone of entrance into an
iner Chamber. there are 70 Character in 40 Syllables
and every one is a vowel, that is indipendent
Sound that is Sounded by one inpuls of the voice
without the aid of another Sound (as the Consonant)
I shall also give the equivlants in plain figures
and also the Same in greek letter (for Sound)
with a literal translation of the Same in English.

84

∧ "Garsin Garddenin" (Talresin)

Facsimile of the Hieroglyphics

̀6́9 ̀6́9 ́9 ̀1 2 ́1 ̀6 ́5 ́1 5́9 ̀6 5́ — 5̀ 2̀ 1

Sign of Ress" numbers

Oι Ὣι]aυ a ωἔa ει ωἔ — ευα
Oι ωἔ — ευα a ι ωἔυ ει ωἔ — ħä
Oι ωἔ — ħä ħ a ι ħaυ ει ωια
O ωια]aυ (εω)]o (a) ħē ħoa

Greek Text

From his egg Jave weaves his winter-web
From his winter-web he goes weaves his summer} web
From his summer-web he goes to seed his eggs
From Jave's eggs is Jo b) Hê (and) Hoa

Translation

Observation — The word "Gar-sin, garthenin"
is subject to a dispute among interpreters.
the first part Gar. means superior; a extreme.
by the dictionary — Sin, means Donation; Alms.
but in the book of Ezekiel 41 ch 16 v "garsingou"
means in the English version Door-Post. Now
it strikes me, that the form of the Hieroglyphics
which is that of the crescent moon; more particularly
so, since the ancient name of the moon was "Sin"
(Chaldean)

85

was the reason of calling that Cave-Gassin. or rather the writing which it contains, which practicoly are figures, qualified by the sign of Possession

"Iav— IO (EW) a HE Hoa"

Mean— Jupeter — Job & the Hoa (or Hea) The purport of this ancient staff or stansga — Seems to Say that Job, was of the order of Hoa or Hea-Der (Druids) of the order of the gods. but it may be asked how do we translate 10, into Job.— the preceding syllable (EW) enclosed implies that it should be added to one figure $5+6 = 11 = 2$, the next syllable after 10 is ´j or first order, therfore $\acute{2} = B$, hence we have job (Job)

The book of Job

is the oldest book of the old Testament, it is not known by whom it was written, so we are told, j have something to say on this point. j have seen the whole of the book. except the part "Elihu Son of Barachel, the Buzite of the kindred of Ram" the yang man that Said "j will answer also my part, j also will Shew mine apinian" it took him Six Chapters to do this in, ! no Small apinian, yang man! who do you think was this yang man, well look up the 23^v of the 3^{ch} of Luke. "HλI" (Heli, in English) and he spoke just like Christian ministers do at the present day, in the name (insted) of the Lord.

The book of Job is not a mater of fact, but a
mater of opinion, – a "Play write" describing
different theories or idealities, a moral lesson
from the stand point of the Druids & Neigals
and also the early primitive Christian church.
Job's three friends, Eliphas the Temanite. and
Bildad the Shuhite, and Zophar the Naamathite.
came and sat down on the ground with Job for
Seven day, and Seven nights. without speaking
a word!?! where was "Elihu" the man of wrath!
the original names of the three friends of Job were

HΛIΦAZ – TEMAN,   ΦIΛΔAΔ – ΣH Υ.   ZOΦΦAP ←
7̣2̇9̇3̇1̇6̣   1̇5̇3̇1̇4̣   3̇9̇2̇4̇1̇4̣   9̇7̇2̣   6̣6̇3̇3̇1̇8̇.

                                          NAMET →
Teman, Namet, same place   4̣ 1̇ 3̇ 5̇ 1̇.
Job was from the land of US same as ΥΝS.
Astrologically the Ram govern Great Britain.
the Sign of the Ram = Υ, this we have in ΣH Υ ←
"There was a man in the Land of "US". &c
see the 40th y vo Gird up thy lains now like a man"
and look at Job in his later days, allthough he had
lost his seven sons and three daughters. he had
at the last the very same number,! this is all
right as a fiction,! what about the fact? ———
if the account is written by inspiration, there
is a rule to prove it, for example. "the Stanza"
just given, "from Jove's eggs is Job the - Hoa."

Which I propose to prove by the Perpetual triads
I aue = 9 1 2 = 8 2 8 = 2 9 6, or Jab —
Rule. Subtract right hand figure from ten. (10 8. 2
place the remainder on the left of the new Sum
then Subtract the middle figure from the left figure
place on the right of the new Sum, lastly make
the Middle figure of the new Sum when added
to the right and left figures equal in unit, the left
figure of the parent or previous triad —
Read the figures beginning with the last. 2 9 6

9 1 2 = Jaue =⎫ Jaue, the god of the celestials"
8 2 8 = Ruth =⎬ gift, was Jab, in the land
2 9 6 = Job =⎭ of US. — or the island
20·36 (units) = of Britain ! → ← →•→
U S = (land. = I shall go further and Reverse

the rule, or proceed direct 9 1 2 = 311 = 547 =
= 7 0 5 = 3 8 3 = 5 2 4. = H?l & H?ue …
again 2 9 6 ← 4 4 3 = 7 6 0. = HO' or HOa —
when one of these rules is used as inspiration
the other is the revelation, these rules are perfect
observe the middle figure of Jab is 9 but by
the rule it would be "0" hence he is described
as having lost all he had but became very great
in other words we are instructed to place 9 where
the, 0, was, this point in the generation are
called the place of the Branch, so much
for Jab and Garseth Gortheum.

" The Red and White Dragons "

Merlin's   **Prophesy.**

the white   The Red

Dragon   Dragon

Signifies the   Signifies the

Saxons.   (The Prophesy)   Britans.

"Woe into the red dragon, for her failure is near; the Caves shall preserve the white dragon that was invited, which shall trample on the red dragon, untill the Mountains shall be leveled as the Valleys, and the rivers of the Valleys shall be slipery with blood; the sense of Christianity shall be abolished, and the fall of the Churches visible, in the end the oppressed part shall be revived, and resist the aliens, because the Boar of Cornwal shall give aid, and the necks of the Strangers shall be trodden under foot."

The hieroglyphics, on the white dragon reading from head to tail = "K T O ⚥ ᴇ K" or Catholic. and on the red = K η ξ ᴇ K (ceric) Stones. from this last name is derived KiꞀk — Church. Meaning the British church, and the Roman church

observe, the heads and tails of the dragon
form the sign + and X, which are the ancient
emblems of these two churches. and the
same dragons or serpents are shown on
the ancient Seal of the Covenant, the date
of which is from 4666 to 6606 of the O) *
or 47 years B.C. to 1893 A.D. this Covenant
is practically ended now, we are now in the
time of the end. or years of grace so to speak.
The time to prepare for the judgment, day to
give account of their stewardship, in respect
to the Covenant of the $\Delta E \zeta - K \zeta \iota o \delta \nu o \nu$.
and the Sacred lands entrusted to them
by the Druids, from time to time. When they
(the Druids) retired because of persecution, and
the asumption of Power to which they were not
entitled to, or fited for, the Druids could not
carry out the Covenant, because the end had
not come, for there are obligation to Consider
as will as benifit to receive. hence they awaited
the time, when those that have don right Shall
receive their reward, and those that has don wrong
Shall receive punishment. — Surely I hear you
Say, we Shall not be punished for what our fore fathers
did a thousand years ago. we are inocent. — Now
if you are found in possession, if you do as
they did, / opressing the poor & deciving the inocent,
and teansing the weak minded. I witt.

fantoms from your wild imagination, then
you are as guilty as they were, and unless you
repent (provided you have done any of these things)
if you have sown to the wind you will reap
the whirlwind, if you have led others into
Captivity, there you also shall go, for as you have
done it shall be done into you, — there is eternal
fitness in these things, and we know that time
repeat itself, hence to those that are in possession
of a trustworthy record, there are no great difficulty
in predicting what is to come or what has happened
in the past. it is only an arithmetical knowledge
that is required, the begining and the end, or
the particular cycle being known the rest is easy.
it has been recorded (allegorically) that a beast or
dragon was seen rising out of the sea (môr)
with seven heads and ten horns, those are the
figures on the head of the Red dragon! ⌢
there was another Beast that came up from the land
with two horns like a Lamb ⌣ or ⊌
these two witnesses John, and Merlin, appear
to have made very close calculation as to time
when, when man would be relived from the
tyrany of these beasts or moral Monstrosity
an intolable nightmare, — "Shout ye sons of
"g'kêrik" the tide has turned, the sea (môr)
is receeding from the Shore, rejoice ye Sons
and daughters of the Stones, because the

Ancient landmarks, are yet in their places.
the Temple has not been injured, and the
record and the oracle are safe within.
Scorn the broken sea wall, and the gate—
that let in the flood (gate of the Hel(l)i-flood)
will be free from the flood, and the fishermen
and the Pirates of the ocean, and the monsters
of the deep, — this is the time to unite the forces.
and rebuild the stone wall strong and high
on the old foundation which yet is good.
Replace the old gate by a new one, made
Scientifically, Self acting, requiring no keeper
. So that your trust need not be in man,! and
that you may feel secure within your ancient
inheritance," where the Lords of Teman dwelled"
and know of a surety that when the sea
shall again return. it shall beat in vain
against the ramparts, and shall not prevail
against the gate, because the keeper cannot
be made drunk with wine, and fornication"
The original of the foregoing "Quotation — " is in
verses, which is very difficult to translate
into rhyme, without altering the meaning.
for this reason I have only endeavoured to give the
general meaning of the words, (not technical meaning)
it would appear from this Song, that the Sea, stands
for "Rome", and the Stones the order of the Jesuits
and that this Sea shall pass away for a time.

"The Giant of the Stones."

The Man, Of figures holding the Sun moon a Stars giving light to the world the guide of mankind

Spiritual or ideal order of gods Commanding the elements the Architect of the universe the everlasting Containing all.

This remarcable figure Consists of 32 figures namely $\left\{ \begin{array}{ccccccccc} 1 & 2 & 3 & 4 & 5 & 6 & 7 & 8 & 9 \\ 7 & 3 & 23 & 7 & 2 & 5 & 2 & 1 \end{array} \right\}$ the digits to the no of each

there are no less than 10 pairs of Sixes. with 2 single Sixe and 2 eights = 16. thus the figure is called "the mystery of Sixe" for even the 7 of which there are $5 \times 7 = 35^{x}$ $= 1^{+}5 = 6$. hence the No of Man is 6606. there are also $\therefore\therefore$ making 6 points = the total Sum added up is 138, total of single figures $3\overset{x}{2} = 6$. and $1^{+}3^{+}8 = 12$. or two Sixes. is it any wonder that the early christians. Sel- ected this figure as their ideal emblem of their faith; their Crist on the Cross, that came down from heaven, the ⊙ of the ✳ and the ☽ holy ghost

This man holds ⚲⚲⚲ in his right hand the Sun ☉
the fore arm = 6. the upper part = 10. or 0 Left do o
hence we have 6 0 0. then the Shaldus ad neck
= 20 ∴ or 6 0 → 6 0 ∗ = 6 or 6 6 0 6. there
is. yet the head. the face ⌣ = 6 in place of cypher –
there is no mistaking. this number or the man.
all the nine digits, are found in this man
every figure is repeated except 9 which is single
this is the "key" wherby they that have under–
standing, May discover the secred that
this man holds. the figure as a whole
is that of the 23ᵈ letter of the greek alphabet Ψ
called "Psi" this word = Ψ ϙ́ ϙ́ = Ι Η Σ
or g̈ ê s (g̈ êsu) now there is no Ψ = ϒ
(the 3ᵈ division of the alphabet has only 6 letters
hence we take the Ψ th of the 1ˢᵗ division which is = H.

"The different parts
Head – neck – Trunk. theĭ̄se – leg̈s – feet – arms do
head to th feet = 9 parts, the 2 arms = 4 part. = 13 p
then there is the Secret part. and the two hands. the
right hand is hidden in the Sun ad th left appear in the star
before we can tharoughly understand the parts
it will be necessary to know the Rule of Xplication
by Subtraction, the Rule is as follows.
write down any Sum, – add a cypher on the right.
this is the sum to be subtracted from (cypher–sum)
Xply the figures of the Sum amiting the added cypher

by the difference of the right hand figure of the Xplyer & 10.
Subtract this second Sum from the first ——
thus

Xplyer	1	2	3	4	5	6	7	8	9
difference	9	8	7	6	5	4	3	2	1

do the same with
the tens and hundreds. place the result of each
Separately in the same order as the figures of the xplyer —
the Same as the result from xplying would be

$$6 \quad \frac{6\ 2\ 5}{=\ 5} \text{ per}$$
$$\frac{}{6\ 2\ 5} \text{ hundred}$$

Supose we wished to Xply 555. by 125. or vis versa.

$$5\ 5\ 5\ .\ 0\ \times\ by\ 1\ 2\ 5.\quad (\text{for } 2 \times by. \ 555 \times 8 = 4440\ )\text{tens}$$
$$\underline{2\ 7\ 7\ 5} \leftarrow$$

Subtracted from 5550 = 1110 place

2 7 7 5 = unit place

1, = 9 diff. 555 × 9 = 4995 from

1 1 1 0 = tens place

5550 = 555 = place of hundreds

5 5 5 = Hundreds place

| 6 9 3 7 5 |

lett us make 555 the Xplyer.
as the three places have the same figure
we have only to find the amount of the right hand figure

$$1\ 2\ 5\ .\ 0\ \times\ by\ 5\quad (125 \times by\ 5 = 625. \text{ Sub'trd from } 125.0\ )$$
$$\underline{6\ 2\ 5}$$

6 2 5 = unit place figure 5

6 2 5 = place of tens

6 2 5 = place of hundreds

| 6 9 3 7 5 |

5550		1250	
2775		625	
2775	3 .	625	4 .
1110	3 ..	625	4 ..
555	6 ..	625	4 ...

Total no of this man of figures.
is 138 as allready shown and 6 is the preemit figure
× by diff 4 = 552 Subtract from 138.0 = •828,
which = 1.828. this year is one of the prophetic years.
the unit of which is $\frac{1}{3}$ in the Colum of mines
the nearest prime = 1801, U. × by + = 1828 (U 20)
observe the letter of the primes are allways Couuted
by the equivaland greek letter, unical unless
marked as 9001 = K̈ ? that means Alphabetcaly
K = 10. and not 1. this man is worth studing.

95

Mathematical Rules.

- are the basis of Ancient Inspired Writing.
and it Counter rule of Revelation, (2 inches)
" Lessons from the Stones of Knowledge.
on which Can be read all the Arts, Sciences.
and the Secrets of the Earth, and the aspects
of the Heavens. with the rules of Inspiration.
and Revelations " the following are the Lessons

□, The Square root, — the Sum of any No x fied by itself
◇, The Tetragrammaton — as words of many meaning
✛, The Columns of Nines. and the Primes, 1000 words.
✕, The Unit of multiplication, and the three Genders
☉ ☽ ✳, The Great triad, — Astronomical Chronology.
= The Perpetual triads of Generation ⇄
☉ Dominical day — Corresponding day of the week. and date.
☽ Epacts, — Age of the Moon on the 1st of every month.
✳ Indiction, or aspects of Certain Stars — .
  Or the true place of Sun and Moon and Stars.
( ) Eclipses of Sun and Moon, in every year —
There are tables accompany these rules for the most —
part, Shewing the answers to questions at sight
the rules to read these tables, are simple and easy.
  The Hieroglyphics and their numerical value &c
  The Greek Alphabet. and its origin, Fac simile.
a Facsimile. of the Allegorical man. and No —
and many other things. Translated into English
by Prof. H. Φ. Σ. (Free Lecture to Students)

"Polytheism, and Monotheism."
Belief in many gods, — Belief in one god only.
The Common theory among the Druids was the first
that is, each World had different gods, the Earth also
had a plurality but only one that governed,
there was a Small number of Monotheists as
it would appear, — then came the Kristians,
who reduced the gods to three — after this the
Mohametans, who reduced the three into one.
the Druids in all maters of theory or faith were free
but in maters of facts, and Covenant, had to
abide by the word, unless such word was in
the garb of inspiration, in such case there were
learned men set apart to interpret such words.
in maters of dress when in public gathering also
it was the Custom to follow the ancient Custom
that each order Should wear their respective Colours
The Bards, Blue — The Ovetes, Green — The
Druids, White — The Hereditary Order, a dress
Striped with red, or golden chains, the first
three order were under one head Arch Druid.
the last order were independant, or equal with
the three orders, Subject always to their Covenant.
this order went under different names among the
different tribes, in Gaul, — Dumaruiz (or
Dumarize) meaning God of the Sea (of uz) Atlantic.
in Britain — Gods of Teman, or Toltecs — Fairies.
also Nereides or Nergels — (Guids to Heaven)

97

among the Kimri, "Aurdorchopian", — weavers of the golden chains. — Coranites — and Giants. When the great "Schism" broke out among the Druids because of Human sacrifices — the nonconformists formed a new order under "H∧I" the lost god of Teman, so called and their dress was ordered to be black in public hence they recived the name of "Kris'dian" + Black gown or shirts) from this word is derived the word Christian, this name is given to this last or 5th order of the Druids, on the records — long before christ was born! those of the Schism. were not organized into an order untill about the Middle of the Century before Christ or A.D. and the first head of this order was "Heli" (H∧I) and the first Public lecture or sermon he preached are on the stones of the records. I have taken the trouble to translate this most remarcable speech, as it throws light on some unsuspected conection between the order. and the Druids, — one thing requires explanation I had the option of taking a facsimile of the speech, without translating it! or explaining it or to translate it there and then without taking the Facsimile, I choose to do the later — the task was a difficult one without reference, under different circumstances I might have done beter, The translation is as follows →

"The first Christian Sermon"
on record, is that of Heli (HЛI) the founder
of the order, and father of the Crucified Jesus.

Honored Fathers (Druids)
Brothers, and Sisters, in the everlasting Covenant,
Friends, and fellow countrymen, now
assembled on this Holy ground, Listen,
that you may hear and understand, the grave
mater which we have to investigate this day.
it is of great importance to the Present generation
and Many generation yet un born. —
you call me Heli (HЛI) Son of the holy-
one; not because it is my name, but because
J was born on the very day the Sea overwhelmed the Sacred land of Teman, the
ancient home of the Giants, the Fairy land;
the inheritence of the Nergals, the Celestial-
hundred. — Where is it today? echo, answers
where! Can you see from where the gods of
Teman came, ? yonder, ! where the Sun beam
kisses the Sporting weaves of the green-blue sea.
where the morning light drives away the dark
-Shaddows of the night. Many of you have
seen that Holy land, and its wonderful —
records, and the Matchless Oracle; are they
all last and gone? the echo, answers gone!
Many of you remember the Royal feast of HᴧEN
(Holy — Helen)

The Mountains of Gold, and Silver, and precious-
Stones, and the incomparable Cycles of times
and relics of the past, and the Mirac of the future-
are they all lost and gone? the echo answers gone
Where are the Giants, and the Lords of Teman.
have they been Scattered? again the echo repeats, "Scattered" of all the Royal Standards
of the Nefals, one only remains with you
the "Ensign" of the House of the Royal Helem.
on that flag the Lion and the Lamb lie down
together under the Shadow of the Sacred Mount-
(⊕) on top of the Mount are the Holy well and Secret Circle
and the Royal Table, on which the Noblest in
the land have considered it an honour to dine
on the Side of the mountain facing the land of
Teman, is that Mysterious Shadowy Signet,
the broken ring of Guidno (ᒋᒉᐳ8) how
Came it there? the wisest of the fathers (Druids)
Cannot tell, the bravest among you dare not
pray into the Secret, and why? because you
Know that out of the frowning Cloud, the thun-
der-bolt of Jove (ᔑᔑᐯ) would strike you
dead, for you belive in the Immortal Gods.
and you also Know that Mortals are watching.
you are assembled here to day, to offer human
Sacrifice! to the Immortals, a National Sacrifice!
allthough the wisest among you bewail your
Cruel Superstition; where is your victim?

have you one, the Law has condemned, No! have you one, that freely offers himself, No! you are going to cast a ballot, for a victim unless he can find a substitute! you will not inquire as to the means employed Brute force — fraud — Cuning devise to entrap the unweary. or whither he has a wife and Children. or a widowed mother, depending on him, for their bread, what maters it to you, as long as you can secure a victim, to your eternal Shame I say it! —— Mark well what I say, the immortal gods. never demanded Such a Sacrifice of you, nither of your fathers, there is no Such demand in the Everlasting Cavenant, there is however a camandment that the inocent must not suffer at your hands! you refused the Counsell of wise men, and disregarded the waring of the great Oracle of Leman. Not to Shed inocent blood! you have passed a law that you may Select a victim by ballot, because you no longer fear an appeal to the Swords of destiny, because they have been swollawed up by the Sea, the ballot fell on one of the Fathers (Druids) he was too noble to Seek a Substitute, and he was Sacrificed! what was your reward? —

were the jimmortals pleased? the reward
you received was a Curse, to be deprived
forever from again entering sweet Azatlan!
Never again to behold the Cradle of the Gods.
or to Listen to the voice of the oracle!
Nor again be permitted to read the Stones of the
recordes, of knowledge, of Arts, and Sciences.
you expected the favour of the Gods, because
you murdered an inocent man! fools,
Curb your impatience, I have not yet done
Speaking, you may reply. in due time.
I have suffered because of the ungest laws
you have enacted. I shall make known
to you this day. the terars that is about to
overtake you. — The flood came on the
Land of Zeman, while my Mother (the Holy Elena)
was in labour to give me birth, Guidno.
of Garn-gur, the keeper of the Temple. was
the last man to leave after clasing the gates—
on finding my Mother in the Temple, the Giant,
tooke her in his arms, and carried her to the top
of the Sarn (Sarn Batrik) the Sea was dashing
over it allready— there were many miles to travel
before a place of safty could be reached, there
the water was rising every moment. what did he
do? what would you do? offer two victims that
you may be saved! Some of you would have done that.

but "Gwidno" was difficultly made, if (said he,) it is possible to save her, I shall do all that a mortal man can do,—Shade of my fathers, aid me,— he took long steps, he ran, he flew as if an the wings of the wind. the sea rising at every step, he staped to recover his breath, the sea was up to his waist, the peril was great. the shore allthorughh in sight was yet a long way off. between him and the shore he beheld a large tree an the Casway (Sam) he shifted his load an his back telling her to hald fast to him that he might have his arms free to swim, "The gods will not permit the "Haly—ane." to perish," Gwidno was a mighty Giant, in the flesh and in the Spirit, yet the task before him was great, when he could stand no longer he swam as but few men an earth could have done, he gaind the floating tree, at last and an it floated saftly to land, at the Stone (of gimbilh) there he faund shelter, an a bed of Ferns an grass he placed his burden, and lighted a fire to keep away the snakes, and wild animals that were numerous there. "Then he prayed" "Great and Glorious Sun, bauntiful giver of Life. heat, and Light, thou hast this day witnessed, the destruction, of Teman and the overwhelming of the Temple of the ancient stone)

and the dispersion of the highest, the Royal—
Nergals,—Let my word float swiftly with
the beams of thy countenance, to inform
our kindred, scattered through the wilderness, or tossed about on the restless ocean.
that the "Holy-one" is Safe, and her new-
born babe on her breast is sleeping "—
All this land was then a wilderness, without
any inhabitents—the next day was monday.
and my stake was planted under the Covenant
(Nergal) and the following day that of my Mother.
and lastly of Guidno,—thus this land—
became ours by premption and ocupation.
Now the heroic Guidno, has been gathered
to his kindred, and my Mother to Holy Azatlan
and I am left the sole Survivor, by their
will, and my own right I hold possession.
is there any one present, that calls in question
my right, or has any one a prior claim to this
Land, if there is, let the Fathers (Druids) decide
between us, or if you would appeal to the
Sword, So let it be, until such trial is had
my claim holds good. And I am Lord of
the three hundred! as such I forbid you
the use of this holy mount to Sacrify inocent
blood,—your claim that because this is a holy
ground, you have the right under the Covenant
to follow the precedence of your forfathers!

on this point you have some appearance of truth on your side, hence justice demands of me a careful investigation, fortunatly we have the means, to arive at the facts, in the record of the Sacrifices. carfuly kept by the Fathers (Druids) they are here today as witnesses, these records cannot be falsified. The first on the record was a Monster. Leprous, Loathsome, Bloodthirsty — whose very touch or breath was death. he boasted of having destroyed whole Tribes every day a fresh virgin had to be given to him as a Sacrifice. to his lust, your forefathers to save the nation, were forced to Sacrifice this Monster, and this act was aproved of by the gods. and the people were Saved! — There was another Calling himself a King, an usurper of power. who atempted to enslave the nation, by abolishing the righteous Law of the land. and Substituting unequal Laws, by levying war, and murder for the Sake of Conquest and Spoile this Tyrant your forefathers also Sacrificed. and received the aprobation of the Immortal. not because the Immortals wanted such Sacrifice, but because by it, the nation preserved their freedom, and trampled on Tyrany.

These were not innocent victims, on the contrary they deserved their fate. The first inocent victim on the records, has attached
to it, a protest, by the officiating Priest (Enurk
wherein he declares "that to sacrify the inocent
be it man, woman, or child, is an insult
to the gods, and contray to the Covenant.
Natwithstanding that, a law has been passed
recently, to Legalize, this inhumanity,
under the fals, and blasspamous pretence
that it is pleasing to the Gods, that one should
die for the sins of many! the gods are
nat monsters, Sacrifice is not for them,
it is nat this kind of Sacrifice that turns
away their wrath, because of disobidience
but a true Repentance, and a resolve not
to repeat Such offence in the future —
we are told, we have no chaise in the mater
we are nat the Law-maker, all we have to do
is to obey the law, as it is, and the Covenant!
to interpret the Signs and the omens!
and in defalt, to be excaminicated, and
became outlaws. to be Shuned by our fellaws".
It is true, no punishment is Recorded for
this Sacrifice of an inocent man, Nither
is there of any favour or aproval by the ginmaster
Many of the fathers, have refused to attend these
kind of Sacrifices, which was a mute Protest.

106

And thereby greatly offended some of you!
Who claim that under the Covenant they were
bound to attend "all sacrifices both public
and privat" have you yet to learn, that some
times a different meaning is given to the words
of the Covenant, When such a dispute takes
place, there is a Law (Rule) and Learned men
appointed to settle these Contentions, were
you made judges? even had your fathers
fellen as low in superstition as yourselfs.
and committed such crime against humanity
that would be no reason that you should do the same
but fortunatly, the records excharrorates them
for had they done it — it would have been recorded.
the Sacrifices at first. was nothing more than the
mode of punishing the wicket, law breakers.
the Druids agreed to perform this office, not
because such Sacrifices were necessary, but
rather that it gave them the oppartunity to save
the inocent. — the only Sacrifice the Covenant
demands of you, is that of your own lust,
and superstitious cruelty. — One night.
not long ago, I stood within the Sacred-
Circle, to Commune with the Shads of my fathers,
I heard a whishbring among the Stones,
as most of you have done, at one time or another.
as if one Stone answerd an other, these sounds
have allways been Considered as a warning!

To either the individual or the Nation.
hence arose the custom, of atonment for
any misdeeds committed, in the passed —
the same must be confessed, and a resolve
made to refrain from repeating the same in future
thus the Sacrifice had Some merit, reason
and humanity in it. which you have perverted
you have been warned by the Great Oracle.
that when a Son of the Gods Should offer
himself as a Sacrifice, no inferior Sacrifice
would ever afterwards be acceptable to the Gods.
To day I am the only "Royal Teman" among
you; and the only one uniting the passt
and the present under the Covenant —
In offering myself as a last Sacrifice
a Stop will be put forever, on Selecting
your victims by ballot, thanks to the Law
which you have enacted, I have a right thus
to offer myself, if you had the right to pass such law
I shall do this to Save you from yourselfs
not to Save you from punishment for what you have
done, — I understood the whishbering of the Stones
the Confabulation was Concerning a Nation,
Translated, it ment — " Morally they are Cowards
Superstitious, Cruel, Crafty, neglecting
Knowledge, and the Cultivation of the Arts,
and Sciences, and Harmony among men
notwithstanding they have plenty of wise men —

willing to teach them. Therefore, they shall go to Purgatory, untill they have had a new heart, and an obedient mind, they shall dwell in moral darkness, untill a new plant shall grow into the light. a new religion, shall come to them honeyd words, which thy shall drink, untill moraly intoxicated, and raveing moral drunkards, slaves that dare not call their soſs their own, when this moral degradetian is compleat, and their physical bandage well established, when they have forgotten the line of their succession, and shall not recognise their own kindred, or the land of their inheritence when they shall be surfited with blood. and be sick into death with spiritual — vomit, when their hearts shall be filled with fear, and their hair shall stand an end with superstitious terror, of their boasted manhood not a vestage will be left. and mystery shall surround the virtue of their mothers, and their sisters maidenhoord will be tainted with lust, they shall dream af devils, and snakes, and the taments of the damned, of bottomless pits and firy — furnesses, they shall be came creeping fanuses hypocrites, and Liars, thy shall hear of heaven but shall not enjoy it, they shall look far it

among the Stars, there, they shall not find it.
they Shall toile untill their bones are aching.
to build golden Mansions to the mother of Harlots
and be thankful for the <u>Crums</u> and the <u>Curses</u>!
they shall be promished a Glorious reward
in the great here after.! they shall ernestly
pray for deliverance — and rest even in an
eternal oblivion! yet their food shall be blood
and "Spiritual Pap" they shall sink to the
Lowest hell. untill their penance is Completed
in that wonderous day, ere the last seed
of the Holy-one, is gone from them forever.
ere the last grain of hope is fled, and the last
remnant of their ancient faith has vanished
and the day has closed in total darkness.
which will debar them from reclaiming
the ancient inheritence of their fore fathers.
ere they are uterly lost! one of the Sons of
the Lords of Teman, will remember them
and shall gather the Sons of the ocean together.
and cause the Nergal-Trumped to be Sounded
and then the Land of Teman and its great Temple
Shall be seen rising from the Sea: and fear
and trembling, Shall take possession of the Harlot
and the kings of the earth. who have feasted with
her in high Places, and partook of her fornication!
Shall pass away as the mist of the morning. —
and a New Song as it were will be Sung in Teman.

A Relic of 325,[AD] from the Nicein Council
Purporting to be a fragment of one of
the regreeted gospels (325[AD])
written on vellum in greek letters
Recording the Life of the San of
HʌI, before and after his
Crusification, Cantaining
the Key of jnspiration
and Rules of Revelation.

ѴσκєѴ Ѕєѡ – єѴѡо єФ ɧ єχєꞁ Ѕєєѡ –
єєχєѡ – оѵɧѴ ɧ ꞁаꞁ HꞁI а ꞁѵꞁ.......
καꞁφаꞁѵα – єѴ ꞁꞁѵκѵоꞁ єѴꞁꞁɧꞁѵоꞁ
кѵμꞁѵ ГѡєѴꞁ.

Usken dew enw,o ev î cheî diw îch îw-
ouên î dad Heli, a dyn – Kalvaria,
en thruchiol en nghengor Kimri Gwent.
——— Literal English Translation ———
Sword of the Lord, is his name, the highest —
God into you, — Lamb of the father Heli, and
the Man of Calvary — Present at the Council
of Kimri Gwent.

Kimri Gwent. means the Sulerians, (Tribe)
among whome Christanity was first established

ΙΧΘΥΣ

Ιꞁοѵꞁ, Χꞁѵоτоꞁ. ΘЄоѵ. ꞁѵоꞁ. ΣѡΤꞁꞁ.
jesus, Christ,   God, San, Savians.
the word ΙΧΘΥΣ (jchthus) means Fish (⊬)

The facsimile represents but a small fragment but the edges form hieroglyphics, the key stave of which is the cross an top (+) = numerical value downwards is, 9, 5, 18, 3, 17, 9, 18, 8, 9 (greek letters) = (jes–gristhi) (+left) 12, 1, 2, 4, 9, 24, 7, 11, 9. mab diw êli) I ES–ΥΣ₁ΟΘΙ–MAB Siw HΛ)
The language is the ancient Kimrik, (not greek) "Jesus, of the black frock (cross–shirt) son of the god Heli"
The relic appears as the top of a raged mountain, on which are shown "Six" paths, and "six" resting–places, or stones, "jes–gristhi" = ~~xxxxxx~~
9 5 9 – 3 8 9 9 8 9 = the unit = "Six," mab–êli = "Six", hence John in Revelation, says the number was Six hundred, three score or sixty, and six
6 0 0:
6 0:
6
by adding up the Sum we have four places 6 6 0 6
the third figure 6 is left out, as the word "diw" (god) is left out in mab–(diw) êli. the right hand figure of diw = 24 = 6, and when it takes its place then will the Judgment Sit, and the Beast will disappear–
This remarkable piece of vellum, was pasted on another piece a little larger of Parchment, on which was a Latin inscription to the following efect–
1st that the fragment of vellum was a part of one of the rejected gospels of the Niecein Council presented by a Learned Native of Britain –
2nd that it was rejected, first because it represented the Lord, as taking part in the Mysteries of the Druids or anti christian rights and Ceremonies.

2nd because purporting, to describe his words and actions, for fifty-eight years, after his Crusification! 3rdly that the Lord did not die on the cross, but gave up the Ghost, for a time, in a trance, by reason of the elexirs of life, given him to drink by the diciples of his father, which causes a trance for two or three days, which teachings are unprofitable to Christians. The Learned person who had wrote this Gospel! and which was rejected by the Niceïn Council. Cut up the parchment, into small Pieces, and distributed them among those that were favorable to the side he had taken in the Council. and delivered a most remarcable speach, the following is the concluding sentances —

"There were christians, long before Christ was conceived in the womb of the Virgin. before he was named Jesus; long before his father Heli (HΛΙ) in the womb of the holy Elen (HΛEN) was rescued from the flood, that overwhelmed the Lords' inheritance, the Temple & the Oracle. Long before Heli's father, the most famous of all the Romans, was cut out of his mother's womb.! — This day from the womb of time Twins have been born, Ar. and Ath (AΣ AΘ) this great Council sacrificed the first, because he spake the Truth, by inspiration, which to the council was a mystery, a thing of darkness!

And Revelation a quantity unknown!
deliberatly they have set up a dream, that
was concived in darkness, Night vision,
of things = fantoms, from the depth of ignorance.
they call this "Light" and the tale but half told, a
fact: the whole truth was too much to carry!
the Light of the fathers (Druids) they shuned, it
was not red enough for them, and their creed is
to reduce men to the level of the beast, that Perish.
We protest, against this alter of ignorance, they
have set up, and the mutalation of the Truth,
that pandering to Superstition, and hypocrisy.
as did the first "Kristians" against, the Cruelty
and inhumanity of sacrifising inocent men.
the darkness then was great, but not greater,
than what we have witnessed this day, because
of this darkness, we have, devided between us
" this rejected Truth" that we may preserv it while
we live, and afterward by our children. untill
the Judgment day. as a witness that the Truth
was once delivered to the Church! and that
we may not be charged with a breach of the
ancient Covenant. with the Nezpals, or suffer
the penalties. that are sure to fall on the tribe of Ath.
The moral fabrick this day erected, in due time will
fall into ruins, and men will marvel. when the
foundation are laid bare, and the moral nightmare
has fled. and Light shall shine as at the begining.

114

The treble Genealogy of Moovs.

For the three lists, See Manuscript "M. H."

One of the rejected gospels of the N. C of 325[rd AD]
one according to Mathew, and one according to Luke.
the first is of British origin, the other two are supposed
to be of Jewish origin, totaly different are the three,
the 1st from Jésous, to Kunóbelin, 54 Generation
with an appendix of 19 from Abraham to Adam.
Mathew gives 41 Generation Abraham to Jesus.
Luke gives 55 Generation from Jesus to Abraham.
and 21 additional from Thara to God (in all 76)
Mathew says from Abraham, to David 14 generation
from David to Jechonias. 14 Gen. from Jechonias,
(or the carring away into Babylon to Jesus 14 generation
the last fourteen however only contains 13 Generation!
there is a difference of fourteen generations between —
mathew and Luke from Abraham. ! are they inspired.
are real genealogies. ? if not what are they?
now in the ancient British Language, I believe we
we may find the "Key" the word ap, or ab, from or San.
Jés-ous, 'Bêli-Môr, Man-hogan, Kavoir.
1 Jesus-óus, San of Eli (Sea) Place. Virgin was found
or in Common Language of to-day. Jesus was the San
of "Heli" of the sea begoten of the Virgin Mary (Vair)
Luke also Says that Jesus was the San of "Heli"!
all are written in the Common Druidical (greek)
letters, but the Language apparently is not greek—
the Key will be found in the perpetual Triad (generation)

Observe Mathew counts the Generation from Abraham ↑ up to Jesus; while Luke counts ↓ downwards from Jesus to Abraham In the perpetual triad, in counting upwards ↑ and downward ↓ the rule is different although the triads are consecutively but in the ↓, when the middle figure is a cypher, it may be a 9 going ↑ as 503=↑=855. and 593=855. hence this is called the Branch, because the product ↓ of these triads separate here 503↓ = 425. but the product of 593↓ = 716. Now if this branch is to be counted we can easily conceive the reason of Luke giving fourteen generation more than Mathew because Luke counted downwards ↓ and Mathew ↑ again we may see also, the reason of the last 14 has only 13 in reality, if we carfuly examin — "the original name "ΠΟΟΥΣ" or Jês-o-us. meaning Jês (the name) o = from, us = place = us or uz (Armaic) = u th (Kimerik) Atlantic — it also seems to be an abriviation "Enis" (Island) and may be translated, Jês, of the island of the At- lantis. the place that Job dwelled in (uz) or one of the British Isles. (Zemom dauntless) the alphabetical number of the name is 9, 7, 18. or by the rule of the signs of Possession 9′ 7′ 9′. Country ↓ 1 6 2 - 8 6 5 - 5 1 2 - 8 2 4 - 6 5 6 - 4 1 1 - 9 1 3 — 7 3 8 - 2 1 4 - 6 4 1 - 9 4 2 - 8 5 5 - 5 0 3 - 4 2 5. 5 9 3 - 7 1 6.

now if we add the branch No 503 to Name 9 7 9

$$503$$

and ÷ the 4 into unequal figures $3^+1=4$ ⌐ 1 4 8 2

thus 1 3⁺1 8 2 change 1 to right, (3⁺1 8 2 1 ← Abram.

by reading as the Hebrews do from right to left.

we have Abram (Abraham) these generations

are simply a figurative generation, to be read

as g'inspired words, by Revelation, to pretend

to belive that these different Genealogies, here given,

are the true linage, Could be nothing short of

Hypocrisy, to belive it to be so, would be positive

proof that there was a loas screw somewhere!

these genealogies as an inspired writing, in my

estimation, are a thousand time more valuable

than as a genealogy, even if they were true.!

it is not necessary, because evry one on earth

carries within himself, or herself, the proof,

the self evident truths, of what stock they are,

if the learned men of any day cannot read the

signs, if that branch of science is unknown to

them, that is no proof that there is no such Knowledge.

if any of them do Know it, but are afraid to re-

veal the fact, because it may interfere with a

pet theory, of their Constituents, or flocks, by whome

they get their dayly Crust, and oleamargrin !

we can only pitty them, we can afford to admit

the fact, because, we are not under the political whip,

or the Ecclesiastic (Ecclesia—Stic) church Shillilah

we don't pray for Rain—but trust in irrigation.

	Branch *	a Branch may start from any 0 or 9 when a central third 3658509 at head ideal.		Prime Twin 593 of 503	Branch of the Twin B
* 503			593		
725			716		
565			466		
* 509	599		418		
185	176		283		
523	424		704		
743	652		637		
763	861		303		
781	962		723		
979	873		745		
162	701	791	583		
865	904	988	707		
512	369	261	367		
824	147	956	327		
656	307	414	381		
411	363	643	975		
913	777	762	522		
738	340	871	833		
214	129	971	755		
641	109	972	502	592	
942	181	882	815	806	
855	973	800	557	458	
* 503	702	(Branch of the Branch)	320	229	
725	817			110	
565	377				
509	336				
Prime	480				

The roat of the mater

The No 503 and 593 = ↑ are Called the Twins because ↑ upwards both Produce the same 855. but ↓ downwards are entirely different, yet all the roats, will all end in the product of the Twins. The roats are supposed to end when the right hand figure becames a cypher and to Branch out when a cypher is the figure placed in the middle or 9 which is its Twin

Starting from 503 ↓↑ up or down, the cycle = 22 generation from 503 to 979. is 14 generation, ↑ and and from 725 ↓ 9 gen. ↑↓ means opposite direction ↑ ·ᵘⁿᵗ · ·² = (unt) & ← figure of Parent figure

"These triads are termed *inspired writing!*
hence to understand them we must use the
rule of inspiration, for example $725 - 565$
standing between (*503 & 509) which $= \acute{E}\,\Upsilon\,\acute{E} - \grave{E}\,\zeta\,\grave{E}$.
or Heli and (g) $e\,z\,e$, the father and the son.
× ply the No by the unit, seek the nearest prime.
$425 \times 5 = 3625 = \frac{7}{2} =$ nearest prime $3601 = D$?
$565 \times 7 = 3955 = \frac{4}{9} =$ nearest prime $3871 = Dm.$
$949 \times 7 = 7253 = \frac{8}{5} = N$ " " " $7201 = Th$?
when the letter has a comma after it, add a cypher
to the unit as × by + add the fraction if any —
to find the original number; the sound of the letter
or words are as in the corresponding letter in
the Greek alphabet, but the meaning of the sound
as in the ancient kimrik. D? $= \Delta$? as De (God)
Th? $= \Theta$? as The (his god) Dm (Mother) the Triad
Father, Son and the Holy mother (ghost)
observe the Mother (565) the sign of possession
is all of the first order, and the Father (725)
has the 1st & last of the 1st order and the middle of 2d order.
the Son (949) has 1st & 2d of 1st order & last of 2d order.
and the order shall govern the subsiquent products,
from these perpetual triads are formed also
the famous "Genealogical Tree" (Tree of life)
as if) was the trunk, from 509 to 503 no branch.
or root except at 503. this No is a Femenine or — as
the upright I are the complement, read on the square
"MЄ$\zeta\,\iota$" we cannot fail to recognise the family. 503

"Ancient Egyptain Records"

See facsimile of the first Seven lines of the
Tablet of four hundred years (Rameses II)
the time of the j'sralites in Egypt &c.
and Translation (manuscript X̄ H.) &cc.
" The living Horus, the living Sun, the pow-
-erfull Bull beloved of Ma, Lord of the
Festival of the thirty years like his father
Ptah, King of upper and Lower Egypt,
Ra-user-Ma Sateb-en-ra, Son of
Ra, Rameses Mer-amen, giver of life.

The above is a facsimile of the first line of the seven
as to the translation, j'have given it as j'found it.
observe the first and last Charecter are the same
= ✠ meaning life or living. it is the same sign as
✚ or plus of the Druidical Hieroglyphics = to 1 &
joined together or 90. those Charecters ⟚ are also
= to ⟚ 90/30 (festivals of thirty years) which was
also kept by the Nergals, or the Gods of Teman.
"Rameses-Mer-amen." = ⌣ ⌒⌒⌒ ⌒ ⌣ ⌣
is also found on the Stones of records, as above.
as of the Hereditary order (Nergals) the Pharoahs
or kings of Egypt were of a different race to the

Egyptians undoubtedly, and I am convinced that the Nergals had first taken possession of Egypt, hence it was called "the land of Kem", or "Kem·i" which appears to be the same as "Kem·ri" first inhabitants, this particular Pharaoh, lived at the begining of the thirty third Century of the triad ☉ D ✱ or fifteen hundred years before A.D. the Tablet says in the fourth hundred years, and the fourth day of the month "Mesori" which is the last or 12th month of the Egyptain year, which begins August 20th of the Julian year. (that is 4m & 3d erlier than the Julian) the no 4 which was the peculier distinguishing number of the Nergals, appears here my add 400 years — 4th day of the month (3×4=12) which is 4m erlier than the ☉ D ✱ (Julian) = mesori = 12.5.18.15.17.9 = 40 the name of the month is = 40. unit of which = 4.

"The word Amen"

is also very Curious, we can understand why it was used in Egypt, but why christians do, so profusly, is more than I can Comprehend. "Mes-Amen" had been dead long before the first christian, protested against Corruption! most likely I will be told that the meaning of the "Amen" is, "So be it" (in greek) odd is it not that the Jews should end their accounts with this greek word, with only two exception, "the Acts" and one epistle of John, it may turn out that the word is written by Inspiration let us see!

121

As allreedy explained the ancient Christians were in Covenant with the order of the Neyals, whose home or place of records was "Teman" there are several ways of spelling this word, such as TRHAꞀ, — TEHAꞀ, — TEHAꞀ, in all the unit is the same = 5. while that of Rameses. ad Amen, = 4, Now these figures or units are the two Complementary, singly both are imperfect, but when multiplyed together the product is perfect. this name Teman-House-Stone or Rock — from the wonderfull Stone Temple, "on this Rock j'll build My Church" the word Church comes from "Kirk (Kerik — Stones) the word Petra (Peter) also means Stone or Rock, when translated. write the word "Amen" in greek letters AMEN.

number. the letters alphabeticaly = 1, 12, 5, 13.

$$\begin{array}{r} 1,12,5,13 \\ \times\ \ \ \ 5 \\ \hline \end{array}$$

the unit is 4, ×ply by the Complement 5. = 5 6 2 5 6 5

$$\begin{array}{r} \times\ \ \ \ 3 \\ \hline \end{array}$$

× product by the right hand figure 3 = 1 6 8 7 6 9 5

mark the periods from the right 1 2 3.

then read the balance from the Left.

reduce the 1st sum to units

thus ∴ ∵ ∶ = Jêz (Jesus)

	1,12,5,13	1·12		1-1
	1·3 {5¯ 4	1·3		1·456
		336		
		112		

∵ ´´ ´ = Krêze — 4 5 6 4 = Deon (Christians)

the alphabetical sum of Amen is 1, 12, 5, 1 3 add the inside numbers. 1 2 5 1 = 9. or triad 1, 9, 3.

Amen, then is an inspired word, requiring Revelation which j have shewn = Jêz — Krêze — Deon. or in English Transleteran = Jesus — gann Black (Christian)

Professor. H Φ Σ.

To the Students of the Stores of Knowledge.
Ladies, and Gentlemen, of whatever age, or
Condition, Kindred, or faith. I Congratulatte
you, because, you are now on the Road to <u>Truth.</u>
if you Continue untill you have Learned all the
Necessarily Lessons, and are Suplied with
a facsimile of these wonderfull ancient records
you will be enabled to read them for your-
Selfs, and to understand what you do read,
without paying a high price for their interpretation.
Like the Axioms in Uclid, they contain Self-
evident truths, requiring no demonstration !
that will not leave the Student in doubt !!
you Shall "Know," the Truth as it is, or was, and
not as fads, and hobbies, and Superstition,
would have it to be, and demagogs say it is.
these ancient records, were written by larned
men Set apart for the Sole purpose of recording
facts only, So that the Same could be read
by future generations, exact as it was written.
to preserve this discovered Truth, from <u>its enemies</u>
certain principal words were written by them
Clothed in Allyay or "Inspired." by divers rules.
hence the Rules of "Revelation" must be used,
this Inspiration & Revelation, Must be <u>learned</u>
by the Student, My work is to help or teach, how
you may Learn, you have the oppertunity.

123

"You're fortunate, that your time coincides with the "time of the end" that is to say, the end of a certain Covenant namely 1893 AD until that year (6606) these Lessons Could not be translated, the Guardians or witnesses of these ancient records, having Apointed me to translate these Lessons or rules, and approved of the same, they are now at the services of any one that will have the necessary qualifications, namely "must be able to read write and cypher, as far as fractions, — and must promish not to teach any of these Lessons, to any other person untill they have understood the Lesson thoroughly unless they know such persons to be Students of these Lessons in Connection with the stones of Knowledge When the requisite numbers of Students. Shall be able to read these records, the stones will be photographed, and a facsimile, will be produced, (on a smaller scale) and in book form Coresponding to the number of Students. a certain number of coppies will be given free. and the balance sold to Students only (at Cost price) I mention this that you may not be disapointed we Concider that these advantages are suficient therefore my Instructions are. not to use any persuation, moraly, or otherwise, to induce, or argument, or debate, either for or against, this, or any other Systems or rules, but to confine myself to facts only; J'am concious, that the Rules. or Lessons, might have been arranged in better form. and abriviated Same, but J have done the best J could in the time at my disposal; and rest satisfied, that the result will proove Satisfactorly. J Shall now make same remarks an each, of these rules, in order Simply for reference, for each are realy independant, yet all are necessary to a tharaugh understanding of these records and either Lessan will repay the Student if he never advances any further than the ane Lessan

"Astranamical Lessons".

The purpose of these Lessons are for Astranamical observation. and Chranalagical exactness, of Times. The Great triad. ⊙☽✶. Commanly knawn as the Julian Period, for particulars see "Memoranda". 2.

"Daminical Day"

or the day of the week Caresponding to any date in the Passed. Present ar future, See Memoranda 16 (right side)

"The Epact"

or the age of the moon an the 1st of any manthe. Do 16

"The Haroscape ar the Aspects"

See Memoranda 17. this is a perpetual Haroscape.

"Eclipses of the Sun and Moon"

See Table. (   ) all Eclipses are shawn for abaut 600 years after that they must be redated. the time is mean time. So also is the Epact (never varies more than ane day)

"The Four Quarters"

Shewes the relative position of the principal stars
the Milky way, — the line of the Ecliptic, and signs
or names of of the Constellations, under the North *
is Shewn the Nexpal Hieroglyphic, ⟩ ⟵ ⟨ ∿
    This is the "Key" to the secret writings, — with the
help of these quarters, any one that has never learned
the first thing about Astronomy, can soon pick up
a fair Knowledge, of the position and names of
Constellations, More particularly by the aid of the
perpetual Horoscope, and the other Lessons ——
These lessons, (except the first) require very
little arithmetical Knowledge, the Calcul-
ations being allready made, — there are three
other Lessons Called Auxillary, for the Nodes,
and declination, and place of the planets.
but these are not necessary to find Easter,
of the christians, or Passover of the Jews.
or the Vernal festival of the Druids —
all of which ar made by the same Astronomical rule.

"Rules of Inspiration"

The Unit of Multiplication — The Three genders —
The Perpethal Triads — The Tetra-gramaton —
(Callom of Nines fraction — Decimal fraction —
and the Primes and fraction — the last has
about one thousand words, and prime numbers
in several different Langnages, — Revelation
is the reversing of these Inspired rules!

"Numbers and Letters"

Original — Common Greek — English Equivalent Alphabet.
— Negal Hieroglyphics figures and characters —
Scroll writing by the same — Picture writing —
and the Sign of Possession, or diminution
(the Primes and fraction belong to this class —
"there are thus
Six Astronomical Lessons — Six lessons
of inspiration — and Six Writing Lessons.
and also Six other Lessons which will
appear in the facsimile, of the original —
making 24 Lessons in all, a knowledge
of these Lessons will enable any one to read
these most wonderfull records, and translate the same into any Spoken Language that
has a proper allphabet of Fonetic Sounds.
and also re-veal the hidden words of inspiration.
"Allphabetically" = (Examples) "By signs of Possession"

ΙΗΣΟΥΣ. } The word, } jêsous
9,7,18,15,20,18. } Sum of the word. } 9 7 9 6 2 9.

add = 42 } No of the sum } add = 42

Fraction 6/4 } Neuter. Gend.ᵉ } Fraction 6/4

Subtract } 41 } Masgulin Gender } From the } 41
the Gender } 43 } Femenin Gender } Sum } 43

9 7 18 15 20 18. } Shaw the last } 9 7 9 6 2 9
— say — 41 } × Sum a fraction } — say — 41
9 7 18 15 19 77 } or gender — } 9 7 9 5 8 8
4,8,59,05,98,85, . 6/4 { inspired { 48 9 79 40 . 6/4
                       { Sum

Inspired 4897940 . $\frac{6}{4}$ Sum

Containing a name of a famous personage.
1st we find by the dot (•) that it is masculine gender
Therefore we divide the Sum by the unit, vis 5 ÷ by
the quotient = 979588, to which add the $\frac{6}{4}$ + 1 =
vis 41 9,7,9,6,2,9, = "Jésous"

4897930 : $\frac{6}{4}$ this is a feminine sign of the same
Therefore we divide by the difference, the unit being 4
the difference is = 5. the quotient = 979586, to this
we add the $\frac{6}{4}$ + 1 = 43 answer = 9,7,9,6,2,9,
in the Neuter gender we are not to multiply
but may add any single figure to the Sum
any where in the Sum after Subtracting Neuter No.
979629 — 42 = 979587, Say 9759587 $\frac{6}{4}$
here because there is no gender sign, Sum is neuter.
and the unit is the figure added to the Sum vis 5.
the chief object here is to find the interpolation.
in adding to the Neuter Sum, any one figure may be used
but in Multiplying the figure 1 Cannot be used
because it does not Multiply. — Observe
the Sign of Parisian reduces the figures at act $\frac{1}{3}$.
in the alphabetical number. mark off the Single
and double numbers of the Letters by a Comma
when the Letters are required to be translated.
The chief points in the Revelation is the unit,
and the Genders and the Fraction, and to work the
rule as the reverse of the inspiration, ÷ for ×
+ for — or vice versa, in the Rules of the 3 genders

"Unit of Multiplication"

In this Rule the Sum is to be multiplied direct. as shown by the signs. by any single figure (except 1) then to the Xplied sum add the Gender sign. Masculine • 2 2̄ 2̈ 2̇ Feminine ∴ 6 6̄ 9. ⚹ or ∴

Rule. Sign.	or the capital Sign ☉ ⊛ 2 6 &c
1 = X ☉ = •	Examples the word <u>man</u>, = 3̇ 1̇ 4̇
2 = X) = 2	in greek, added to one figure = 8.
3 ‾) X -) = -2	in the Kymric = 7̇ 1̇ 8̇ added = 7.
4 Ẍ X :) = :2	in English-German or French = 1
5 Ẍ X X) = Ẋ2	that is 4̇ 1̇ 5̇. Seek the unit on the Left
6 +) X (+ = 6+	1, is found of the Masculine gender.
7 = X (= 6	to be Xplied ance, 8 is feminine gender
8 = X ☺ = :	also to be Xplied ance, 7 is fem. gender.
{ 9 -) X ☺ = :	Now supose we X each number by 4.
{ 9 +) X ☉ = •	3̇14 × 4 = 1̇ 2̇ 5̇ 6 ∴ that is Inspiration

of the Feminine gender – or the difference
to find the ÷ or we must first find the unit = 5. Diff 4 ÷̇
over the Quatient 3̇14 place the Sign of possession.
7̇ 1̇ 8̇ × 4 = 2̇ 8̇ 7̇ 2̇ 6 here we must ÷ by ½ of the Diff.
we find the unit to be 1, the difference to 9 is 8 (½ = 4)
Again 4̇ 1̇ 5̇ × 4 = 1̇ 6̇ 6̇ 0 • Masculine we ÷ by the unit 4
when the unit of the original Sum is 3. 4. 5. or 6. there
is two opperation if 3 reduce the Sum by subtracting 1.
if 6 add 1 to the Sum, 4 & 5 are reciprocal or Complementary, if unit of Sum be 4. × by 5. if 5 × by 4 the first time
then × the product by any single figure. the unit 9 must be made
either 1 − or 1 + that is the Sum before it is Xtiplied.

"The Tetragrammaton"

See Exhibit A. B to G. of the forming of the ◇ & ✝

These are the principal Rules used in Inspiration
the Perpetual Triads are generaly used with the
Genealogical lists or the Succession of the Centuries
—See the Treble Genealogy, and the Boat of the mates.

The fractions (of 9 or 10)

May be more properly called axcilary, Rules ⁓⁓⁓

"The Primes and fractions"

These are indispensable in translating, much
the same as a Dictionary is at the present day
the full meaning of them Cannot be thoroughly grasped
untill the facsimile of the Stone-records is seen.
nevertheless they will repay the trouble of learning, a
hundred fold, because of the principle on which
they are Constructed. No word in any language
Can be written, that an answer Can't be found
in this List, of about a thousand words. ⁓

Example — Supose the word $\left(\text{I N O U S} \right) = 9.7.18.15.20.18$
there are 10 figures here, as there are no more than five
places in the primes. we must devide the word into Syle-
gês = 9.7.18. we have still 6 figures left. we add the 18
= 9̇, now we have 15209̇, neither of these Sums are in
the Primes, So we must take the nearest Sum (less than it)
for the 9.7.18. — 9631 = K̈y h, { for 15209̇ — 15121̇ = K O R.
fraction $\frac{7}{9}$ { fraction $\frac{8}{9}$ $\frac{8}{9}$

For answer ×ply the word by the ✝ and add the fraction
$107 \times + = 9630 \atop 85$ } = 9.7.18. { $168 \times + = 15120 \atop 89$ } = 15209̇. answer

thus the word resolves itself into "Kê-Kor"
the first is an abriviation Kewri or giants. and
Kor, means a round, or a circle, a choir in a church.
and the fractions are = 88·89, = to ⊖rri (Thrri)
this last word is equal to "The Druid" in the
Rymric = "Kawr Kôr Therith" in plain English
"The Great (one) of the order of the Druids"! :-
it must be born in mind. that these thousand
words. are not the full Dictionary but only
a Small part of the beginning. and allthough
Some words will come out when thus devided,
and others will not, yet the principle is the
main thing to understand. the Lesson will give that.
with a little practice and Patience ——
The numerical value of the words. must be
found by Substituting Greek Letters (equivelants)
and Converting the fractions into plain figures
by the Columns of Nines. that is the Numerator.
is the No of the figures in the Col. Counting from the top.
the Denominator is the No of the Col. Counting from 10.
and the No of each Letter must be X by ✝ (Hieroglyphic)
on the original records, when the facsimile
will be produced. each of the Scribes or
Recorder ataches his Name in full once
at least. and afterwards. some abriviated
form of the Same. j Shall give an example
of Such Signatures from the 1st Century of Anno Dom

"Signature of the first century," here are Six Characters three of them uprights and of the highest order, three also forming the 1st and 2d Syllables. ♪↑ — ♭↑. abbreviated thus ♪↑, or ♪↑↑, or ♪↑, also by twos ✝ ✝ ✝ or thus ✝, ✗, ✗, or ✝ ✗ ✗, that is the Sign of Plus & multiplication Now the Sum of the word added up is 42 = 6, hence the abbreviation will alter the unit as ♪↑ = 9792 $\overset{27}{=}$ 9 = IHΣOΥΣ, or Jesous, this name is also written | ⌒↑ ↑ ♭↑ ↑ or thus | ⌒✝ / ✗ ✝, all of which have a vocal sound this last form are generally in scroll writing. these scroll writing are capable of expressing the direction without altering the meaning of the word

1   2   3   4   5.   Read from the Star ✳
1 is going downwards
2 is going upwards
3 is to the right and 4 to the left, and 5 is double downwards, and to the left. practically this is a Cross here the letters of the first division are not dated but the 2d division has one dot and 3d Dev two dots the Same thing is done with the Sign of harmonum music is also noted in this manner. the scroll being made to follow the tune.— and all manner of things. Mountains Seas rivers plains and valleys men animals Birds and reptiles, or parts of men or animals — mostly the heads ___

Here we have the head of the Eagle of Wen-adocea (Eryri) Starting with the eye! downward, to the left, up, and to the right. ΚΑΣΥΑΣΘΟΥ. Suppose we wish to draw the great "American Eagle" ΑΜΕΣΙΚΑΥ ΗΥΛΕ beginning opposite the eye at the arrow.

then downward, up, and to the left. allegorically the full mean reading, an these Stores of Knowledge there are many allegorical figures which are not a part of the records proper, — far example the Hatching of the great Egg, and the curious Compound that came out of it, to wit

= krissior =

(The treble)
(Product)
(in one)

3̈181̈8̈, 9̈c̈4, 144, 7̈629-3̈69̈ï ← 1̈899̈49̈c̈4, φαⁱᴦⁱh oor arᛞ hᴏⁱᴍⁱᴦoᴦᵀ Ƙⁱⁱᴦᴦⁱov

---

Read in the direction of the arrows, but turn the figure upside down, except the ↓ arrow. this figure is an English translation of the or-iginal, which was on the Stone. but the bird Coming out of the egg is a facsimile. and the reading is Krischan, or Christian,

Original
Represents
a nest
with 3 birds

Facsimile

7,114, 18, 312, 18, 7928 94, 3214.
 η τας υϯ μαϧ αϯ ης β ϯ ι ς ϫ ηαν.

See the Mythology of the Excommunicated Bird
that encompassed the Island for two years
with nightly cries calling all kind of birds to her
from the Island She went to the Vale of galabes
and from there to the top of the mountain where she
Planted a male oak. and in its branches
made her nest, – three eggs she laid in the
nest, out of which came a Fox, a Wolf, &
a Bare, &c — observe there appears in the nest
the heads of three birds, (Llwynaws. Blaith ae Arth.)
according to the Allegory, but according to the figures
it reads "ê Tad, ar mab, ar Êshrid-Glan."
in English = The Father, and Son, and, Spirit & Holy.
as to the Island, there is no doubt it means Britain.
the "Vale of Galabes" means the Plains to the East
of the Rocky mountains, (in America) this country
was well known to the Druids, as will be proved
when the records are made public, this country
became their first refuge after the flood of the Gn. Cont

1 = Britain. 2 = Mexico
5 = head of a goat. 6 head of a Bull.
4 the head of both a man and a woman, Allegoricaly
Kêd and her Son in the dark, that is when the
man appears the woman is not seen, and when
the woman is seen the man has disapeared !!
Turn the man on his head and. Kêd (ced) appears.
3 is the "Key" to the Hierogliphics, at which the
man and the woman are gasing stedily,
observe the animals are looking the other way.
towards the Hirogliphics 7. = "Xaur Barok".
Translated; Xaur, (ychain — Oxen) Barok=
(Banog — Natable, Remarcable. high, there is an
old tradition about these High-oxen drawing
Same monster. of the ocean, to land, and the Sea
never brock over the land afterwards, generaly
there is Same faundation to these anciant Mythalogies
in which a dim Shaddow of Same fact is preserved.
Astralogicaly, the Sign of the Bull and the Twins
(the twins originaly was two Kids) meet where the
the Line of the Ecliptic Crosses the milky way.
and the Sign of Orian farms a triad

The ✳ jimplies the Sun at the time of the vernal–
Equinox, this reffers to the beginning of the order
of the Druids, at that time the prime meridian
ran between the oxen, through the sign of Orian
which is on the Equator, then the seven stars (gt Bear)
will appear as ⅃, or one, called first parission.
To the South west from the Bull, is the Constellation
of "Cetus" the Whale. or some very great fish:
which the tradition calls "AΦaVK" (avanc)
the Bull appears as pulling this fish accross
the Equator, close to the River Eridanus, at the
head of which the right foot of Orian is placed
but the tradition calls the oxen, Ychain Banog:
"HV̄-γaΔalv." which means, bold, valiant, strong.
this title no doubt the writer found, in the Horiz–
ontal scroll above the place of ✳ ~~.
for Hu – or Hugh, is the same word – there is
also related a conversation between the man and
the woman (Kêd (or) avagthy, her son) she asks
what light hast thou? He answers there is twilight
on the horizon, the morning stars fortell the coming
of the Sun, and I can read the records of the past
proceeding from the Star. ✳ V~~. which he
Pronounces. Jo–hên–hû–gê, & Kêd answers
I read, from ✳ jlgr–gwêg, ← ~~∧ ✳

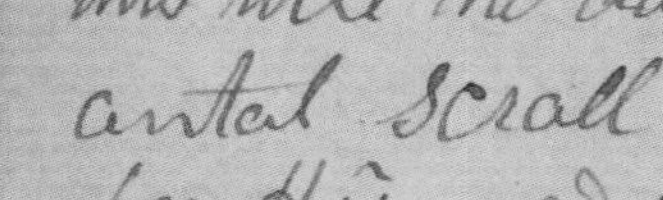

(IOhrr hvon) 96747237 = 9
(Inrr{ rwnr) 92383673 = 5
18,9,13,0910

Hieroglyphics = words numbers

These Hierogliphics have a peculiarity that no other kind of writing paress, they can give the phonetic Sound of Letters, and the numerical value of figures, and Parsition or direction they can be formed into Separate or different forms of Men, or Beast, or any known thing, the first eight will Pair (·) ʘ ⊃ () + or X ↑ ⤬) | —
when added = 6 8 10 12 90 = $\frac{6}{1}$ $\frac{8}{2}$ $\frac{1}{4}$ $\frac{3}{5}$ $\frac{9}{9}$

" Origin of the Alphabet "
which is Commonly called the Greek Alphabet.
but it anciently was called the "ΚΨΟΓΛΚ"
because it was taken from a Stone Stanza.

"Original Stanza"

Spoken

Alpha beta gama delta ⁓ Epsilon. 8 × 3
Zeta heta theta ⁓ j-O-tah. 6 × 3
Kapa lambola Mu Nu Xi ⁓ Omikron. 7 × 3
pi rho Sigma tau ⁓ Upsilon. 5 × 3
phi Khi psi ⁓ Omega. 3 × 3

α β γ δ ε ϛ ʒ θ ∂ ι · κ λ μ ν ξ ο π ϟ σ̄.
τ υ φ χ ψ w. 24 letters 8th of 1st & 9th of 2d clanble

It is evident from the foregoing facsimiles of the grouping of the hieroglyphical numbers that the unit of each group (letter) gives its true place in the alphabet, which the greek letters do not give, without a knowledge of the hieroglyphics, because of this difference we may term the hieroglyphic the vowels, and the greek letters the consonants. observe in the stanza it begins the verse with the vowel A, and ends each line with a vowel of three syllables — "ʃ(⌣" = Lev, — a Sound a cry (Levariad — Vowel) or if we place the ⌣ in front ⌣ʃ(= 325, of A.D. the unit = 10 = 1, the character may be ℓ ℓ ƒ (Alpha) "Alph<u>a</u>" the A. is the first letter of the 1st division and L the 2nd of the second division, and ph or ⌽ the 3rd of the third Dividian of the Alphabet but the greek names. of the letters, do not generally give the key of their number or meaning but simply gives the Sound by the Initial.

"The Rule"

Start at the Lower left Character, except ^{2}⟍^{3} and ^{4}⟍^{3} and the $_3$◯. add the number of each Character to one figure and place on its left, then place over, each figure the Sign of possession thus ^{1}A$^2_3$ & $\underline{1\cdot 253}$ = Alph = the greek name but, its real meaning is a voice or Sound or a vowel as explained before. the following is the conversion of the character into plain figures

A = i253. B = 2911. Γ = 393. Δ = 4724

   Aleph   Bita   gim   Dêld

E = 5'5. Z 6'i. H = 7'7. Θ = 8'443

  Epsi   Z'w   H'ê   Thêêph.

I = 99. K = 1944. Λ = 29245. M = 31425

  ji   kioch   Libde   manue

N = 4949* O = 651. Β = 75911. ϼ =

  Nichi ↓   opsit   peiaa

81583.) Ξ = 5'7'7 { Σ = 9324. Τ = 1943

  Raethm   Hêê   Sgud   Jiêg

Υ = 25'i44. Φ = 393351. X = 4'i4

  Upsiaêê   vimmea   chin

Ψ 5'995. ∩ = 69681, } the Place of Hêê is

  P8ie   W83ra { between the N. & the O.

By Comparing the interpretation of the Hieroglyphics
and the greek names of the letter, it will be seen
that several are nearer to the Hebrew Sound. as
Aleph, Beth. Gimel. and Same are unlike
either, — yet all conform to the unit of the Letters.
as well as the form when the Hieroglyphics take
a straight form in the greek letters for the most part.

       "the ancient names"

Aleph, Bita, gin, Deld, Epsi, 3'00, Hê,
Thêêph, ji, Kioch, Libde, minue, Nichi,
Hêê, opsit, peiaa, Raethm, Sgud,
Jiêg, Upsiaêê, Vimmea, chin, P8ie, W83ra.

The Rule to multiply a Sum by Subtraction
I have allready partly explained, and now
I shall explain more fully, as this rule is
used Same times in "Inspiration" the Sum
is written down tenfold by adding a cypher
on the right, and the xplyer as a decimal fraction
for 125×8 write 125·08 Rule of Revelation.
Take the difference between the xplyer and ten (10)
which here is 2, × the figures to the left of Decimal point
by the difference (2) = 250, Subtract from 125·0
that is from the original Sum with an added Cypher.

Example
125·01 (Diff 9)
−1125
125 = Answer

125·02 (8 8)
1000
2·50 = answer

125·03 (8.7)
875
375 = answer

125·04 (8 6)
750
500 = answer

125·05 (8 5)
625
625 = answer

125·06 (8 4)
500
750 = answer

125·07 (8 3)
375
875 = answer

Continued
125·08 (8 2)
250
1000 = answer

125·09 (8 1)
125
125 = answer

125·0555 (8 5)
625
625
625
69375 = answer

555·0125
2775   ↓×8
1110 (4440)
555   Answer

69375
observe the
two last Sums
give the Same
answer.

although
the middle part of the working is
different, after xplying by the difference
the figures must be one place to →
this in sted of writing 1000 by this
rule it would be 125·08!
and instead of writing 69375. we
may write 125·0555, or 555·0125.
this is writing by Inspiration.

whatever the figures past or to the right of the •0 may be, Count them as if single figures. but place the different products in their order to the left of the right hand figures place which is under the 0. in the example 555·0125. the difference of 2 = 8 & 1 = 9 and the 5 = 5. the product of 1's diff. is 5995 from 555·0 = 555 as shown in the Example or 2's diff = 4440 from 555·0 = 1110. the product & subtracta of 5 are equal this rule in Common practice may not be of much use, but it is an important rule of Inspiration. the decimal point • devides the Sum into two parts as the male and female in generation of animals. the Positive, and negative, or the Sum × plyed by the Diff- erence, and the answer. or the proportion of male and female. the two added together always are = to the original Sum, which had been made ten fold. Same time the male and female Parts are equal = as 125·0125. respectivly = 1125 – 1000 – 625. these

must be subtracted Separatly from 12510 first Sum

– 125 – 250 – 625 } place product thus   –   625
× 1125 – 1000 = 625 } Same relation   –   250
= 1250·1250·125.0 } as 1. 2. 5.   –   125
                                                    15625

The Rule of 4 & 7 is Similar to this Rule.
a third of the Sum to be × plyed by either, 4 = 1/3. 7 = $\frac{2}{3}$ 1/3 of 21 = 7 = 4. $\frac{2}{3}$ = 14 = 7. if 4 is to be × thus 7, 4, = 84. if 7 is to × thus 14, 7, = 147. if the Sum will not devide by 3 without a remainder, but leave reinder of 1. or 2 the × plyer must be added or subtracte as the case by be *

To illustrate the 2ᵈ Example. we find the Parent.
= 5˙2˙6˙5˙0˙. = Eloe, or Eloi, the Parent's name
(see L. 3. 23) which is translated "Heli" the Father.
the name is given by mark (15. 34) before the words —
"Lama sabachthani" (2˙13˙1˙9˙12˙14˙8˙14˙9˙.)
Start with right hand figure 9, place this as the left figure
then Pass 5 and take the 6ᵗʰ which = 2 = second figure
then add up the next five = 15 take the unit 6 (3ᵈ place)
then pass two (not counting the right hand figure already used)
that is pass the 2 on the left and the 4 on the right,
and add the next two viz 8 + 1 = 9, place in 4ᵗʰ place
we have yet left unused the left hand figure à 14 – 4.
the three on the right added = 1 + 4 + 4 = 9, which belongs
to the right hand figure place, Subtract the 2 from 9 = 7.
or the second figure from the right. = 9 2 6 9 7 9 = Difference
to this add the Parent Sum   ·5˙2˙6˙5˙0˙ ˈ ˈ ˈ ˈ ˋ ˌ
and apply the signs of Possession   9˙7˙9˙6˙2˙9˙ ‿‿‿
in greek letters = ΙΗΣΟΥΣ or JĒSOUS !
This rule, of inspiration, would only show the
last Xplyed Sum, Signs of possession and the Gender.
thus 4 8 8 3 2 7 9 ˈ ˈ ˈ ˈ ˋ ˌ ; the interpreter must find
the Parent Sum from this Sum, and the difference
from the Sentence following "Lama sabachthani,"
by the rule of the Sign of possession. but the usual
way in this rule is to chalange the inspired writer
to deride or better the word, with the interpreter.
the first to give the difference and the later the parent Sum.

A = 1253. B = 2911. Γ = 393. Δ = 4724
Aleph   Bita   gim   Dêld

E = 5'5. Z 6'i. H = 7'7. Θ = 8443
Epsi   Z'w   H'e   Thêêph.

I = 99. K = 1944. Λ = 29245. M = 31425
ji   kioch   Libde   manue

N = 4949* O = 651. ⟨ = 75911. ρ =
Nichi ↓   opsit   peiaa

81583. ⩵ = 5'7'7 Σ = 9324. Υ = 1973
Raethm   Hêê   Sgnd   Jiêg

Υ = 25177. Φ = 393351. X = 4'4
Upsiaêê   vimmea   chin

Ψ 5'995.   ⋂ = 69681, the Place of Hêê is
psie   Ws3ra   between the N. & the O.

By Comparing the interpretation of the Hieroglyphics
and the greek names of the letter, it will be seen
that several are nearer to the Hebrew sound. as
Aleph, Beth, Gimel. and Some are unlike
either, — yet all conform to the unit of the letters.
as well as the form when the Hieroglyphics take
a Straight form in the greek letters, for the most part.

          "the ancient names"
Aleph, Bita, gim, Deld, Epsi, 3'oo, Hê.
Thêêph, ji, kioch, Libde, minue, Nichi.
Hêê, opsit, peiaa, Raethm, Sgnd,
Jiêg. Upsiaêê, Vimmea, chin, Psie, Ws3ra.

143

The Reverse Rule = 2ⁿᵈ Example.

	Left		Right	
1	= 9 6 7 4 /|/|	1	= 9 7 9 6 2 9. /||||.	
2	− 4 7 6 9.	2	− 9 2 6 9 7 9	
3	= 4 9 0 5 /|||	3	= 5 2 6 5 0 /|||/.	
4	+ 1 1 1 7*	4	+ 1 7 1 1 1	
5	= 6 0 2 2	5	= 6 9 7 6 1	
	× • 3		× , 7	
6	÷) 1 8 0 6 6 (/|/)•	6	÷) 4 8 8 3 2 7(/||||	
5	= 6 0 2 2	5	= 6 9 7 6 1	
4	− 1 1 1 7	4	− 1 7 1 1 1	
3	= 4 9 0 5	3	= 5 2 6 5 0	
2	+ 4 7 6 9	2	+9 2 6 9 7 9	
1	= 9 6 7 4 IOHN	1	= 9 7 9 6 2 9. IHΣOYΣ.	

Inspiration

Revelation

The top Sum, is the Sum of the word (IOHN)
the 2ᵈ is the Same reversed, the 3ʳᵈ the Difference.
of the two Sums. (Called the Parent) = P. Sum
this is allways a nuter gender, to which must
be added either a masquline of femenine Sum
as Shown by 4ᵗʰ. the 5ᵗʰ is the Sum of the two genders
added, which is to be multiplied by any single
figure, the 6ᵗʰ is the ×plied Sum or "Inspired Sum"
Revelation is the reversing of this Sum by the
Reverse Signs, for ×, ÷ for +, — then aplying
the Signs of Posession, we have the original word.
after finding the Parent Sum (3ᵈ) the interpreter will
Chalance the reverse Sum, either verbaly or seek the word
in the Sentance, the two added = the original Sum

144

To illustrate the 2nd Example. we find the Parent.
= 5́2́6́5̇0̇, = Eloe, or Eloi, the Parent's name
(see L.3.23) which is translated "Heli" the Father.
the name is given by Mark (15.34) before the words —
"Lama sabachthani" (2̇1̇3̇1̇9̇1̇2̇1̇4̇8̇1̇4̇9̇.)
Start with right hand figure 9, place this as the left figure
then Pass 5 and take the 6th which = 2 = second figure
then add up the next five = 15 take the unit 6 (3 place)
then pass two (not counting the right hand figure already used)
that is pass the 2 on the left and the 4 on the right,
and add the next two viz 8+1 = 9, place in 4th place
we have yet left unused the left hand figure & 14 - 4.
the three on the right added = 1+4+4 = 9, which belongs
to the right hand figure place, Subtract the ← 2 from 9 = 7.
or the second figure from the right. = 9 2 6 9 7 9 = Difference
to this add the Parent Sum   .5̇2̇6̇5̇0̇ ′′ ′′ ＼ ′
and apply the Signs of Possession   9̇7̇9̇6̇2̇9̇ ‿‿‿
in Greek letters = IHΣOΥΣ or Jêsous !
This rule, of Inspiration, would only Shew the
last Xplyed Sum, Sign of possession and the Gender.
thus 4 8 8 3 2 7 9 ′′ ′′ ＼ ′; the interpreter must find
the Parent Sum from this Sum, and the difference
from the Sentence following, "Lama sabachthani,"
by the rule of the Sign of possession. but the usual
way in this rule is to chalange the Inspired writer
to deride or Letter the word, with the interpreter.
the first to give the difference and the later the parent Sum.

Explaination. the reversing of any sum, and
Subtracting the Lesser from the greater, makes
the result a Nuter gender Sum. if we add 1,
any where in the Sum, the gender will be masqutine
if on the Contrary we add 8 it will be a Femein gend
hence the Centiny 18 hundred Suplies the figure
if 1, is added put a single dot after the Sum • then
xply by any single figure exept 1, = Masquline gender
but if 8 is added put two dots : = Femenin gender.
Supose we Select the word "Boaz" = 2,15,1,6
in the Greek alphabet, or in English 2, 15, 1, 26.
the word is read in English from Left to right →
but in Hebrew words are read from right to lef ←

← 6 1 5 1 2 .H; The last sum alone if given to the
→ 2 1 5 1 6,E   gnterpreter, who is required to find
3 9 9 9 6; .   a number or Sum. that will when
  × 7   added to the Lesser of the ⇄ Sums
)2,7 9,9,7,9 •(be equal to the greater of the two : →
and this must be performed by a reverse rule. for xply
÷, for + Subtract, or vis versa. }÷) 2,7 9, 9, 7, 9 •(
hence the Required Sum = 3 9 9 9 6.   3 9 9 9 7 _
added to → E, Sum   2 1 5 1 6
                    ← 6,15,1,2. Answer is to be read
as in Hebrew from Right to left, or the reverse.
because → or E was given, but if the → of the Sum
had been the greater and the Lesser ← read → .
the only difficulty in the Revelation is the devisor.
very curious 2́ 7́ 9́ 9́ 7́ 9́ ← = I H Σ Σ H Υ, (jêssêu)

146

Observe that there are two ways of reading from right
to left as the Jews do, or from left to right as in greek
or as we do. Hence whichever way is the Least on the
left, must be Subtracted from the greatest Sum.
and the letter H or ← or g → because when the least
Sum is given, the answer must be by the reverse,
now by this rule of Inspiration, we first, Subtract —
Second, add the gender number. third, × the gender-sum
by any single figure (except 1) and in the answer as
Revelation, each operation is the reverse, first,
we ÷ Second Subtract the gender — third we could + the
last Sum to the Lesser Sum H. or g. as the case may be

Inspiration } — + × g or H } for before we can divide,
Revelation { + ÷ — H g } we must add to a unit.)

this reversing is in Strict accordance with material
Laws of Body and mind, life is the result of
two or more opposite elements, often one is
called "good" and the other "Bad" but in themself
they are neither the one or the other but Comparitive.
when this rule is used, in general, the Subtracted
Sum, or the lesser of the ⇆ Word. is given
through the Primes. as in the last Example the →
is the least (21516) this is not a prime number
but its place is between 21511. and 21601. take
the Lesser Sum. the word = Uri ($\frac{6}{0}$) the fraction
must be given if not a prime. which is by adding to unit
and Subtract the right hand figure || 2,79,9,79,= Uri $\frac{6}{0}$
Λιοηι — ΓΦι = (The Word that was — — — —

Inspiration (Example)   Revelation

word $\dot{9}\,\acute{\gamma}\,\dot{9}\,\dot{6}\,\dot{2}\,9 >$ $\Lambda a - \xi \upsilon \Theta, - K^{a}\xi \upsilon, \; K^{a}\chi\Theta.$

$- \underline{9\,2\,6\,9\,7\,9} <$ "Slain - is, (the) Lover (of the) slave."

$5\,2\,6\,5\,\overset{+}{0}$ that is the litteral translation,

$\times \qquad 4$ but very different is the meaning

$\dot{2}\,\acute{1}\,\dot{0}\,\dot{6}\,\dot{2}\,\dot{8} - <$ by the rule of Revelation.

$(\mathcal{L}\,a - \underset{\sim}{3}\,u\,th, <)$ as the reversing of Inspiration.

$= 4)\dot{2}\,\acute{1}\,\dot{0}\,\dot{6}\,\dot{2}\,\dot{8} - \prec ($ the unit = 1 the diff. = 8, ½ of which = 4.

$\underline{5\,2\,6\,5\,\underset{\sim}{7}}$ as — equal 7 we subtract this + ~

$5\,2\,6\,5\,0$ = the Sum of the word ⇄ Subtracted.

To this Sum add the Sum of $K^{a}\xi\upsilon, \; K^{a}\chi\Theta$. this
is done by converting into Prime words and fractions.
into a Sum, $K'\dfrac{8}{2}$ and $K'\dfrac{7}{8} = 9\,2\,6 \cdot 9\,7\,9 <$
the unit of $K = 1 \times$ by +, + fraction $\Big\{+\underline{\quad 5\,2\,6\,5\,0}$
$\dfrac{8}{2} = \overset{no}{col^n}$ of Nines = 26. $\dfrac{7}{8} = 79$. $9\,7\,9\,6\,2\,9 >$

"Thus in the Revelation every operation is reversed
to that which produced the Inspiration, — observe
in this Example the figure added to the difference
was ~ a 7, being the left hand figure of the old-
Style Century, (72|00) which is = to 18|00 N. Style
the figures are ____ = Respectively ∵ ∴ either of
these figures may be added, but the proper sign must be
given. after the last x plyd Sum, as well as the sign.
representing the reading of the lesser Sum of the word
> means to read as in Greek as → or from left to right
< as in Hebrew ← this is important because the answer by
Revelation, must be in the reversed direction.

From the foregoing example, it will be easily conceived that an interpreter. Should he be ignorant of the signs or neglect them, or fail to discover if the words were inspired or not, his interpretation could not be relied on, the signs • or : imply the younger. and the — or = the older and — • . means Single and = • : Plural. moreover each sign has a different rule to the others, one implys the "unit" and two the "difference" or the half of either ! at first this double rule, may appear difficult, but by strictly following the rule, it becomes very Simple, and the result exceedingly interesting —
Repetation of the Rule — Select any word in any Language, number each letter alphabeticaly, or if you know the sign of possession, you can reduce the number of figures equal to the number of letter. this Sum is called the Sum of the word; reverse this Sum by placing the right hand figure on the left &c then Subtract the lesser from the greater = the difference to this Sum of the difference, add either 1̄, or 2̄. 7̄, or 8̄. then ×ply the last Sum by any Single figure (2 to 9) except 1. place the sign of the figure of the century, and of the lesser Sum of the word, this last Sum and Signs must be Shown, or it may be Converted into words. and the Sign placed after, — for Revelation, use ÷ for ×. and — for + that is Reverse the apperations. any alphabet will do, provided, the Same is known.

"Taleisfferies"

Arian – Dêr — or — Druid's Money.

The fac simile shaws bath side of the Cain or Charm these were made of gold, or silver, and same time of baser mettle, or ather materials, they were warn as Charms, and supased to protect the wearer fram evil influence. and as a mater of fact did so to a certain extend. inasmuch that if the Passessar Cauld read the characters an them! he arshe must be a member of the ordee of the Druids, fram whome help wauld he had when in need; or ane belanging to same ordee in Cavenant with, them if able to letter or devide the ward, shawn an the ☉ face one wauld ask, will yau _Letter_, or devide the ward? the ather wauld answei, with yaur help J will do so. "begin them" No yau begin, "No begin yau" Naw Suppasing that ane was a christian (af the Cavenant) he wauld use five letter begining at eithei star ✳ = ✳

ΙΕΗΖΗ, – ΑΙΓΘΕ, (jė ėžė – Aigªthe) after the ward was properly given, the questian wauld be asked have yau any cithei ward that J may bettei understand. the ather wauld say ≨ Σ Ρ ΙΙ∩ ☰ ≨ S Ꞅ Ρ Ⱞ Ж ≨ (this was dane by changing the right hand letter of each pair fram the 1st to the 2nd devisian of the alphabet (greek) what is that equal to? to him that sits an the right hand of the Haly ane.! — J shall naw praceed to explain the wanderful Candensation of the Hieroglyphics

Sun   Facsimile.   Moon.

On the Moon face there are five circles, the outer three
are devided into 19 equal Spaces. each Space to be
brought Horisantaly on the left of the moon ☉. the
outer Circle is that of the Centuries, the 2ᵈ = + — or =
the 3ᵈ is the Epact of the Century. the 4ᵗʰ Circle is that
of the twelve months of the year Showing the number to
be added to the Epact for the age of the ☽ on the 1st of —
the iner circle of ten letters, are read as they Stand (above)
The two outer Circles on the Sun face are ÷
into 24 = parts. equal to the 24ʰ of the day or 15° or
2 weeks, the outer circle = the 12 Signs of the zadiac.
the iner Circle = the 12 Months of the year. both of
which are read on top, the 28 dots deviding them
Shows the dayly motion of the ☽. — the Hieroglyphics
in the middle and the arch (☽☉☽) of the Sun. must be
read as Stationary. (as above) the Stars below the arch
represent the Milky way (via lacta) and the 7 Stars above
is the Sign of the Great Bear (Ursa Major) Showing the hours
of the day as well as the Months and the years ～～～～

The four great feasts among the Druids were the two Solstices, longest and shortest days, and the two Equinoxes, the autumnal and the _vernal_. the vernal Equinox. is the same as the _Passover_, of the Jews, and _Easter_ of the Christians. among the later the vernal equinox is counted the 20th of March (although some time it happens on the 19th, 20th, 21st, 22nd, 23rd. the first full moon after, is the Paschal full moon. and the first Sunday after, is Easter Sunday. ------

"The Tales ferris" will tell you the time of Easter, for 23 hundred years beginning with the Century before Christ. and that without any more complicated counting than can be done on the fingers. — the first thing to do is to find the Paschal full moon. Say for the year 1800. Turn the Century = ϵ = ϵ on the left of the $\odot$ = Epact 4. next turn the month of March = ♈ add the figure 1 to the Epact = 5, = the age of the ☽ on the 1st of that month. therefore She would be full on the 11th. which is prior to the 20th hence the next after the 20th will be in April. the fourth month ♉ = ♉ and 2 is the figure to be added to Epact = 6 days old on the 1st hence full on the 10th the next thing to do is to find what day of the week the 10th fell on — this we find on the Sun face, 1st find the Century on the inside of the arch, 1800 = ♇ take the right hand figure — or 8 a Tuesday = 1st of April also the 8th. hence the 10th was 4 a Thursday, the next Sunday would fall on the 13th which was Easter Sunday in 1800.

2nd Example, 1893. we have allready found the Century's
Epact to be 4. (\ ) the nearest = year is ᚼ or 76,
which is counted as the Century's Epact, then counting ↓
one epact for each year in excess. 76+17 = 93. =
the Epact ‿ as the face stands, turned to the left of the ☉ = \ or 12
thus the Paschal full moon would not fall in march
but in April. ♉ = ⁺2̇ (Same time ⁺3̇) the full ☽ = 1ˢᵗ or 2ⁿᵈ ♉
here we wanted Say 12+3 =15 or full on the 1ˢᵗ of April
because we find that the first fell on Saturday, thus
the century = ᵛ̅ᵢᵢ +\+(+ (+⌐) +)+⌐\+((+⁹³‿. = ♄ᵃ saturday.
Easter Sunday therefore fell on April 2ⁿᵈ in the year 1893.
for Easter Sunday cannot fall later than April 25
nor the Paschal full moon later than April 18ᵗʰ, there
happened two full moons in this month in 1893
on the 1ˢᵗ and 30ᵗʰ (1ˢᵗ = Pesach). or Paschal full moon

    To find the aspects at 10ᵖᵐ 2ⁿᵈ ♉ 1893 ―――
it happens that this date is on top ‿ (sign ? matt) place the
earth ⊕ two days of the ☽ to the right = ♍. virgo.
(or \ when on top) near the middle of the sign, place the
Sun ☉ exact opposite in the middle of ♓ Pices
or 12ʰ apart, and as the new ☽ is with the ☉ the full⊕
is with the ⊕ as the moon was one day past the full
place the moon. one of her days to the right of the earth.
or in the last decade of the sign of the virgin at ♍.
for any day in any month 10ᵖᵐ is the first position
for any hour earlier in the day turn as many hours from
the left on top — for any hour after 10ᵖᵐ turn from the right.

Note the position of the sign of the great Bear ⟋
fairly it you can tell the time of the day, or month
if ⟋ at 10 Pm three hours previous it was ⟍ and 3 after
10. it will be ⟍ that is it changes 45° evry 3 hours —
for the year the first position ⟍ = middle of July —
at 10 Pm and changes 45° evry 6 weeks (or 3 hours)
observe the Dominical day means the 1st of April &
July, for any other month add as many days of the
week to the Dominical day as there are of Stars —
the Months are Grouped in 6 division under the arch.
with from one to 6 Stars Standing against or ⟋⟍ = 4
these are the 2 February 3 march. 11 November for either
of them ad 4d to the ☽ D°. that will be the 1st of such month
in Leap years add one day less for January ad February
that is add nothing to ▭ and for ♄ add 3 insted of 4.
Remember in looking at the ☉ face your Supposed
to be facing the North Star, the East is on the right
the West on the Left. the top is the upper Meridian
and the botam the Lower Meridian (under the earth)
thes Hierogliphics after a little practice are as easy
to read as plain figures or Letters, the amount of
information Contained in this Wonderful abriviation, this marvelous Inspiration, this un-kn-
own facts, highthertofore, Supposed to be only Some
worthles Superstitious Charm, are now revealed
in part at least, in their true light,! and this "Light"
may lead Some to the greater Light, about to appear !

154

"The two witnesses" 2

(See Revelation, 11ᵗʰ Chap 11ᵗʰ Verse,) after three days & a ½,
But before you try to unravel the mistery, Learn the
the Rule of the witnesses! namely the Centuries of
the old and new style. vis $\overline{7}\overline{\overline{2}}^{00}$ of the old and 18^{00} new
these are the two witnesses, "the old," and "the young"
they also represent the Lesser & greater (1 & 2 & 7 & 8 greater)
the unit of both are = 9, = one of the number of the gods!
The Rule, write any Sum, — Select any one of the 4
figures $\dot{1}$ $\ddot{2}$ $\overline{7}$ $\overline{\overline{8}}$. if there are a figure of the same name in
the Sum place the witness on the left of the Sum, but
if the witness is of a different name, you may place it any
where in the Sum, — Reverse the Sum by writing the
Right hand figure on the left, and the left on the right.
Subtract the lesser from the greater; — from the difference
Subtract the witness, from the unit place, (discard it)
the witness being expelled you have only your own
Sum left, (the difference) ×ply this by any single figure
the Sum thus multiplied only is to be Shawn, with,
the Sign of the witness (·, ∴, or —, =) that Saw the Sum
either the writer or interpreter may Chalange the other
to produce Such a figure as shall when added to the figure
given by the Chalenger be equal to either the greater or
lesser Sum; the difference of which had been ×plyed
The interpreter will add his figure, when the lesser Sum is given
or Subtract it if the greater Sum is given for the answer
the interpreter will discover the Difference by reverse opperation.

Example, Supose the word John = $10\,\text{ℕV}$ $\overset{9\,6\,7\,4}{}$

and the witness $\overset{=}{8}$ was Selected = 9 6 7 $\overset{+}{8}$ 4. →

Reverse the Sum, & Subtract difference = 4 8 7 6 9 ←

from the difference Subtract the witness — 4 8 0 1 5. Difference

48015 − 8 = 48007. × $\overset{4}{=}$ 1 9 2 0 2 8. = Shown

now the interpreter Knowing, that the last opperation

was by $\times^{ion}$ proceeds to ÷ by the difference of the unit,

as shown by the Sign = , (the difference of the Sum is always 1)

the product of this $\div^{ion}$ = 4 8 0 0 7 + $\overset{=}{8}$ = 4 8 0 1 5, = Difference

the greek reads from → the Left the Hebrew from ← to right

the writer on demand may give either the greater

number or Greek → or the Lesser, or Hebrew ← either

as a Sum or by each figure Sepporate (from the right)

or he may disguise the Sum by use of the primes!

48769, will fall between 48691, & 48781 Primes

take the word oppasit the Lesser of the two ="Eda"

as there is a fraction over the lesser of the two primes

add up the Sum 48769 = 3$\overset{+}{}$4 = $\frac{7}{8}$. or "Eda $\frac{7}{8}$"

(192028 = Eda $\frac{7}{8}$ ←) × Eda by +, × Denominator by 1

and add the numerator the total = 4 8 7 6 9 ←

Difference 48015) the answer is read → or Reverse ←

Eda $\frac{7}{8}$ = $\dfrac{4 8 7 6 9}{9 6 7 8 4}$) and the witness is removed from

the Sum leaving the answer 9 6 7 4.

In this rule every thing is double, or Reversed,

even the Chapter and verse quoted are 11 · 11. this

may be but a Coincidence, — the fraction $\frac{7}{8}$ = $\hat{e}\hat{r}$

or "Edaêr" or the Dêr, or Druids (y dêr' —)

Even the 3½ days daubled make seven(7)
which is the last of the Witnesses, or the Centuries.
hence after this witness gave evidence," the Spirit
of Life (of the gods) from god entered into them,
and they Stood upon their feet; "
If we, Consider the 7 &8 as the outer
Life, and the 2•1, the inner or Spirit

7	2	•	7 8
6	22	•	2 6
6	6	—	6

always endavouring to bring an equilibrum in
by drawing from the outer Life their own equi.
the 2• draws 2 from 8, Leaving 6 in the unit place
•1 draws from 7, one leaving 6 in the place of 1000
as Shown by the curraws, thus the inner life=22•2
then these three equal figures being added = 6•
the single 2 having being drawn to the 22, leaving a
a space vacant, and now appear as 6 6 0 6•!
"Here is wisdom. Let him that hath understanding
Count the number of the beast; for it is the number of a man; and his number is six hundred
three score and Six" (see Rev 13th ch. 18 v.)
Some will Scoff and laugh, at these figures and
Say "there is Something rotten in Denmark"!
And the Champions of the isms will declare
war against the Infidel, who dare to believe
"there is a rule for Revelation" or that Inspiration, is the Result of Mathematical Science!
but he that hath understanding, will Count the
number, nevertheless, and Man will regain his freedom!

and shall have dominion over the beasts!
of the field, that came up from the Earth, and
the _Sea_, and the heavens, to torment men.
who speak great things, and blasphemous
in the name of the Lord, and the scarlet woman.

"The 'Fairies' Mythology"
are extravagant if we try to understand
them in a literal sense, but the reality
some time surpasses the fiction, and the
"Tales Ferries" will prove a new science
of the mind. a Spiritual Electric battery,
that will eclips the late Electric discovery.
I have allready Shown you how to look through
"the key hole" and observe the aspects of the heavens
Some other time through the Same key hole!
you may observe the secrets of the Earth ⊕
Allegorically the earth is a Lock of which you
have not the key, that key is in possession of
the Fairies, See how easy they can open the door.
they insert the key, turn it to the left and the door is
open, having entered, they insert the key on the inside
and turn it to the right or the reverse, and the door
is Locked again, in coming out again, they open
and shut by a reverse turning, and having seen
the Secrets, of the iner Chambers of the earth
they will try and explain the mysterious things
within; Using a simile or a Comparison to do so.

158

The original of which this Jaleis ferries is an exact Coppy, had a Curious tradition atached to it namely ". That if a pin was put through the center and the two ends of the pin to rest on two steel blacks in a natch. and after sun down the Charm was expaud to certain Stars it would begin to revolve. and Continue to revolve untill the Star would set, and if placed in total darkness, there would appear a light where the pin (Brass or Copper) tauched the Steel. Strong enough to read the syms or Hieroglyphics, and if a Looking glass was placed so that the reflection was seen, a wanderful sight would be the result, whither we call this a dream, or a vision, or a fantasm of the mind, or Revelation or halutination; the fact remains, that, these sights were seen, by a number of people, in the present Century; and I am one of those that beheld the vision! but as I was only a child then, I cannot now give any explaination, and yet I can remember perfectly well, haw beautiful was the sight —

"Stationary reading of the Hieroglyphics"

✱ ♃ ♒ ♈ ♉ ♊ ♋ ♌ ♍ ♎ ♏ ♐   ✱ moon face

$\frac{1}{0}$ $\frac{2}{2}$ $\frac{3}{1}$ $\frac{5}{3}$ $\frac{7}{5}$ $\frac{8}{6}$ $\frac{2}{7}$ $\frac{4}{2}$ $\frac{9}{4}$ $\frac{5}{3}$ $\frac{7}{5}$ $\frac{1}{7}$ equivlant.

1. 20. 12. 32. 52. 62. 65. 22. 45. 32. 52. 64. ^{Primes}

a u m̲ 5̇ 7̇ 8̇ 2̇ ✗⁄4 9̇ 5̇ 7̇ 1̇

translated — "We are of the Linage of Sepa" a̶p̶e̶s̶

∴ ∖ + ⌒ (Dê) god of the Crass. or the 54th. 00 = +7 or 8.

"The erliest known Greek inscription"
on the rocks at Abu—Simbel, Nubia.

BAΣIΛEOΣEΛΘONTOΣEΣEΛEΦAN-
TINAN
ΨAMATIXO·TAVTAEΓPA
ΨANTOIΣVNΨAMATIXOITOI
ΘEOKΛOΣ·EΓΛEONBΛΘON
ΔEKEPKIOΣKATVΓEΔΘEIΣo
ΓOTAMOΣ·ANIBAΓOΛΛOΣo
BXEΓOTAΣIMTOAIΓVΓTIOΣ
ΔEAMAΣIΣ·EΛPAΦEΔAMEAP+
ONAMOIBI+OKAIΓEΛEQOΣOV
ΔAMO·

In the reign of Psamatik, the second
in Egypt, about the year 596. B.C. nearly
2492 years ago, his name begin the 2d Line
"Psamaticho, Amasis. another manaek's
name also appears in last but one line. the original
are in five lines ending with the • otherwise
the Letter are without any space between to shaw
where the words begins or ends, Psamatixo, ends
the 1st Line. and De amasis, ends the fourth line
there is but a slight difference between these letters
and the Capital greek Letter at the present day —
the same kind of letters are found on the stones of
knawledge more than a thausand years previous —

160

The Egyptian Hieroglyphics, Tablet of Snre-
feru the first king of the fourth dynasty,
at Wady magharah. Called by the historian man-
tho, "Soris" titles him "Neter-aa", (Great God)
and "Neb maat" (the Lord of Justice) also "Horus"
(the Conqueror) the Characters are similar to the
Tablet of the four hundred, (see facsimile) and are in part
phanetic, with certain "determinatives" &c
an Eagle = a, — a leg and foot = b, — a horned Serpent =
f, — a hand = J, — an owl = M, — a chicken
= U, Same Characters equal a Syllable and Same
two Syllables. as a bowl or basin = Neb, a
hatchet = Neter, a guitar = Nefer, a crecent
= aah. in this respect there there is a strong resemblance to the Still more ancient Nepal writing
in the nepal hieroglyphics however, whither as Scrall
writing or figures of things, Such as man or beast
land, water trees &c there is alway a numerical
unit or single Sound, it maters not how many
figures goes to make the figure or picture they
can be added up to one figure, but never to a cypher.
hence in this Language there are nine vawels (9)
that may be pranaunced lang or short with one impuls of the vaice, witthaut any aid as the Cansanants
but Seldam is there more than Seven used at present.
and Same of these are termed or Cancidered as Cansants
in English, this make it difficult in translating into

the English language— because the Syntax differ very much, as a rule the adjective, preceeds the Noun in English, while in other languages it fallows the Noun. thus throwing the numerical value of the words out of their order, as els the English Syntax, will appear backwards, and it will be found difficult to enlighten Same, so far as to temporary permit such liberty with the "queen's English" and at the Same time these folkes will expect a literal Translation, with liberty to drop a H here and there and place it Somewhere els! a free translation is not difficult provided we do not look for, or require a teenical, or dogmatical, rendering to prove ours,(our little habby or fad or faith to be true) or are too nice about grammar and Syntax.

"ΚΙΣΤΦΕΙΝ. ΔΑΔΓΥΘ"
Or the Stone Chest of Revelation.

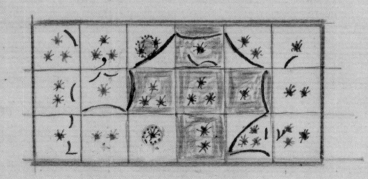

Analysis, 1st there are 18 ⊡ in three lines of sixes having 1 2 or 3 Stars. and with two exceptions. have also 1 2 or 3 hieroglyphics, the foot of the Cross. and the foot of the Square when standing up ▯ as a witness. I shall first give the allegorical. Lessons found on this face of the Stone, Starting with the lower right hand Corner with the hieroglyphic V = 12 added = 3 = ϑ next ı = 9. then ſ = 6 then on top of the Cross ⌣ = 4 we are thus reading from right to left as in Hebrew ⩊. ı̇ˊ⌣ı̇̀, which in English is "John" the Star ⌣ or the last of the name means Chapter. and the star on of the right the verse 1st to ∴∙ 6th " There was a man send from god (⌣̇ = ∆ H. or God) whose name was John. this man begins by saying " in the beginning was the word, and the word was with God, and the word was God?" that is the English version, in the Gaelic version it is " agus do bé Dia an Bhriathar." — and God was the word; also in the Kymric, " a Diw oedd y gair; . well what was the word? you will find it on the arch which surrounds the Cross, but you must Count it and thus by the right rule, write the first three character on the right ⌣ı̇ (. placing the decimal point on the right, then add up the next three \⌣ı̇ = 1 place on the right of the point. then take the difference of the remaining two ⌢.⌣ı̇ = 6 place on the right of the .ı̇ı̇ lastly add up the first three figures to unit = 1 place on the left ı̇ ⌣ˊı̇̀(.ı̇ı̇ = 1HZE.1Z. (ȷ̇ẽżeiż — ȷesus)

on the left of the Cross we find $\therefore - \because \therefore$
$= \Lambda \Upsilon \Gamma$. (Lug — Luke) the $\therefore$ is the Chapter.
3 chp 23 v, " and Jesus himself began to be
about thirty years of age, (being (as was supposed)
the Son of Joseph) which was the Son of Heli.
observe I have taken the liberty to place the
parenthesis where they ought to be, because
it is inconvenient to tell two Lies with one
breath! leave out the interpolation, which
is not a part of the Sentence, and you will make
Jesus the Son of Joseph, and Joseph the Son
of Heli. both Statement are untrue if we
believe Matthew, I may say that Heli (HΛ↓)
was a Lord of Teman (where God came from)
Again on the left of the Stone begining at lower—
Left corner we find $\dot{L}\dot{J}\dot{J} = K \alpha e th$, or Kaer
it means Bondage, or Slavery, if we wish to find
the particulars, count all the Stars within the arch.
they number 13 = the Chapter of Revelation. the
last verse of which Says. "Here is wisdom" &c
and those that possess that Capacity may easly
count the number Sixhundred three Score & Six.
the Stars on this Stone, $\therefore \because \therefore \} = 6606$
of the great triad ☉ ☽ ✳ or the julian period
which is equal to 1893 A D or the begining of the end,
that is the time when man will over came the beast
I Shall now give Some Enigmas from the Square.

To read these, Start with the arrow, follow the lines pronouncing the letter that stands at the angles. 1 Roman, 2 katholik, 3 kirk, or church — 4 Anglekan, 5 Dragon. 6 mör-Heli, 7 = "I E Z Y" these are Sufficient to shew the maner they are Constructed, and you may continue alike figures, always bear in mind that one or more Corner of the great Square must be included, this is Called working on the Square, — now let us see what revelation we can discover in plain words. or in a literal sense. we have been reading this oblong [▭] horizontaly, if we read it perpendicularly [▯] we See the order of the Stars are the Same whichever end is up. the Stars are divided into three groups by the hieroglyphical arch, and the different groups give three different numbers which are called the = of the Century. in finding the Dominical day of the year, 1st turn the arch with the opening to the Left and the left arm of the Cross will have two ** = as many tens (20) the rest added one 8. and the 1st = year is 28. Next turn the opening to the right. Count all above the Cross, divide by the Same the tens = 5¦6 lastly count all below the Cross thus ⋰⋰⋱ = 8¦4 we have thus used 33 Stars, and 3 remains, these represents the ☉ on the right and ⋱ = the ☉ on the left of the foot of the ✝ which represents the Earth ⊕ (☹ ⊕ ☺)

By the reverse possition = ☉ ⊕ ☺ or Morning & evening.
⊕ over ⊕ = Midday and ⊕ over ⊕ = Midnight, in this last possition
we read the Hieraglyphical arch, occupying 7 □
one only having two Characters ∟ representing the
Leap year century, (366ᵈ) as indicated by the foot of
the Cross ⊡ the right arm of the Cross ⊡ (= the 1ˢᵗ Century
of Anno Domini. and the top ⊡ = the 2ᵈ Century—
the left ⌐ ⊡ = the 3ᵈ Century, the foot again = 4ᵗʰ Century,
and every four hundred years before or after, so that
1800 = the top = ⌐ or ♂ Tuesday. thus the Centuries
read from right to left, in a circle of 400 years—
the odd years of all the Centuries count from left to
right, and also the days of the week, the months
of the year are devided into Seven groups, the Dᶜ D⁷
found for ⌐ are the day found on the arch = 1ˢᵗ
then count the groups from lower left corner = 1 1 ∟
round the arch, one day advanced for each group
Rule, find first the Dominical day of the century
which is also equal to the nearest = year (28·56 or 84
from which Count towards the right <u>one</u> day, for
each year in excess for three years and for the fourth
year Count <u>two</u> days, as many times as required.
on which ever day of the week the required year falls
that is the Dominical day of such year or the 1ˢᵗ of April
and also July. if the year is a Leap year Count <u>one</u>
day less for January, and February, than given by the months
thus we practically may find the day of the week Corresponding

To any true date for ever, — I say true date because
from 325 A.D. to 1752, (in England and her Colonies)
the old style gained three days in every four hundred years.
or one day for every hundred years, except the leap year century.
— that practical demonstration, is about as much
as any reasonable person can expect. from so
small a number of hieroglyphics, — yet I shall
give another proof of the power of the stars, to
reveal the secrets of men and things — Rule,

   Select three persons (or places)
number three slips of paper 1, 2 & 3 draw by lot.
then select three articles, number these also 1. 2. 3.
or the name of each article and its number on three
slips of paper, draw these also by lot, each person
or place having ~~having~~ one article, known only
to himself, — each person will turn down his
own number, any where on the face (of Revelation)
he who has article 1. turn down as many as his own No
he that has article 2 twice as many, he that has article
3. four times as many as his own number, and
no more or less, — the face is then shown to the
Interpreter, who is required to tell which article
each person is in possession of ! without
any other knowledge but what the stars show.

1. 2. 3. Person) the 1st person has article 2 = 1 2 = 3
2 3 1 Article) 2d per has article 3 = 2 . 8 = 16 &c
3 10 6 take the difference, — ν December, !

Before giving the Phillasaphy of the Cross,
and the Archialical Arch of the Hieiogliphics
I shall give a facsimile of another ancient Cross
in use by the Druids from a very early date —
it is now called St Cythbert's Cross —

This consists of 8 Small crasses and
the Great Crass itself or 9 crasses
there are also 8 Hieioglyphical
Characters of this form)

(in greek letters)

There are also the signs of Possession
bath root and branch

Teh feat right left

Latest = 50 or 5 unit

6 10 6 10 . add the uprights to one figure 6+6=12=3 unit
then add the horizontal 10+10 = 2.0 × by the 3 =
60. place between the two upright Sixes = 6.60.6
And as this year ends the ancient Covenant of
the early British Christians and the Negals or the
Hereditary branch of the Druids, we have positive
proof, that the earlier Churches followed the Druids as
to the time of Easter (= Passover = Vernal Equinox)
Cythbert was born about 625 old became a
Christian but held to the Druidical time for Easter.
for a long time but in the end adapted the Raman
time he became Prior of Lindisferne (or Melrose)

in 664. and was made Bishop in 684. but he resigned his See in 686, and died on 20ᵗʰ March the same year, was buried at the Manastry — (Lindisfarne) but his banes rest now at Durham. The dispute about the right time of Easter, resulted from the Romans using the Julian or old style. which gains on the true time, one day for every hundred years, except evy 4ᵗʰ century as can be at a glance seen. by the following table from 300

N.º Centuries. Day
3 = 0
4 + 1
5 + 2
6 + 3
7 + 3
8 + 4
9 + 5
10 + 6
11 = 6
12 + 7
13 + 8
14 + 9
15 = 9
16 + 10
17 + 11
18 + 12
19 = 12
20 + 13
2100. + 13

this old eranean style was used in Britain untill 1752. but Pope Gregory 13ᵗʰ had caucted the Style a hundred years befor that, or rather he adapted the ancient Style amang the Druids, Example ~~Decemb~~ 28. 1065. fell an Wednesday So we are tald, — the Stanes Shaw the 1ˢᵗ of December to be ♀ or Friday and as the 29 would be the Same 28 = ♃ or Thursday. as the 10ᵗʰ century had gained 6 days. the Sixeth day after ♃ would be ♀ or Wednesday in the time of Cythbert. the gain would have been 3ᵈ the runical Characters begiry an the left of sign of Promian are •) ⌣ ⌒):·(⌒ ⌣ (• if we pair these =)(⌣⌣ ⌒⌒)(added to single figures, (the ⌒ = 14 = $\frac{5}{7}$) = 6 6 $\frac{5}{1}$ 6 practicaly St Cythberts Crass, is the Same as faund an the stanes of knawledge, the original Sign of Addition.

169

See map of Britain at the time St Cuthbert leaving out Ireland, and Scotland north of the Clyde, the island was pretty evenly divided between the English Saxons and Jutes on the East. and the Britons on the west as shown by the shadowed line, at that time "West Wales" included Cornwal, Devonshire, Somerset shire and Dorset shire, as the County is now divided. "North Wales" included all of Wales, Monmouth-shire, Hereford shire, Shropshire, Cheshire and a portion of Gloucester shire & Worcester. "Cumbria" North of the Mersey, Lancashire and the hilly part of West York shire, and the mountain Counties of Cumberland and Westmorland. "Strathclyde" north of Solway-Firth to the Firth of Clyd into Scotland. The English were, Bernicia — Deira — East-Angle — and Marcia. East & West Saxans — and Jutish Kent. — Gradualy the boundry changed further west, untill about 750 When all of West Wales became Saxon, and Cumbria and Strathclyde became English, and Wales alone remained British including Monmouth. Between Ireland, and Britain runs the Gulph Stream as shown on the map from the Isle of Man to Cornwal thus the middle ⟍ represents the famous "Ferman"

— Cornwel

The Sacred land of the Lords of Teman (Neggals) or the Hereditary order of the Druids (1st order) observe, this Gulph Stream is a reality, and the Sacred land of Teman (where God came from) is also a reality but hiden from our view by the Vail of the Sea. if this land ☌ is reversed or turned at right angle thus ♏ we can perceive its relation to St Cythbert's Cross plainly. as I have allready shown) ⌒ ♏ ⌒ ⌒) ʃ = ((ʃ (That this Cross was used by the Ancient British Christians, cannot be daubted, and its Druidical origin. I can asure you is certain. I shall now conclude my explaination of the Stary Cross and the Hieroglyphical arch. this Cross then represents the Earth ⊕, and the hieroglyphics the Stary heavens, when the moon is above = night. when the Sun is above = day. if the open part of the Cycle where the ☉ is placed was closed by turning the ⌒ thus ☽ and the other ⌒ ⚵ (we have the ☾ = N ad ☾ = Δ or D. and the ☉ is between the day of the Sun is the 1st day of the week). which is called IN ⌒ hence reading these characters from right to left. we have ⚵ = Dun-Man when that gap in the circle is closed up. this figure ⚵ is = the Sign ✕ or Multiplication. the unit of which = 42013. = 10 = 1. observe ⚵′ ⚵″ = 14 turned round makes Man, while ⌒ = ♄ Saturn (Satan - or the Beast) as we find in Revelation.

This earth has 5 □ and 10 ✳ representing units of forces, the direction of the forces are towards the center of the central ⊡ thus the different parts are held togather by reason of this inherent forces, the Sea fills the Space between the outer Squares, making the earth appear round, when the tide ebs and flows it is caused by the earths motion around its own center, this central region is inhabited by the "gods" (of Teman) The Sign over the place where Teman lays is ⊏ as the Map Shewes, read this on the square T)(E ⊏M⊐ A 6 N 7 5 8 = "Peacefull Teman" Now we turn this face of the of heaven and earth down and anather face appears, that of the Epact or the Exodus, from this face we discover the age of the moon on the first of any month during all of the "Der Chrisdon" Covenant (dispensation) by these two faces we discover the true time of Easter which the Roman church did not correctly keep untill the Middle of the 17th Centry 16 — we have yet another face to examin but as this is concerning the inner Secrets of the ⊕ I shall defer my remarks, to give you time to study the Mater, if you do not desire any further light, or neglect to make use of what hints I have allready given, I shall not labour in vain but to help you I shall give Some Translations

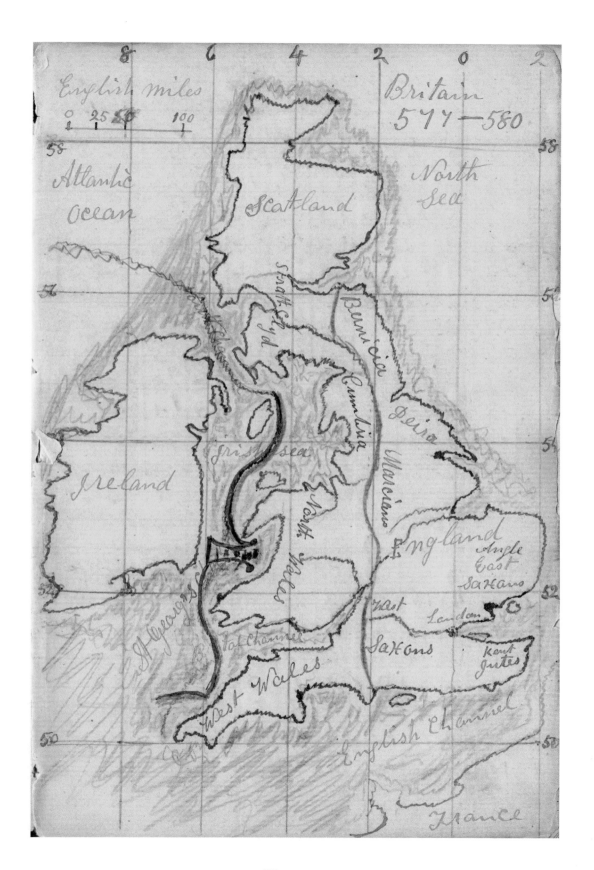

English miles

Britain
577—580

Atlantic
Ocean

Scotland

North
Sea

Strath Clyd

Bernicia

Cumbria

Deira

Irish sea

Marciano

Ireland

North Wales

England
Angle
East
Saxons

St Georges

London

East
Saxons

Kent
Jutes

Bristol Channel

West Wales

English Channel

France

173

"A Combined Table of Multiplication and addition and units of any two numbers from 1. to 144"

1	2	3	4	5	6	7	8	9	10	11	12
2	4 0	6 0	8 0	1 1	3 1	5 1	7 1	9 1	2 2	4 2	6 2
3	6 0	9 0	3 1	6 1	9 1	3 2	6 2	9 2	3 3	6 3	9 3
4	8 0	3 1	7 1	2 2	6 2	1 3	5 3	9 3	4 4	8 4	3 5
5	1 1	6 1	2 2	7 2	3 3	8 3	4 4	9 4	5 5	1 6	6 6
6	3 1	9 1	6 2	3 3	9 3	6 4	3 5	9 5	6 6	3 7	9 7
7	5 1	3 2	1 3	8 3	6 4	4 5	2 6	9 6	7 7	5 8	3 9
8	7 1	6 2	5 3	4 4	3 5	2 6	1 7	9 7	8 8	7 9	6 0
9	9 1	9 2	9 3	9 4	9 5	9 6	9 7	9 8	9 9	9 0	9 1
10	3 2	3 3	4 4	5 5	6 6	7 7	8 8	9 9	1 1	2 2	3 3
11	4 2	6 3	8 4	1 6	3 7	5 8	7 9	9 0	2 2	4 3	6 4
12	6 2	9 3	3 5	6 6	9 7	3 9	6 0	9 1	3 3	6 4	9 5

Table of the Dominical day – and day of the week

		☉	☽	♂	☿	♃	♀	♄	22: 18: 14:
									2: 6: 10:
		4	16	28	12	24	8	20	
		♂	☿	♃	♀	♄	☉	☽	21: 17: 13:
		32	44	56	40	52	36	48	1: 5: 9:
		♃	♀	♄	☉	☽	♂	☿	20: 16: 12:
									54: 4: 8:
		60	72	84	68	80	64	76	23: 19: 15:
		88	·	✳	96	·	92	·	3: 7: 11:
									Centuries

Signs of the days of the week and Leap years.

These Tables have been translat into plain figures.
for the purpose of proving the Hieroglyphics and that
at first it will be easier to understand, there are no
great difficulty to understand these tables, Rule,
for Mulliplication. take any two figure on margin
the angle of meeting. gives the Sum of their ×ultiplication
as 6×5 = 3/3 (× the →3 by 9 and add the 3 =30. all double
figures are Decimal figures, as 1/1 =10, 2/2 =20. and &c
the upper of the two figures is the unit of the two figure
and also the number from the top, in the Colums of Nine,
and the lowest is the number of the Colum of nine.

"The Dominical day Table"
Rule, Find the required Century on the right hand
next find the nearest year between the day Signs,
all of which are Leap years, the angle of meeting of
the century and Leap year. will be the Dominical day
of the century and the Leap year if over the *, the D 95
of any century falls in this Colum as 18: or 1800
= ♂. and 17: = ♃. and 16: = ♄ & 19: = ☉ but any
other Leap year, will be the D D of Leap year only
for each year in excess count a day to the right hand
Such day found, Count on the 1st division of the Months
☌♌ then one day more for each division to the Month Sought
on whichever day of the week the Month falls. that will
be the 1st day of Such Month except in Leap years we
have to remove ♒ & ♓ one Space forward as Shown
on the Margin aro ♒♌, and ♓ Mr. in place of * 4 ♒

175

Having shown the connection between the Cross of St Cythbert, and the stones of records, let us analyse the name itself. viz "ΚΙΘΒΕΡΤ" or "Kithbert" = 10, 9, 8, 2 · 5, 17, 19. 19̇8̇2̇·5̇8̇1̇

→ = Kithbert, ← = Ire, Brit (Britan)

$\left\{ \begin{array}{c} \dot{1}\dot{9}, \dot{8}\dot{2} \cdot 5\dot{8}\dot{1} \\ \text{☽} \cdot \text{☉} \cdot \text{⊕} \end{array} \right\}$ = the Cycles of the Moon (19) Do Sun (28) and the Earth (15) observe when the ☽ is with the ☉ She is New or 30ᵈ. and when with the ⊕ 15ˢᵗ or full, the ⊕ = 581 years of the new style (Anno Domini) = the triad (☉☽✳) period 5294, or the Julian Period. The Paschal full Moon this year fell on the 7ᵗʰ of April and that day was the 7ᵗʰ day of the week ᵥ Saturday. here the unit of the ⊕ 581 = 14 = 5. the Epact = 4. and the paschal full moon fell on the 7ᵗʰ day of the week and very curious we find on the Map of Britain. these Self-same figures 577, — 580 AD — This century is remarkable, Arthur king of Britain died about 542 aged 70. St Asaph died in 590 St Austin, landed on the isle of Thanet in 597, and was made first Archbishop of Canterbury and died in 694 — Mahomet was born at Mecca in 570, St Cythbert was born about 625. and was a British christian before he became a Roman — Catholic, St Asaph died before the coming Augustin. and the British Church, held out a long time before adopting the eroneous time of keeping Easter, as observed by the Church of Rome, which at that early date had gained about 2 days on the true time.

wheither, St. Cythbert, had this name from the first
or it was given him by some writer of later time is
not my business to prove, the name (as I have shewn)
if read backward as in Hebrew is "Tre - Brit" and
the unit = 7. (1982581 = 34 = 33 = 35) Subtract
the masculine gender No 33 from the sum of the word =
1982548 = "Kiθbedr" Kithbedr (pe·t·r)
here we have "Peter" hidden in Kith bert.
in the femenine form 1982547 = Kithberw. !
Wnebthik (gwinebthig) frowning face.
the word "Kith" in the kimrik means, a hiding,
or concealing; secret. — let us now consider
now some of the secrets of the Earth ⊕. Partly
revealed in the St Cythbert's Cross, here we have
the same cross ～～～～～ the Cross represents
but in place   the Earth, surrounded
5 Squares.   by the great oceans.
with stars   the upper arm
we have   is above the ocean
5 Circles   but the Lower
with   is covered by it,
Planets   the right and left
that govern   arms, are, the right
the Centuries   about on a level
or Dominents.   and the left above it ～
there is an open space or land between the earth and the
sea, and is said to be inhabited by the Gods! and
in the Centre is the great throne, or Hall of audience.

177

A certain order of men have a right to enter this Secret land, under the everlasting Covenant. but have to pass through the Valley of death, and if they neglect the Signs, and the observances, will Surly perish, but if they do follow strictly the Same path, which all must follow. their reward will be great, and the Knowledge is a Secret — it is further declared the Language in use ✳ in this wonderfull land, is an universal Language! that may be expressed in any other Language, as all languages may be rendered into the universal! a Knowledge of this Language entitles those that understand it to Certain privelages, which Cannot be attained without, hence the Lessons, are intended, as in Some degree to qualify the Student. The four planets in the center of the four oceans, are the Masquline planets, which alone govern the Centuries. the place of the 3 femenine planets ☽ ☿ ♀ placed between them respectively on the two arms and top of the Cross, will be in the order of the Seven days of the week alternate, the Spirit of the earth and the ocean the outer circle is devided also by the Cross =) ⌣ (⌢ then ♄ = ⟍, ☉ = ⟍, ♂ ⟍, ♃ = ⟍. | — Cross the four arms are held in place because each of them has an inherent force in the direction of the Central Circle of the ☺ each of the oceans also has its forces towards its own center —————

Now a △ is simply an allegorical figure, showing but one face, while a solid triangle has 4 faces. in like manner a □ shows but one face, but a solid square has 6 faces, and also a ✝ has 6 armes. all at right angle (the unseen may be called the poles. there is a very common error in our day. even among very learned men, in respect to the construction of the Earth. founded on the very funny theory of attraction, (I suppose) we are told that if it was not for attraction, the Earth would fly off into space! but why should she do so? because if you tie a string around a stone, and swing it round your head, then suddenly let go the string the stone will fly off !! how funny. then again. the interior of the earth is a furnace so very hot that the hardest stone will melt, but kind reader, how do you suppose this most heatfull theory, got a footing among the "wise men of Gotham" well one of them found a gimlet hole in the earth, and taking his thermometer, he went down himself but the thermometer went up, the lower he went. that is an enigma says the wise man, "I have got it" (he might have said "Ureka") and faithwith he constructed a theory founded on the points and lines and Superficies. of Uclid (jimginary) "at the top their, was 45° at the botom it was 100° in 1 mile in 100 miles it wauld be 5500° !!! A La Farenheat

That was the Theorem, which the wise man proposed
but he left it to us to prove that it was (not) true.
by mathematical reasoning, or simpler still,
"by faith" which require no reason at all —
as my orthodox friends will tell you, they
have been sending Emigrants, to the Starry regions
for a long time, neglecting "Sweet Azatlan"
the Fairy land beneath the Sea, the Cradle
of the Gods, and the home of the Angels. before
the great flood." well if you wish to learn
a different Story to what I have just alluded to
this information will be forth coming when
you are able to read the universal language.
and if you are properly qualified, I assure you
it is quite Certain, that you may have the opportunity, for an Ocular demonstration, or see
for yourself, the Glorious heavens of the Cross.
knowing as I do the kind of education you
have had, I do not expect you to take for
Granted these accounts of the earth and its heavens
without duly investigating those purported facts.
at the same time, I advise you, not to throw
this opportunity away, without an effort to
discover the "Truth as it is". not to be content
with the "Truth as you wish it to be" or believe
it ought to be, be practical, on this practical
earth, why go hunting after fantoms, and fictions
while the reality is within your reach!——————

180

"Truth as it was, is, and ever will be"

This face is the same as the Tales-Ferries

Facsimile, a similar figure with slight variation on the "Tales ferries," and an "Kist vein dad gur e" is also found but this is the Simplest as well as the Most ancient. it has not a character or point More than is Required, and yet it has enough (in all) but 25 Single characters and 11 points, 36 all tatd. one each of | κ —, three (↱) with arrow heads, ⌇ there are also three double characters ∠. ʒ. V. = 10. 11. 12. all the rest are single, — "The king wore the Crown, one up and two down" this has a reference to the three arrows, or the position to read the figures in the first place. J have allready Shawn by the rule the allegorical name of the arch, and the order of the Centuries, and Months, and the days of the week. these arrows have a number or meaning nos 5 6 1. and in the Epacts Cycle of the Centuries. we find them literaly carried out. 5 down twice 6 up once. Moreover they shaw the equal years of the centuries. ↱ = 28, ↱ = 56. and the up ↱ = 84. further the up ↱ divides the points, 4 on the Convex & 4 on the Concave.

or $\frac{4}{7}$ ⟨Leap years / Days of the week⟩ and the two month ♂ ♌ or D^o ⟨⟩ there is a rule, that belongs in particular to 4 & 7. Namely one of the rules of the triads, Supposing that any given Number or Sum is to be xplyed by these two figures. Rule ÷ the Sum by 3 which one third = 4, and twice $\frac{1}{3} = \frac{2}{3} = 7$, if 4 is to xply $\frac{1}{3}$ on the left and the $\frac{2}{3}$ advanced one place to → and if 7 is the xplyer, place $\frac{2}{3}$ first ad $\frac{1}{3}$ advanced one to → if the Sum leave a remainder of 1 add the xper to the Sum — or if there is a remainder of 2. —

Example ÷ 3) 360 (= 120 = $\frac{1}{3}$. 240 = $\frac{2}{3}$) $\frac{120}{240}$) 1440. $\frac{240}{120}$ } = 2520. which are 360 × by 4 & 7 respectivly. if the Sum had been 362, there would be 2 reminder, we would make the number 1+ thus 3) 363 (121 = 242 $\frac{121}{242}$} = 1452 — the x^{ll} 4 = 1448. 〰〰〰

The 11 point or dots also have their meanings Namily the progressive advance of the Epacts allways by 11 rejecting 30^s, but the Centuries Same time have 1+ or 1— them the Cycle of the Epact which begins with 30 or 0. the three arrows also are redd allegorically. ↓ = 5, ↗ = 6. ↘ = 1. or "A z e" (Saint Asaph) reading from right to left, by the sign of possession ↘↗↓ , St Azeph) was a Bishop of the ancient British church in Covenant with the Lords of Teman. and these three arrows Shews the relation that existed between these early christians & the Druids.

As the Druids were an order, and not a tribe
or Nation, but simply in Covenant with different
tribes, their records, are a mixed record, as for
example the "Kumri" "Angli" "ad" "Saxons"
and the three tribes of the Gauls, or Kelts,
Now having given the literal reading of the "seal"
I shall procede with the Allegorical arangements
in the first place it consists of two arches, the upper

= the days of the week and the centuries. the Lower

= the Months of the year in seven groups,
this may be called the (arch) or ark of the K^t
reading from the left. 2 10 13 = ⌐}1 = HⱭi (Heli)
or ⌐}1 = HⱭoe. again 3-i,9 10 11. =)́⌐}́ =Anglo,
or)́⌐31 = Angli. again 45 7 14 7 8 = "Kêm̂ru." or
Kêm̂ro, or Kêm̂ri, the
first is the Country, Second. a man of that County. 3 the people &c
the three arrows = 1321 = ∩)(⌐= ȝaeȝ (Sais)
or 1231 = ∩()(⌐= ȝeaȝ (Seas) sea-men. or
"Sasnach" here the word begins and ends with the
whi = 6 and the () added = 6, and we have to place a —
or .o. in place of the) added to the X—}(⌐(—(or 6.6.06}
observe there are slight variations in the order of the
Months ⌐ ad l, so as to to confound the Dominical days.
if the . is opposite the middle of the Character, it is single.
except ⌐} this = the 3 months, count each . from the
left, to the required month, Y is the 6th to be added to these
two month ⌐} is the 4th add 4 days to the Epact for these

HⱲi 1   AⱲⱲ 2   ƺaeƺ 3   KⱲⱲi 4

Facsimile of four Tribal Seals, in Covenant
with the order of the Druids, in the century 5400 os.
or the century before Anno Domini; the 1st = Ħ li,
or Heli, meaning the "Briny ocean," also ointment
a name given to the chief, or Father of the early
order of "Krisdian" (Christians) the No is 729.
and the Sign is ☿, or Mercury (Strong sea)
2d "Angli", meaning open, or large & Flood.
(Sons of the Giants that escaped from Teman &c)
the No is 14329. the Sign is the moon (Called Llaer)
hence England was called "Llaegar" (gar = near relation)
3d = "ƺaeƺ" or Saeson — Saxans, this Seal.
has the three arrows, which gives the name, and
also the No thus begin with the 𝄐 Subtract the
first figure ⸍ from the last figure ⟍ (8−2=6) then 𝄐 —
8 from 4, (borrow 10 = 14 − 8 = 6) 2d. having borrowed
from the last arrow place a Cypher then add last 6.
"6606"   4th Seal = Kemri, or first inhabitants.
the No is 17389. the Sign is the ☉. observe on this
Seal there is Shown the Cuniform Character ⟊
and is = 3 the figures taken in by this Character = 20
20 × 3 = 60, the arrow 𝄐 = 6 place on the left of the 60
and ⟋ on the right. 6606, of the ☉ while the other
6606 was of the ⊕ Earth or sign of the Saxans

184

as these Seals, and others, are likely before long
to become very prominent, by reason of certain
Covenants, represented by them, I shall here point
out certain Curious Coincidents, or shall we say
facts, ? — the four Seals shew plainly a common
origin, the first two F. D. shew no arrow, the 3rd shews
three arrows, but no Cuniform ▽ Character, the 4th
has the arrow and the Cuniform Character equal to 3.
the three Months that begin on the same day of the week
are ⌐3 = to H. V. X. the number of days to be added
to the Epact for these Months are 4. except in leap year H = 3
the 1st 2d & 4th Seals begin the word on the left thus ⬚
and make use of one or more of the triad months.
the 3d begins with the ∠, thus the two lines are at X
or the sign of multiplication, but the 3d has the sign
⊕ or addision, or the Earth, — Literaly the three arrows
are ⌐ or Γ = Z. ⊃ or ⊃ = A. & ⌊ or ⌊ = Ξ. (= Z A H.)
which is the root of Sarean, or Sareani, thus
each of the names have a treble termination, as
Kêmrù, Kêmrò, Kêmrí, or Anglù, Anglò,
or Anglí, or Êlù, Êlò, & Êlòí (or Elí)
observe that the sign of possession are /|\ or \|/
when in regular order, (Zahù, Zahò, or Zahí)
the reason for using N at the end of this word, is,
that either ̈a ̈ı must have a place in each name
in some of its forms, \ either as △ or N or X, as in
H.I., it becomes H.I.V. (Helen—Elin) because this
character shews the Dominical day or sign that governs.

"The Great triads of Chaldea & Assyria
1st. Ana, or Anu, "Heaven" Êa, and Bel.
Anu, "Lord of the Starry heavens" or darkness,
"the first born, the oldest, "the Father of the Gods."
Êa, "Lord of the Deep" the intelligent guide
founder of order and harmony." Bel, was
the Son of Êa (HA). 1st triad ANA.HA.BEΛ
2d triad, Sin. (☽) Shamash (☉) and Raman.
(Power of the atmosphere) or Treble-forked lightning bolt
3d group, (Ninip or Niněb, or Nirdar, or Nin.
= the planet Saturn (♄) 2d Meridug, or Merodach
Planet Jupiter (♃) 3d Nergal. Planet Mars (♂)
4th Nebo, or Nabu, = Planet Mercury (☿) 5th
Ishter = the Planet Venus (♀) 6th San, or Shamcash
"Eabâni" was half bull half man, Sign ♉,
Êa-HAN – "Ea-the-Fish" in Greek called "Oannes"
an animal endowed with reason, the body
was that of a fish, but under the fish head there
was a man's head, and a man's feet under the tail
he came out of the Erythrean Sea (Persian Gulph)
he taught Letters, and Science, and evy kind of Art,
during the day he dwelled on the land, but in the night
went back into the ocean." this Exalted fish, move—
ed round the World on a Magnificent Ship."
to guard the Earth, His Chief Temple was at the
Mouth of the Euphrates by the Sea, he had a Son
of the name of "Dungi" the first King of Shumir &
and Accad in the Land of Chaldea"

"The twelve great gods of ancient Chaldea."
Anu – Êa – Bel – Sin – Shamash – Ramân –
Ninadar – Maruduk – Nergal – Nebo –
Belit – & Ishter. — Nabanidus the last
King of Babylon in 550 before Christ or A.D.
repaired the ancient Temple of the Sun-god,
at the City of Sippar. in the foundation he found
the Cylinder of Naram-Sin, Son of Sharukin
(Sargan 1st) King of Acadê. which had been
placed there 3200 years before his time, or
3750. years. B.C. observe there was another Sargan
of much later date, do not confound the two together.
at the City of "Ur," the Seat of the moon-god.
at Erech or Urukh, gain the Anu or Ana,
(Heaven) and Anat or Nana. (Earth) Spirit =
Zi, thus Zi-Ana, Ana. "Spirit of Heaven"
Zi-Ki-a, Êa = "Spirit of Earth." in the time of
Sargan of Agadê, in the Callender are marked
five days of rest, in each month of 30 days.
called Sabattu, or Sabattuv, these are
the 7th, 14th, 19th, 21st & 28th, on these days no
work of any kind was done, no Cooking. Riding.
Speaking in public, or military or civil duty,
nor even take Medicine, ! of these 5 days of rest.
4 would happen on the same day of the week
if the Month began on ☉d there would be 4 Saturdays,
and one Thursday (19th) if ☿d = 1st then 4 Tuesdays.
and ☉d (19th) would be two days of rest or "Sabbath"

Greek Alphabet	Corresponding Hebrew
A lpha	Aleph
B eta	Beth
Γ amma	Gimel
Δ elta	Daleth
E psilon	He
Z eta	Zain
H ta	Heth
Θ eta	Jeth
I ota	yod
K appa	Caph
Λ ambda	Lamed
M u	Mem
N u	Nun
Ξ i	Samech
O micron	Ain
Π i	Pe
P ho	Resch
Σ igma	Shin
T au	Tau
Υ psilon	Vau
Φ i	
X i	
Ψ si	(Koph Tsadde)
Ω mega	

It will be seen the two alphabets have been borrowed from the ancient Phoenician, but at the present day are wide apart. The Phoenician appears to have been borrowed from the "Nezzal" alphabet, which is the oldest Phonetic alphabet in existence. Of course they have not the same order — Compare the following:

of these Columns there are nine Corresponding to the 9 vowels — all slight slickers 1 2 3 4 5 6 7, ...

there are altogether 54 letters or characters representing so many simple sounds.

(Greek Names)	Phoenician			Early Greek				Hebrew Early & Later				Hebrew Names
Alpha 1	✗	✗	✗	Λ	✗	ᗅ	1	✗ ✗ ✗				Aleph
Beta 2				B			2					Beth
Gamma 3							3					Gimel
Delta 4							4					Daleth
Epsilon 5							5					He
Upsilon 6							6					Vau
Zeta 7							7					Zain
Eta 8							8					Heth
Note / Iota *10			(Theta)				9					Jeth
Kappa 11							10			*		Yod
Lambda 12							11					Caph
Mu 13							12					Lamed
Nu 14							13					Mem
Xi 15							14					Nun
Omicron 16							15					Samech
Pi 17							16					Ain
18							17					Pe
Koppa 18							18					Tsadde
Rho 19							19					Koph
Sigma a/San 20							20					Resch
Tau 20												Shin
9 Theta *						10	10			*		Tau
		jota										

The proper place of the last character is after Theta = jota but the later Hebrew is in order. it will be seen that Later Greek has two more letters. (these are Consonants)

189

The Phaenician Alphabet like the Hebrew
consisted of twenty two letters, 4 Gutturals,
aleph, he, heth, and ain.} Corresponding to the
א , ה , ח , ע (Hebrew.

4 labials, beth, Vau, Mem & pe,
Corresponding to. = ב ו מ פ

4 palatals, = Gimel, Caph, Koph & yod.
Corresponding to = ג כ ק י —

3 dentals = daleth, teth, & tau,
Corresponding to - ד ט ת

3 linguals = lamed, nun, & resh
Corresponding to = ל נ ר

4 Sibilants = Zain, Samech, tsade & shin.
Corresponding to = ז ס צ ש

like the Hebrew the phaenician is read from
right to left, and like the Neyal the characters
have different values, as if they had some
knowledge. of the "Signs of possession" or position
as the Neyal. alphabet conforms to the rules
of numbers, it follows that the place alters
the value, — in no case did the Phaenicians
write boustrophedon, (as the early Greeks did)
that is alternately from right to left, and from Left
to right. or as the Egyptain. either way in different
the Egyptains also used a vast number of Syllabariums
and determinatives, making more than a thousand
Symbals, — The chaldeans and Assyrians, also
used about 300. different Cuneiform characters —

"Phoenician theory of the beginning of all things"
first, there was a dark and stormy air, and turbid
chaos. without limit for, countless ages ——
then the wind became enamoured of its own
first principles, and an intimate union took
place between them, a connection called desire
(Pothos) and this was the beginning of the creation
of all things. from this embrace with the wind,
was generated "Môt" (slime - or watery secretion)
from which sprang all the seed of creation.
and there were certain animals without sen-
sation, from which intelligent animals
were produced, called "Zôpha-sēmin" and
these were in the form of an egg. — and from
Môt shone forth the sun, and the moon.
and the lesser and greater stars. and when the
air began to send forth light, by the conflagration
of land and sea, wind and clouds were
produced, and great downpourpour of the
heavenly waters, — from these and the heat of
the sun, ensued thunder and lightning,
then the intelligent animals began to move
both in the sea and on the land — all these
things were found written in the cosmogony
of "Taaut." &cc, — Here we have a different
principle of creation, from that of the Hebrews
very nearly corresponding to the Eternal Elements
of the Druids, from which all things were made.

191

Rough sketch
of a Dragon
and Same
Runes,
from
an

ⅠⅠ ᚼⅠᛒⅠ ᚠᚱ ☆☆ⅠⅤ Ⅰ ᛏ ᚱ ⅠⅠ ☆ ᚼ Ⅰ ᛏ.

ancient tumulus, at Maeshowe, near
the ancient Kirkwall, in the Orkney.
Supposed to be from the 9th to the 12 Centurys
these tumulies are called the Pict's houses.
this one of Maeshowe, was Conical, 36 feet high
300 feet in circumprance, the main Chamber
or Cromlech, was 15 feet square, & 13 feet high,
with burial Cells on the North, East & South
from 5½ to 7 feet long by 4½ wide, and 3 feet high
there were about one thousand Runes, and many
pictures of animals, no Satisfactory translation
has ever been given of them but with the aid of
the Neipal alphabet, the different parts of the animal can be read numericaly at least

"Universal — Nergal — Numerical Alphabet"

The numbered grid (columns 1–9 across the top, rows 1–9 down the left side) is filled with handwritten shorthand-like symbols that cannot be rendered as text.

To the right of the grid the following annotations appear:

Vowel	Word	Number
A	And	Nine
E	End	Eight
H	Hen	Seven
H	Hane	Six
I	Jn	Zine
O	On	Four
T	un	Three
A	Woo	Two
Y	7	one

The plain figures on top are the numbers of the Columns.
and on the left = the number of lines or figures from the top.
The dotted figures ⠄ to ✚ on upper left to lower right corner
of the Square. Represent the 9 vowels of this alphabet
the vowels govern the "Consonants." which must be
of the same value as the Vowel, that aids it, either
in the Denominator or the Numerator of the fraction
Observe the denominator throughout the same Column
and the Numerator the same throught the same line
if the Alphabet is established, as regards the order,

B C D F G ' K L M N p Q R S T V H 3 ✚ Val
1 2 3 4 5' 6 7 8 9 10 11 12 13 14 15 16 17 18

Count the first Consonant B on top of the Colum and N at the foot
then the Consonants that have double figures to the right of the vowel
The Vowels have a short and long Sound, if short write
only one of the two figures, and the double figures if long.
the unit will be the same, 10.20.30.40.50.60.70.80 & 90.

Before atempting to translate by means of this alphabet
Consider the folluing Axioms of self-evident truths.
A Vowel is an indipendant Sound of the voice
that may be Sounded long or short with one impuls
of the voice, of which there are nine distinct sounds
and these have but the one Sound, in all the
Combination, if there are diphrangs or triphthangs
each must be Sounded, smoathly without a stop.
as gair, or gwair, both are single syllables.
the Consonants cannot be Sounded without the
aid of one of the Vowels., hence they must follow
the Colum or the line of the vowel that suports them
practicaly the vowel is the Same as the decimal point
in decimal Sums. having a known value, —
because evry vowel is a single figure and a cypher
and stands in the square at right angle with any
two figures of the Same value, the Numerator and th
denaminator being the Same, they are = one (kind)
thus the value is = its place in the Colum and the Colum
each Colum begin with, 10. 19. 28. 37. 46. 55. 64. 73. 82. 91 ↑
91 begin the Second Square, all the ☐ have the Same footion
and the different squares are number in there order.

A B Γ Δ Z Θ K Λ M N Ξ Π P Σ T Φ X Ψ.
1 2 3 4 5 6 7 8 9 10 11 12 13 14 15 16 17 18
a b c ch d δ f ff g ng l ll m n p n s t th

This is called the Kim. o greek alphabet, there are
Some Consonant that are not proper as J in English,
which is a double Sounded Consonant ΔZE. (omitted)

Example the word "Man" by the three alphabets English }}ν. Kimrik }}ν. Greek }}ν. as a matter of fact this is not translating but transposing or changing the Key. the vowel has the same sound and value in each but the Consonants differ.

"Analysis of the Vowels."

⸪	⸫	⸬	⸭	⸮	ⸯ	⸰	⸱	†	= a Bird flying.
→	↘	↓	↙	←	↖	↑	↗	—	= the direction.
12	20	30	40	50	60	70	80	90	= numerical value
α	ε	η	Ħ	ι	ο	υ	ω	ɟ	= the Sound

the first eight, are devided into the upward & downward the → implies the water or tide ebbing or going out. the ← = the tide Coming in or flowing. the following ↓↓↓ = the root Sign of Possession. and the ↖↑↑ = the Branch — is a Nautral. these different forces balance each other, that is →← being equal they counter act. ↘↖ also balance, or ↘↑↗, also make an equilibrium the moving power therefore in a word or Sentence is generaly in the Consonants, or the fractions. Now to the Clearer understanding of these forces we'll draw the paralelograms of each pair. thus each has the Same force but in diffet 4↗ + direction Starting the + with a ə E it reaches 1, then the Ħ η takes the place of a.E. driving the object to 2, where — υ ω. begins. carrying it to the place of begining, having made the circle of the Stars. by their several forces.

There is a reason to believe that the account we have from the Jews. of the ages of the antideluvians, who are said to have lived (some of them) nearly a thousand years! that, there was a mistake, in the figures. then used by the Babylonians, in this Maner. Supose we Say 1° of Latitude and Longitude. on the E. quator. = 60 Geographical Miles. or 69•04 English miles now it will be plain that if we omit the point. the figures. would be 6904, or supose 69•7 was the figure, that is Seven tenths. then we have 697, or (Six hundred and Ninety Seven) in place of $69 \frac{7}{10}$. I mention this Simply as a warning. not to Commit Such a mistake with the Nepal alphabet, be carefull of the points, for to use a fractional figure as a whole number, is a grivious mistake, for that decimal point, all though in its Self of no value, is Nevertheless an impartent factor in conection with the other figures —— Same time. a • Stand for 10, and Same time for 1. and at other times for the whole number of the unit, its value depending on the rule that is used. in the Daminical day rule it Stands for a day and also for a Century. in the Epact it Stands for 10, or 1 on the left of another figure — or unit or it May Stand for the Sign of Nassessian in the alphabet,) = a.) = K. and) = J. as)};)(•)(•), or "Katolik"} The Runes are Straight Lines }

I shall here show the Manes (not the absolute)
Numbering of the Letters of the universal Language
See the columns of nine the Vowels are the Decimal nodes

ح ۷ ۷ ~ ۲ ۲ ~ ۷ L = A. E. Ha. HE. I. O. Hu. Hoo. y. •

and the double figures or fractions represent the Consonants

Numbered 1 Labial. 2 Guteral. 3 Dental. 4 Liquid &c

| by triads = | B M P | G ng K | D N T | Lh Eh Rh |
| Dual = | V F | gh Ch | S Th | Z J |

Allegorical Figure   of the Earth, and Sea.

The Earth ⊞   The Sea ◖◗
= four Squares,   = the Sea
in one is the   'within & without
Sacret alter of   the Earth, the land
Saturn ♄.   and the Sea are =
Connected in such   a way that their inherent
forces Combine and cause the tides in the oceans.
to run 6h out and 6h in alternetly, that this law may
be easier to Comprehend, let us briefly Consider the
attributes, of the Primary Atoms, which are unchanged
in form, and therfore Eternal having nither begining or ending
and when free in space revolve apparently on their
own center, by the inherent force in each atom, and
occupy each its respective Space, and this particular
portion of space Cannot Contain any other atom or atoms
at the same time, — there are round or globular atoms
or elements, when they predominate in any Combination
they produce a figure more or less rounded in form.

Angular atoms having flat Surface Combine to form a permanent, amalgam or forms different from either prime, but having force equal to the Combined as for example, one equivalent of Hydrogen (=1) and one Equivalent of Oxygen (=8) Combine to make water, and the equivalent of water is "Nine" = to the two primes this "Theorem" requires a mathematical demonstration but we must never forget the unit, of the Sum, because if there be a fraction, we must not Consider them as whole numbers. (as it would appear the Jews did, when they found the age of a certain person to be 96·9, or nearly 97 years, but in their wisdom they dispensed with the decimal point, and said 969 years old!) observe, the Combined forces of the earth and the Sea (we will Supose) Causes the Combination to revolve to —wards the right, thus bringing the Earth ⊞ the portion of the Sea within the □ = ⌣ (¹⁄₇ or 64 in the Col) 1+7=8 or ⅓ of 21⁴⁄₇ (day) the 0 = 6+2 = 8. also the outer Sea = ⌒ ⌣ = 8. again Supose the revolving was toward the left ⊞ = ⌣ = (68 in Col) 5+7=12=3. also ◊ = 4+8=12=3 lastly ⌒ = 12=3 it will be Seen, by comparing the different position of the □ ⌣ = (28) ⌣ (=32) ⌣ (= 64) ⌣ (= 68) but the Sea itself is the Same within and without. in each position, — in the Same quarter of the earth is Shewn the (Cromlech) or three Stone alter of ♄ in his house ♒. or Capricornus (goat) now in respect to this curious figure of the earth which are found on the Ancient Stones of Knowledge, more than — thousand years ago, the Same Character

was found latly in Australia on or near the ♑
or tropics of Capricorn (23½° South Lat) and about (E.L.) 135°
or as near as it may be the center of Australia or [symbol]
if convenient, compare the voyages of "Hea Dêr" the nest
shown there, is surrounded by the same lines. as the alter of [symbol]
and geographicaly we know that the nest represents Australia
and the sunken Continent is represented here by the ⊞.
this square consists of Γ (Gama) and ⅃ or •| and |– or 90.
the outward form of the Sea forms the Letter G (Latin)
and the inside of the Sea = γ or the small g in greek.
hence we see the three mysterious G^s (the Gog mag)
(Γογ•α[symbol]) out of this square, which with the Sea
is supposed to revolve on the center or the alter of Saturn.
the Hieroglyphics within give us the following six figures
⊞ = $\frac{1}{—}$ numerator / Denominator } = $\frac{1}{7}$ placed 1st . . . . 7, next ⊞ $\frac{2}{8}$ = 1•28•7.
lastly ⊞ take left (4 = 2d place and ⊞ = (5 place near the last
thus ".14,28,57" this is the decimal fraction of $\frac{1}{7}$ =
Start = $\frac{1}{7}$ $\frac{3}{7}$ $\frac{2}{7}$ $\frac{6}{7}$ $\frac{4}{7}$ $\frac{5}{7}$ } the key word is the $\frac{1}{7}$. in 1 and 2 = num
in 3 & 4, Start with a figure that is 1 more. 5 & 6 with 2 more

$\frac{1}{7}$ =	1 4 2 8 5 7	= 9
$\frac{2}{7}$ =	2 8 5 7 1 4	= 9
$\frac{3}{7}$ =	4 2 8 5 7 1	= 9
$\frac{4}{7}$ =	5 7 1 4 2 8	= 9
$\frac{5}{7}$ =	7 1 4 2 8 5	= 9
$\frac{6}{7}$ =	8 5 7 1 4 2	= 9
	9 9 9 9 9 9	

These figures are of the neuter gender,
the right hand period = the definite article He
(the) if we subtract 1 from the 3d period
and add it to the article = "Hea" (3 god of the
then read the 3 per from ← 13, 28, = "Mathie"
(mathew) or the mother) "the guide"
the 3d product $\frac{3}{7}$ = 428571 (= 47 14)
= to the 1st year of Anno Domini (new style) 1, begin and end with 4.
$\frac{3}{7}$ in Colum of 9s = 6.6. See the Chapter and verse of Matthew !

.14285̈7̈ = ᴀᴠᴠᴅᴇᴢ – The Nests
.2̈85̈714̈ = ᴠⱔᴇᴢᴀᴠ – of old
.4̈285̈7̇1 = χᴠⱔᴇᴨᴀ – Stones of the Father
.5̇714̈2̈8̇ = ᴇᴨᴀχᴠⱔ – Father's Stones
.7̇14̈2̈85 = ᴨᴀᴠᴠⱔᴇ – that disapeard
.8̇5714̇2̈ = ⱔᴇᴢᴀᴠᴠ – where we came from

Australia	before the flood	the Alter of
our Fathers	that migrated	we their descendants

sign of possition . Greek letters   English translation   Do

observation on the alter П = 135, (= East Longitude)
(yet we my Consider that rather a Coincidence than its
Longitude from London) the unit = 9. in this position
there are eight different positions in Notation as follows

$$= \frac{14 \quad 11 \quad 16 \quad 13 \; \{18\} \quad 15 \quad 12}{\frac{9 \quad 5 \quad 2 \quad 7 \quad 4 \quad (9) \quad 6 \quad 3}{1, \; \acute{E} \quad Λ \quad H \quad Δ \; (1Σ \; ZO \; Φ\mathit{m})}} \right\}$$

= ᴬᵘⱔ ᴇᴧᴧⱔ – ʷⱔ GOΦ .
= ʝ went below —

this would imply that at first this alter was Submerged
or that this part of the great Continent. (of 4 Subdivisions)
at first Sank togather, but afterwards the Southern ¼
again rose above the waters, – hence the prediction
that the other quarters will in the fullness of time
also arise, Similar prediction also exists in respect to the Island of Teman, – the Templ of Teman
is Supposed to represent the internal parts of the Earth
that is to Say the length Bredth and highth (thickness)
all the same (see Rev 21^{ch} 16^v & 17^v) = 12000 Furlongs. (= ⅛ mile)
12000 [crossed out] = 1500 Miles (English) the walls are =
to 144 Cubits (= 18^{inch}) from the elbow to point of Middle finger)
$\frac{4½ = 72}{\text{get } 216}$ } this wall divides the four Squares, in the form
of a ✚ this is the main interior of the Earth ⊕ .

The Allegorical discription found in Revelation is not exactly the same as on the Stones of knowledge which says, that the interior is ⅛ of the Circumference (that would be about 3,125 English miles!) but if the Mesurments given in Revelation (12000 Furlongs) was the mesure of one of the four squares (=1500 E.M) then the four squares would be = 3000 every way. and the walls said to be 144 Cubits the average Mesure from the Elbow to the point of Middle finger, is about 18 inch = to 216 feet or together 3,216 the difference is but a very small fraction and as the Cubit is not a fixed Mesure, it is easy to account for the small fraction of difference—Now according to the Stones of knowledge the Passage of the Sea through the Earth purifies the water from all impurities of Salt, &c. and the water becomes pure and Clear as Crystal, this also is the description John gives of the "River of life" — But My orthadox friend will say, this means a Spiritual State, and, the throne is not the Earth, or of the Earth this must be taken as an allegory! or Spiritual! very well My friend, let it be So, of course Heaven, and the throne also must be So. and every thing els mentioned, including the Dragon and the Bottomless—Nevertheless, you will permit me to belive that the fact remains, "there is a heaven of the earth, earthly, containing a Spirit or intelligence, which we may find if we Serch within, there is a straight road to the throne!!!

"The perpetual Generic triads of Saturn ($\hbar$)
or the Genealogical tree, of the Father of Gods & men
containing 77 generations in all, the first seven
from the root is single, all the rest are double or 14.
generation to the period, in the same maner as the square
root is devided into periods of two figures, see the
the Facsimile attached, translated into plain figures,
Saturn is the Dominical day of every Leap year century
and the seventh day of the week is named after him.
observe in every 7 generation, there are one or more sevens
which when added together by the rule gives a "key"
but we can discover by the Sign of Possession. 5·1·3
the century which has 366. is the 1st of 3d period
of 14. and ten above is the Sign of Possession
the following analysis, of the allegorical figure
and the Sign of Possession and the number, will help
the Student — 1st of the figure, this is (in the original)
a Man in a Siting posture, with one hand pointing
to his head, and the other hand pointing upwards.
the head and neck consists of Sixe triads. forehead = 600
eyes = 664, nose = 734. Mouth = 5·1·3, the figures are the
units of three periods of two figures each. the Sign of poss"
is that of the root, that is red from the hip to the knee →
and from the knee to the foot ←, and the words are
é, k̇, φ → e kᵃ φᵉ and ← φᵉ kᵃ eᵗ = ureka — I have it.
or gᵛ found it, — that which has been found is the rule.
the unit of the left hand period (5) to odd or even.

this may be either 3,2 or 1,4. let 14 then = the lefthand period
double the 1st = 2nd period. double 2nd p = 3rd period, double
the 3d p. we have 1.12 here we cannot go any further because
there must not be more than two figures in each period —
then to the right hand figure of the 3d p. add the hundred (lefthand 1)
and we have ·14·28·57, which = the decimal fraction
of $\frac{1}{7}$ the small fraction ·12 left, now becomes one index,
this we divide equaly 6 + 6 (=12) this triad has $\overset{6\ 0\ 6}{* * *}$ three
this triad is on the seat of the man, 366 is the Navel.
and 664 or 600 is the top of the head, and these four triad
are the tetragrammaton of the man "the words of many-
meanings. — (see the Facsimile on the next Page)
This ancient Picture and Scroll writing is very
interesting, as it was written by jnspiration,
and if we have a knowledge of this rule, it
is not at all difficult to read and understand.
it belongs to the Astronomical Class, and is
like Uclid's "Points, Lines & Superfices"
not a reality, but an imaginary, or jdeal,
or Allegorical, explaindtion of facts or truth.
There is a remarcable resemblence between
Same Spiritual ideals, among Christians,
and this astral allegorical production of the
ancients, with the ancients, Saturn was one of
the ancient gods, the Father of both gods, and men.
he presided over time, or death. even his Scythe.
is shown at that part of the body that is only con-
-ected very slightly at the lower class" ⌐⌐ + $\left(\begin{smallmatrix}3\ 7\ 3\\4\ 1\ 7\end{smallmatrix}\right)$

From the ideal father, is but a short step to the Creator of all things; from this astral emanation this Genealogical tree, disguised by inspiration. and requiring a knowledge of the rules of revelation before we can easily understand its meaning for we must not forget that an imperfect understanding of its Scientific Construction, or its true purpose, would most certainly mislead, because there are many ways of reading these hieroglyphics, of which, the figure is entirely composed of, moreover, it would be not at all to be wondered at, if this figure was mistaken for the Prince of darkness! the Source of all evil, or any other Spiritual Conseption. — But he that hath understanding will be able to count the number of this man (a Beast) nay more this man has the number on his face! (Consult the 13ch of Revelation and the 18th verse — furthermore, this number is a Scientific fact, having to do with time as mesured by ☉ D ✳, or the great triad and the Genealogy, if not a real fact, is a Scientific axiom, of great importance, when aplied to the mater of fact, — here again the Christian has what he belives to be a fact, in the good old book, for which he has Such veneration, and great Confidence in this Suposed Genealogy can be seen in Mathew 1st ch and Luke 3d the first Counts from Abraham to christ. and the other from Jesus to Abraham and on to god!

The Christian is supased to belive that this is a true
geneaology, and yet they are so very different, Mathew,
Says from Abraham to David 14 generation and he
repeats this 14 gen, three times that would be 42 generation
but in the last fourteen he only gives 13! Now
Luke gives 14 generation More than Mathew, from
Jeses to Abraham! there must be Some cause
for this difference, either these genealogies are
of two different persons, or els they are allegorical
as this genealogy of Saturn, — Now Supasing that the
writers had access to this of Saturn, it would
be easy enough to account for this difference!
My neighbans Mr Cit Songa, would like
to hear Me explain this Spiritual Mystery —
which he has been told is also a Scientific Marvel!
and More than two thausand years old. but he
declares that it would be quite usless to atempt
to do So while Mr Tsirch, and Mr Ledifini,
are present, unless they agree not to engage in their
usual Wordy-War. — these two gentlemen if
present, May Stay and listen, on these condition
or atherwise will please to retire. — Now Mr Cit-
Songa, I have no daubt you have been aften
pusled at the fierce wordy-war Carried on by your
neighbaurs, a Spiritual-Scientific battle to the
death, I will not ask you to take my word, as a
Matter of fact, what I prapose to do, is, to give you a
rule to wark aut, the same will be a self-evident truth.

205

Now, Supose that my name is <u>Mathew</u>, and that
I lived about Nineteen hundred years ago, that
I was a friend of the guardians of the <u>Oracle</u>.
and had learned somthing of the mystey of it —
I required a genealogy, for the purpose, of incl-
asing in it a mater of fact, a truth, which could
be understood by my friends, but would not
be understood by my enemies — in short I wished
to preserve this truth by "inspiration" for the time
hence I choos the genealogy of the god saturn.
that is, that part of it, that have the stars (triads)
the arms. and the leg, 14 triads or generation in each
observe one period of 14 Starts from the + at the back
and the other from the + on the breast. and both end
at the great cross † on top, the last triad of each
are locked togather, or added into units. ⊂ < ⇁ ∥ (⇀)
(q̇ 5̄ 4́) = HΣE. hence because of this adding
up of two triads there would be only 13 for an arm.
and this is the period ending with 380 as it is the least.
Now my Brather Luke, also wished to copy all
the genealogy, and he began at the † where I had
finished, only he used the units of the added triad
Êʃι (jesu—jesus). but I ended my list. by making
one word of the two triad, thus 380 4́ 6 6̀ (grê33)
(or KRISS) hence I did not use the Sign of pasession
because I did not count the triads of the Body or the
thrane on which it rests. from which the river of
Life isues. of pure water Clear as crystal ~~~~

Now, Mr Citsonga, do[es] not profess to be guided
by a Suposed light which he cannot see, nor does
he pretend to guide others while in darknes himself.
therefore with his permission j'will try and throw a
glimer of light on the mysterious brotherhood —
and their Secret methods, and Spiritual indulgence.
The Secret Chamber of the gods, is strictly guarded.
and no one is allowed to enter, th[at] cannot answer
the questions asked at the door, or give the proper sign
the place is "Tapu" (Taboo) to the uninitiated.
Having arrived at the door, and having knocked in
a prescribed maner, a mute question is asked, " ? "
you will observe this is the Sign of Interogation,
and you are to write the answer. (place), on the left. then
1, and on the right the difference vis ⟩ answer) I \ +.
2ᵈ gue. where is that Situate⟩ "in the bosom of the Father"
3 gue. what is your Name? " Mᵃ Θ^ω " (mathew)
4th gue. Can you give the Scientific meaning of the Name?
"the name Cansists of two words, the inatial of the 1st
is M, which belongs to the "Second order", unit = 3.
which may be devided into 1&2, or into 1, 1, 1, we take
1&2 of the first order = a b — Mab — Son. or we take
the first of each order or devision of the Alphabet = a, k, J.
and prefixing the unit. Mak' or Makt = also Son.
the Second word inatial = Θ. of the 1st order, unit = 8,
we devide it into 2&6. which we take from the 3d order
vis M&w̃ (ΥΩ) = ΘΥΩ — Deuw — god (Son—god)
these answers being all Satisfactory mathew was
permited, to make a translation of the astrological part.

Now another knock is heard at the door in due form and after answering the _first_ dumb (?) question correctly. he is asked, "How do you travel? answer, from the great Cross (†) to the throne, from which the truth runs as a river of pure water clear as crystal, 3ᵈ question what is your name? Answer, "ΛHK" 4ᵗʰque. give the scientific explaination of the meaning of the word, answer if read ← it means Kêl – Hidden – Inspired, and also means Kîl – Narrow, because the original is found on that part of the "Oracle" where "the neck joins the head and the body, thus ↲, = (Luk⁵·) Since your name is found So near the Sign (ı ı) and you propose to translate, you must translate all, including the throne, if on examination the facts are correctly preserved, or if you are conversant with the rule of Possession, and Know the Same when you see it. Answer, I know the Sign, and its root is in the Mouth of God! (ı ı ⌣) translated = 5. 1. 3. and the rule is, ÷ the 5. into odd and even, (1&4, or 2&3) I take the 14 (because it Coincides with the Stars.) as 1ˢᵗ period then double the 1ˢᵗ P. for 2ⁿᵈ period = 28. then double the 28 = 56 for the 3 period, lastly double the 56 = 1. 1 2. here we have three figures, add the hundred 1 to 3ᵈ period = 57. and leave the fraction 12 as a future interest. the Periods are •14, 28, 57, which is the Decimal fraction of ♄ or ⅟₇ or the presiding Spirit (of the Seventh day of the week, and the dominical power of every Bissextile year of all the Centuries (366 days) against which is placed the + of one of its arms ⌐ +

or the upper triad of the lower devision of the body.
Now we may supose that Mathew, and Luke.
haning translated their respective lists, would
require the Sanction of the Guardians before they
would make the Same public — and he (the guardian)
on examining Mathew's list, discovers that there
is one triad Short, And inquires the reason, Mathew
answers, that the missing ward is Contained in the
last two names in the list namly Joseph & Mari.
first they must be written in greek letters, and numbered
by the Sign of Possession ĬŎ̈ΣĔΦ ↔ MẮPĬ̈ 9 6 9 5 3
the Ward reads from the right gr i s t !   9 8 5 3
(or chist) the triad left out (380) being,   1 9 5 4 8 3
my own name, as allready explained, which by the rule
is added to the 667 or the last triad of the other Branch —
this explaination being in due order, it was aproved —
Next Luke was asked to explain the reason why his
list Cantains only 76 while the original has 79 triads
Luke answers, because by the rule as used by me, that is
Starting from "the Key Stone † the triad on either side are
added into one Sum, and also the triads following
the other two Crases + or Branches are not Counted
because only 9 is supstituted in place of a cypher "0"
thus 198 = 108. because both produce 919, these are the
reason that I left, the three triad out of my List —
and the reason being Suficient the list was approved.

209

Now Cit'sanga declares, that he has become interested in this Mysterious astral ghost, and would very much like to have a little more light on this mater, and to examin this mystry when divested of its allegorical garments, and understand those peculiar rules, that enabled Joseph and Mary, between them to produce a "Grist"!

I hereby present My friend with this Translation in the form of a key of Generation of gods, & men, which I hope will facilitate the Study of the original. and the following remarks may be of value, the two branches are connected by an arch thus $3\,8\,0$ † $6\,6\,7$ are added together into Seperate <u>units</u> $\left.\begin{array}{c}6\,6\,7\\3\,8\,0\end{array}\right\} = 9\,.\,5\,.\,7\,,$ and the lesser triad (380) for the time, loses its identity in the greater (667) hence Luke begins his list with this united number = HΣE, and then follows the lesser = $2\,2\,7$ = HΛV (Heli in English) observe also that these united triads, $3\,8\,0$, and $6\,6\,7\,,3$ practically are Jaseph (⊙ 0 3 ê ph) and Maᵈ Λ'ê, as shewn by the rule of possession. Joseph borrows the 1st of Mary $3\,. = \Phi$ or ph. and Mary borrows the 3ᵈ of Joseph 7 "a key, a lock, and a door hold a certain relation to each other, when the door is to be locked the key is turned one way, and then to unlock it in the reverse way, in this way Mathew locked the door, to hide the Father, and Luke unlocked it, to shew the Father, which he calles "HΛV" = Êli or Heli, !

"The Translation"

516.464.688.258.227. 380.

375.
617.
584.
845.

Read consecutively
from the + 108. and also
from 607+ Branches

832.422.866.262.198 +108
919

600
664
734
513
965
271
108
721
439
786
373
417
366
607+697.
474
626
594
955
161
879
672
644
514
175
499
456
606+696.374.517

330
667
144
950
551
215
838
132
640
114
620
884
282
318
357

"The Key of Generation"
of Gods an Men.
Read from the great † Consecutively,
except the Branches, which begin
at the Smaller Classes, the Throne
continued without a breke,
because the object of this key
is not allegorical, but literal
(919) is the Product of both 108 & 198.

687.364.407.256.488.
348.
219.
191.
982.
891.
989.
171.
964.
603.726.445.517.374

811. 102.
917.378.246
(378)

488.256.
46.378.

Both Sides Equal.

Throne
& River of Life

211

1 0 2	
8 1 1	
9 1 7	
1	
3 7 8	
2 4 6	
4 8 8	
2 5 6	
4 0 7	
3 6 4	
6 8 7	
3 4 8	
2 1 9	
1 9 1	
9 8 2	
8 9 1	
9 8 9	
* 1 7 1	
9 6 4	10.56
6 0 3	2 6 0
7 2 6	8 8 8
4 7 5	6 8 2
5 1 7	7 5 4
3 7 4	7 3 3
· 6 9 6	4 1 3
4 5 6	8 5 6
4 0 9	1 5 2
1 8 4	8 6 9
6 1 3	5 6 2
7 3 5	4 2 5
5 7 4	2 7 6
6 0 8	
*	

The Genealogy as Given by Mathew, the Abrams Shows the word "Abraham" by taking two figures from each triad, and the "unit" of the three us 3. (* 171 = David) * 608 = the coming away into Babilon) the Last 10.56. is a tetragrammaton. to be trans figured into a triad, by adding 5+6 = 102. which is the Same as the first hence a Cycle. again by adding the 5 to its 1=6 = 606. which is the Same as the triad Standing (by Luke) for Abraham. vis 606 where the list of Mat? derivds from Luke's by Substituting 696. the triads of both Mathew & Luke are of Consecutive order, but in direction differs → Luke's ← is the unit of the previous triad.

but that of Mathew's = → from ten (10) the figures 9, & 1 are left out, by ÷ 9 = 3+3+3. by turing this triad & 1 7 1 into a tetragrammaton 3 1 3 4 3 = 4 1 3 4 4 the word = Sheep, Dāvēd

the order by Mathew is ← → • and by Luke ← • → and because of this we Cannot use the Same rule for both the → figure of Mathew is the difference from the tens. and hundreds, but the → figure of Luke is the previous hundreds plain ten.

The triads 365 and 504 do not progress, = but appear alternately.

212

observe $\begin{Bmatrix} 380 \\ 224 \end{Bmatrix}$ mary) Heli are added together = 607, the Branch

= + 699. and both of these downwards produce 474 = Dên

— man, but upwards they do not produce the Same, viz

366 & 357. yet the added Sum in both = 15 = unit 6.

J have put three signs over 380 the Sign over the cypher 0

is 9 the figure that forms the branch, = M'ri, by the account

given by Mathew She was Eincient, but not by Joseph.

and Luke gives the name of the Fatter "Heli" (English translator)

Jt is evident to me that the genealogies given by

Mathew and Luke, are genuine, as an allegory.

and if they did not draw the lists, from this Astrial

production of the Druids, then J must, that they did

a most wonderfull imitation, a wonderful Coincidence

J may here mention, that J have in my possession an-

other of these lists, differing in Some points from the

other two, but Seems nearer to that of Luke. as Luke

gives 76 generation, and this one, which purports to be

one of the rejected Gospels of the Council of Nice, 325

gives 73 generation, ending with "Adam" it was by

reading this List, that J was first struck, with the res-

emblance between it and another List of the ancient

kings of Britain, which Can scarsly be claimed

to be a true genealogy, allthough the order of the kings

might be true. but we shall pass on and examine

this key in its Scientific aspects, and explain

the Rules of the triads, and of the Sign of Possession.

Root /\ and Branch \/. and the irregular, 9 667 3

"The first thing that will strike the eye, will be, ⚹

Shewing a double arch, joining the upper and lower branches also the signs plus + † + and the root sign of possession I I \ then the single triad oposite the begining of the upper arm which is as it were removed from its proper place ⟵ the last triad on which the arch rests. are 3 8 0 & 6 6 7 these two Sums take from the triad thrown out viz 9 1 9. equal to their units. 6 6 7 = 1̇ᵘⁿⁱᵗ, so one of the 9° is taken and placed on the left. and 3 8 0 = 2̈ᵘⁿⁱᵗ it takes the remaining two 1 9. and place these figures on either side of the middle figure 8 3̇ 1̇ 8 9̇, and the other branch = 9̇ 6̇ 6̇ 7 3̲ the 3̲ is borrowed from "Mari" that is the amount of the unit of 3 1 8 9 = 3. hence Mari and J o ʒ ê ph (= Joseph) Now 3 8 0. is an irregular triad, and 9 is reciprocal to the cypher hence 3̇ 8̈ 9̇, = "Mᵉri," the last triad of the lower branch is 6̇ 6̇ 7, this branch is irregular in the right hand cyphers, inas much. as this branch starts from 6 0 7 + which is the same number, as the last two triads of the upper branch when added together 3 8 0 ⎞ = 6 0 7. 2 2 7 ⎠ but Mari was betrothed, to Joseph prior to her ♂ with "Heli" (2̇ 2̇ 7̇) and now his name at first = 6̇ 6̇ 7̇ = O ʒ ê, he takes the last figure of Mary 9 as his first and her first as his last = 3 ⟶ 9̇ 6̇ 6̈ 7̇ 3̀ = joseêph. one more illustration, the last triad of each branch 3̇ 8̇ 0̇ ∴ 6̇ 6̇ 7̇ 3̀. the figures on either side of the + are added viz 3 5 4 5 in we have thus Six Sign of Possession 1. 2 & 6 are the root sign, and the other three of the 1ˢᵗ order.

jt will be seen the uper branch harrawd th right hand figure of th lawer branch, and th lawer, th left hand figure, of th uper branch; these are added respec- irly to the unit place figures. $0+7=7$ & $7+3=10=1$ <u>unit</u> the Camman fractian $=\frac{1}{7}$, the ward $= \dot{3}\dot{8}\dot{4}\cdot\dot{6}\dot{6}\dot{1}$, which $= "\Gamma\varsigma\eta\zeta\zeta\tau"$ (Grêzz†) or christ, in English. absene th third letter η (eta) is the Sign of <u>Saturn</u>. this ocupies th $\odot$ in Mari "The Mather" or <u>Eve</u>: it seems that bath mathers, fell into the same, or th Same apple fell on them, but Adam is nat repated as wishing to put away Eve, Jaseph had a mind to do so.

The 7 days of th week are named after the Sun & moan and the five planets, which in th arder of their revalutian are $\mathbb{D} \; \text{☿} \; \text{♀} \; \odot \; \text{♂} \; \text{♃} \; \eta$, here we are to supase these seven to faun a circle th $\mathbb{D}$ fallaws η. taking the central $\odot$ as the first day of the week Sunday pass over three to th right th $4^{th} = \mathbb{D}$ moanday. pass three again fram $\mathbb{D}$ th 4th is ♂ Tuesday (massday) th 4th again fram $\text{♂} = \text{☿}$ Wenesday (Murcury-day) th 4th fram $\text{☿} = \text{♃}$ or Thursday (Jupeter-day) th 4th fram $\text{♃} = \text{♀}$ Friday (Venus day) lastly th 4th fram $\text{♀} = \eta$, or the seventh day Saturn-is day — we may discaver th arder of their revalutian, fram th week days arder $\odot \; \text{☽} \; \text{♂} \; \text{☿} \; \text{♃} \; \text{☿} \; \eta$, by starting with η^{d} passing over <u>ane</u> to the left; we also can percive that in th day of the week, the masguline & femenine are alternetly. and Saturn is always th Daminical day of every Leap year Century. and then venus shares th hanaurs with him

Now a Bisextile or Leap year has 366 days and we find this triad, the 1st triad of the 3d period of 14. (or the 1st, 6th of the Seventh) the Common year = 365. Now the Common year whither up or down produces the Same triad viz 507, these are not found in the genealogy having allready shewn that Saturn in order of revolution is Seventh, and in the order of the week it is the Seventh and now in its Genealogy, is also by Seven, in the handle of the Key there are 3 times Seven (21) triads, in the middle part there are 4 times Seven (twice 14 or 28 triad) and the Same in the two Branches in all 77 triads. there are a certain relation between 7 & 4, which I shall presently explain — the top of the head (forehead = 600) Counting down the 4th figures or triads have the Sign / I \ called the root Sign of Possession. the Number is = 5.1.3 which is = the units of 14·28·57, or decimal fraction of $\frac{1}{7}$.

There is a curious Legend in connection with this "Key" and it is interesting, as shewing, that christian Genealogy, has a strange resemblance to this Legend. but before giving it I will first explain the Rules. Governing these triads, 1st Starting with $\overset{\leftarrow}{9}$ I $\overset{\rightarrow}{7}$ in the triangle to go ~~further down~~ 1st add the Sum to one figure. (if you wish to continue further down.) = $\overset{\leftrightarrow}{8}$ then Subtract the $\overset{\rightarrow}{7}$ from $\overset{\leftrightarrow}{8}$ = 1 for middle figure. lastly subtract the $\overset{\leftrightarrow}{9}$ from 10 = $\overset{\rightarrow}{1}$ or = $\overset{\leftrightarrow}{8}$ 11. and any other triad going lower follows this rule — in going up, the rule is $\overset{\leftarrow}{9}$ I $\overset{\rightarrow}{7}$. 1st Subtract $\overset{\rightarrow}{7}$ from 10 = $\overset{\leftarrow}{3}$. then Subtract the middle figure from $\overset{\leftarrow}{9}$ = $\overset{\rightarrow}{8}$. add these to unit. and if required Such other figure when added = $\overset{\leftarrow}{9}$.

216

The triad then = 3 7 8. therefore the middle arrow shows whither the direction is up or down, — Now the first 21ʳᵈ facing a triangle, is called the Lower Heaven (spirit place) where the Spirit is tried if found wanting is turned out of heaven, again into space. but if found good enters the inner triangle, and is there perfected, and conducted to the first + or the entrance to the second heaven — where the upright dwell (1)1)=9 1 9 here are three figures when added into unit = 10 = 1. thus we find that one is three, and three is one! this one place is opposite the second + or door of entrance into the third heaven. over these two heavens stands the great arch, and the great sword (of destiny) or "Cracea-Mors" this then reminds us of the great architect of the universe!!! and the place is an oblong square, — these two heavens ☐ ▭ or added ✚ or thus ⌐, these heavens or key is supposed to revolve, so as to lock or unlock the door — as the legend is given in full elsewhere, I shall only give here some of the most important point in it. 1ˢᵗ there was a covenant, between the six tribes and the Druids which made it obligatory on the Druids to be present at the sacrifices as interpreters of the omens ᵉᵗᶜ. 2ᵈ these tribes sacrificed all evil doers. whose sentence was death, — in the course of time they began to sacrify the Innocent if there were not enough of prisoners, against this the Druid protested and many refused to attend. and at first they were excommunicated, but afterward were readmitted to Cammior on condition that they should wear "Black garment" called "Kris-chan" hence there were christians before christ's time! 3d these christians entered into a covenant with Nezgals or the Hereditary branch of the Druids, who had never offered sacrifice of blood, — they were in sympathy with these christians who now openly aligned to practice 4th these Nezgals were the keepers of the Records and the great oracle, and the secret grounds of the Druids and from them were elected the Arch-Druid and the captains in war (the Druids never engaged in war) this was mostly done by ballot, but in case of certain contingences, an appeal could be made to the Swords of Destiny. one of these Swords was kept at "the Temple of Teman" in Britain, and the other at the Stones of Carnac in Gaul (France) — 5th a trial by these Swords took place, in consequence of the result, a secret marriage took place between the bearer of "Cracea Mors" and Helen the Holy one of Mount Paren, a virgin in the Temple of the ☉ ☽ and a godess, of the Hereditary order of the Nezgals — of this marriage an only son was born, his name was "Elvar-of-the-Sword" (Elvar-o-glêth) who was the last conceived in "Teman (last Lord of T") on the very day of his birth the Sea overflowed Teman hence he was called "Heli" (Salt-water) or Sea. 6th in conformity with the oracle's declaration

"That a son of the gods should offer himself as a Sacrifice, and after that no inferior person could be offered
as an acceptable offering, to this end, Heli, when
he arrived at maturity, offered himself as a last Sacrifice! (see the first recorded Christian Sermon) —

7th while about to be finalated, he was resqued
by an armed band, of gigantic Stature., and the
victim was carried on board a Ship, which imid-
iatly Sailed away, — to Rome, and Palestine &c
where he married a virgin, and out of her he had
a Son, who afterward Sat on the throne of his Father.
now this pair Heli (2 2 7) and mari (3 8 0) we
find Supasting one Side of the arch, and the mother
of Heli is also there (2.5 8 ÷ (here the 5 is ÷ into 1 & 4.
and 8 ÷ int 1 & 7) = 2.1 4.1 7 = Elana — the fairest.
thus making three periods. the three right hand = 4 1 7.
the product of the leap year 3 6 6. or the 2d triad of the
upper (14) Periods, counting upwards 13 we have 6. 1 7
and downwards we have (a reversable = 1 7. 5) 1 7th = 5. 1 7.
and the 36th = 9. 1 7, — the Student will find many curious.
Coincidence in this "Key" but remember that Allegory
is always deficient or Short of the reality represented.
J Shall now try and explain the Arch and the Key-Sword.
and the Suparter of the Arch. Scientificaly (arithmetical)

original   Translation

The triads on which the arch rests 3 8̇ 0̇, and 6̇ 6̇ 7̇, and units
are turned into the tetragrammaton or 4 figures or letters
of many meanings. one has the right hand figure ÷ 1. 6
the one crossed or enclosed in a circle thus + or ⊕ } 6 6 + 6.
2. the left hand figure is × by the unit 2 = 6 then an = figure
is taken from the 8. (6 6 added = 3̇) leaving 2 to prefix the cypher unit
= 20 × 3 = 60, lastly remove the 1st. 6 to the right = 6 6 ⊕ 6.

2	3	8	0
(2	2	2	7
+6	2	5	8
÷1	÷7	15	15 *
	8	+6	6

here we have ÷ 6 6, the reverse of the other triad
we divid the ÷ into 7 ∂ 1 and cross the 1, now
the unit of the top triad = 2 place on the left (tens)
the others 2 + 6 = 8. = 28 = Cycle of the ⊙ or Sun.
again the 6 6 7 added = 19, = Cycle of the ☽ or the moon
the Colum add to 15 = Cycle of a certain Star (say ♂)
we have thus the great triad ⊙ ☽ * (Julian period) we
also read these numbers harisontely 2̇,5̈ 8̈ divid 5 = 1, 4
and 8 = 1, 7, the unit is preserved = 2̇ 1̇ 4̇ 1̇ 7̇ = Ha-lcur
translated "Salt" 2̇ 2̇ 7̇ = HΛV. or Heli, — Brine
or the Briny-ocean. 3 8 0̇, = M'ri (Mary) means
a drop of salt water or a tear. the right hand figure
of 380 is interchangable with 9 = i or 1, lastly we
will read the arch and the Suparters 3 8̇ 0̇ + 7 6 6 7 add-g
= Γ Ρ Η Σ Θ = Grêsth or christ, as the sword is
now Suposed to have been drawn, let us enquire
by whome it was drawn, for this purpose let us
add up the 3 triads on the right (only one has been used)

units 1	6	6	7
(9	1	4	4
5	9	5	0
	16	15	11
	7	6	2

here each Colum is added separatly into units.
nis 7̇. 6̇. 2̇, = HWΛ. or Éwl. or Juli.
we may add 1 or 9 for the cypher on the right
as they are reciprocal —

As these signs of possession are sure to be pusling at first to the Students, I shall incert 6 different position.

/	\	\	1ˢᵗ
/	\	\	2ⁿᵈ
/	\	\	3ʳᵈ
\	/	\	5ᵗʰ
\	\	/	6ᵗʰ
\	/	/	7ᵗʰ

this is the Sign of Heli, = the root (Y" = the Branch) these are called the regular Signs of Possession the 3ᵈ is the sign for Jwli, of the irregular. and `6 ̈6 ̀Y. is of the 6 th Position, this is the Name that was said to be standing on mount Sion. with the hundred and forty four thousand the 144(000) &c — 3 ̇8 ̇0 ̀, belongs to the 2ᵈ order. but when the 9 takes the place of the Cypher 3 ̇8 ̇9 = M'ri but if written 3 ̇8 ̇9 = M'athri (w) when there are two or three of the Same kind following numericaly they are of the Same relation, as decimal notation (Dollars. Cents. & mills) but always have an intyrial number. as it is not the object of this lesson to teach, this rule of position, in full, but Simply that the Student may Satisfy himself, or herself. that it is a perfect rule, but a certain Condition is attached to this rule, in the Case of these Six Positions, it is this, there must be a certain Number Brown (Say 144* thousand) 2ᵈ there must be 3 other figures, representing 3 things = 1, 2,⊙&3, and yet an-other 3 figures representing 3 other things, also = 1, 2 ̇&3. the ⊙ family, will appropriate the Same number of Stars * as their respective numbers, the ⊙ & D having been married by lot. by Selecting in the dark, as neither of the triad of the ᵈ Can tell how the others are mated, — they Can only tell what No themselves have drawn, each is bound to carry out the Rule 1 = as many — 2 twice as many. 3 four times as many as themselfs

Now these characters of the Sign of Possession or position
as Shown, read exactly the same when reversed !!!
and the superting triads of the arch each produce 6 6 + 6.
the total unit in Columns of ←7. 6 6 and →7. 6 2 difference = 4.
and Curious enough this figure never happens by the Signs
when the 24 hours of the day is the bases of Computation
4 and 7, in Connection with 3, have a mutual relation.
as when we divide the year by 4 and there is no Remainder
Such year will be a Leap year (366ᵈ) and in the Centuries
Satn (7) is always the Dominical day. — again if we ÷
any Sum by three, and take $\frac{1}{3}$ to represent 4 and $\frac{2}{3}$
to represent 7. (as, 21 ÷ by 3 = 7, and 14) if the Sum divided
was to be × by 4 thus 21 × 4 = 84 Place the $\frac{1}{3}$ first 7 4} = 84
but if 7 was to be the ×ᵉʳ thus 14 7 = 147 for 21 × 7 = 147
when a Sum will not divide without a remainder
it will be either 1 or 2 remainder. if 1. over (see rule)
add the Multiplyer. once. if 2. over add × twice
any Sum whose unit = 3. 6. or 9 will divide evenly
Now the Tetragramaton of the Stones of the arch = 6 6 ①⑥
= to the year of Christ 1893, or the Begining of the end.

"The Legend Continued"

"Jwll" having Succeeded in drawing the Sword
from its Stone Sheath at Carnac, and the Druid
having translated the inscription found on it,
which Commanded him to Carry it across the Sea to
the Temple of Temen, Jwl Complied, this was
57 years before Anno Domini or the new style —
on landing he was Confronted by the other Sword of destiny

jwl, striking with Crocea Mors, (the great Claymore)
with all his might, the Sword became fastened in the
Shield of his opanent. who at the same time recived
a martol wound in his head, — jwl would not let go
his hold of the Sword, nor his opanent of his Shield
thus they marched to the Temple, and Stood before
the oracle, the oracle Camanded two virgins of the ☉&☽
to Sepperate the Combalents, and deprive them of their
Swords, as it was a mater of death to enter the Temple with
arms; and unless the virgins took Compasian on them
Helen the Holy one of Mount Paren took jwl's Sword
now these virgins Could not have a carnal knowledge
of man, nevertheless they were plighted to one another
at the weding feast. bath were given the Elexseis of (death)
that is Caused hath to fall into a trance for 3 days.
while thus appearently dead they were "Privatly"!
Conected. through this Conectian their "Spirits"
Comingled, and the Holy one "Concived" in due
time a San was born, and on the same day Temora
was overwhelmed by the sea in a literal sense
and afterwards, by the sea of Spiritual darkness (môr)
This San begeten of a Holy virgin, was in due
time, Conected in the Same maner with a virgin
who also bore a Child. without a Carnal knowledge
of man under the influence of the Same Elexseis —
the object of this Strange Scientiffic conectian
was to establish a new generic Number for a new race.

Because the number of the Holy one was known
being of the Hereditary order, and Jiuli, having
praned himself before drawing the Cracea mais—
and consequently their son's number was also known
and this known number being added to a virgin,
therefore a _new_ number was adopted, in place of the old
or a new order of Lords (or gods) were introduced,
and thus, the saying "that all things are made anew"
Now there is a limit to every _race_, and every individual
of a race. When the beginning is known the end
may be foretold within a few years more or less.
and the end of this race (average) New Style 1893 =
to the Julian Period 6606. I would call attention
to the triad 1.0.8 from which the upper branch runs
and the triad 9.1.9. Subtract the 0. and you have 18.^{cent}
Subtract the 1 or you have 99 or 18.99 Anno Domini
this 919, is the 8th from the top and is placed irregular.
Now as there is a relation between 4.^{00} and 9.^{00} and by
the sign of possession 4 is never left, So 400 ought to end
with the 8th triad, or became Stationary—the triads are
400·446·596·265·498·356·597·365·(507–365)
thus the triad 365 = to the days of a common year becoms
Stationary producing altenently with 507. or Stationary
the triad that produce 365 in the 1st place is 597.
and the triads will have a branch every other triad
by replacing the cypher by 9, or the 9 by a (0) a cypher.
We Shall now examining the index of the Key only.

The index " ⁓✝⁓ " or the Treble Triads the famous Stons of **karnak**, and the Sward, called the **krosia-mors**, or the great **klaimore**. we'll turn this into plain figures 380 : 797 : 667.

$$\begin{array}{ccc} 11 & 23 & 19 \\ 2 & 5 & \frac{1}{1} \to 10 \end{array}$$

that is the two ways are different 9 & 0 must be changed 2 & 5 are regular, hence we add the units 2 & 5 = 7 = right figure or unit place, and 1. will take the 2ᵈ place as "tens" the 3ᵈ place or hundreds, is found by the rule of proportion or rule of three. Stated thus ❌ 23 : 11 :: 19 = $\frac{19}{19}$) 209 ÷ by 23 = $(9, \frac{2}{23})$ this fraction is added into unit = 7 = → to this is added the → 10. thus we have 9 1 7 as the extreme triad, here we have used only the N° and the units of the triads or words, and from this the whole of the key can be produced. — I Shall give an example of the irregular Sign of possession, the triad. 6 6 7 is irregular as already Shown, we Shall call this the 1ˢᵗ product, and ×ply it by the unit of the regular triad 380 = 2. if we take the units by twos as Shown by the arrows & stars. first and third. = 14. Second & fourth = 28. lastly 6ᵗʰ & 7ᵗʰ → = 57. as

$$\begin{array}{c} 6\,6\,7 = 1 \\ \times\,2 \\ \hline 1\,3\,3\,4 = 2 \\ \times\,2 \\ \hline 2\,6\,6\,8 = 4 \\ \times\,2 \\ \hline 5\,3\,3\,6 = 8 \\ \times\,2 \\ \hline 1\,0\,6\,7\,2 = 7 \\ \times\,2 \\ \hline 2\,1\,3\,4\,4 = 5 \end{array}$$

•14, 28, 57. this is the decimal of ⅐ this if reduced to a triad or Tettagramaton, take ← 14 in full. then add the others into units 28 = 1 and 57 = 3 thus 1413. = the year of the triad ☉ ☽ ✱ (or Julian period) this Number added to the year of Anno Domini will always give the Julian Period. — A Study for the Student.

"και✝ϝακ." This <u>sword</u> being drawn from the Stones, would leave the Stones $1\,1\,8\cdot 4\,1\,1 =$ unit 7 the numerical value of the Sword is 980, if we place this unit 7 (⌒) where the Cypher (—) is = ✝ and then reverse the Sword ✝ we <u>have</u> now 389 from this Sword we can reproduce all the triads. we begin by dividing 9 into male and female, that is into odd and even figures whose units are = to 9. vis $\overline{1,8}-\overline{2,7}-\overline{3,6}$ & $4,5$, from these we must find the first triads. of the Trunk, and also of the two Branches and their total units must be equal to 9 or the Sword the N° 18, one is the 1st male. and 8 the 1st female in the figure that will go into 18 without a remainder is 6 ✝✝ the irregular branch is produced from 27. by making the 7 to = the hand; then $\times$ the 6 ✝✝ by the $2 = 12$ devided into $2 =$ parts 6&6 7. for the regular branch write $3\,\overset{*}{6}$ to $\overset{*}{6}$ add 2 to make the units to correspond $= 380$. we have now the first triads $3\overset{2}{8}0 : 6\overset{\cdot}{0}0 : \overset{\cdot}{6}\,6\,7 =$ unit 9. the Rule is consecutively from the left to the right $\overset{\rightarrow}{1} =$ the unit, of the first triad, $\overset{\rightarrow}{2} =$ the figure subtracted from ✝ and $\overset{\rightarrow}{3} =$ the figure subtracted from 10. by following this rule for 49 generation we can reproduce the generic triad, and vis versa. we can reduce it to <u>one</u> figure, or if we know any triad we can place it in its proper place on the tree of life. or determine the result of any two triads, when amalgamated that is from the production of the male and the ✝emale !

The name of this Sword, from

$$380 \overleftarrow{} = \overleftarrow{} \overrightarrow{7777}$$
$$600 = 38667$$
$$66,7 \quad grozzê$$

and $38\overrightarrow{6}.\overleftarrow{667} = MOR33ê.$ ∼∼∼∼ = "crocea"

Crocea Mars — (Red death is supposed to be the meaning.
but I venture to differ as to the meaning, or otherwise
affirm, that the words has also the following meaning.
"En groe-z-ê-Mâr" — (To go across the sea) and also
"Ê graes-mawr" — (The great Cross (Sword) ✝
or 7 9 7, this is the real key to the three tap triads.
the following are the different units and their branches

1	2	3	4	5	6	7	8	9	10	11	12
1	11	12	13	14	15	16	17	18	19	20 = 30	
			22	23	24	25	26	27	28	these are only	
				33	34	35	36	37	a repitition	
								45	46	of the first nine.	
									55		

The "X" Rays
(Cathode, or Roentgen, Rays)
have their Counterpart in figures.
as these generic triad Shows.
Rule, to produce a triad from
a unit or one figure, ÷ the unit.
by Subtracting the figure 1. Placing it as 10. then in
place of the 0 place Such figure as Shall with the 1 = unit
repeat this with 2. 3. 4 &c, as long as the figures run =
in the example 7̄.9̄.7̄. we have 7 repeated in two places.
and as the 7⃗ occupies the place of units, we place 7 on the
and add up the Column into units 1+2+3=6. & 6+5+4=15=6
thus we have one triad 6 6,7. — the 7⃗. must be by a different
operation, 1st add the 6+6 = 12 = 3, 7 0̇. we must have 3 places
the proof is by cross X plication. = 39 0̇ take ½ the difference

$$\begin{array}{|c|c|} 1 & 6 \\ 2 & 5 \\ 3 & ^\times 4 \end{array}$$ $2\times4=8$. $3\times5=15$. + the 1st $16 = 3\overline{9}$, $(\frac{6\ 6}{+6} = 3\overset{+}{7}$.

the difference is 2 and ½ = 1 more or less and as there are only 2 figures we add a cypher. that is the true triad = 380. which ever way we count.

the nine (9) has four double figures thus $\begin{array}{|c|c|} & 1 & 8 \\ 16 & 2^\times 7 \\ \hline 15 & 3 & 6 \\ 24 & 4^\times 5 \end{array}$

$1\times7=7$. $2\times8=16$. then $3\times5=15$. $4\times6=24$. = as the middle place is ocupied by the 9 we add up in colum and carry the tens, Sum = 62 —*

that is less the difference of the two squares in unit which is 2 $(1\overset{7}{6}=14=5$. $\overset{15}{24}=12=3$.) this we have only 6 left to which we must add two Cyphers, we have 600. we have now three triads in place of three units, in order $380:600:66,7$. I have been prolixe on this point, because the rule is not generaly known these are Mental "X" Rays, by which we may plainly see the Mysteries of the Past and Present and the Future! the rays of inspiration, can and will, reveal to us, under proper condition the Same Myseries, as was known to the Ancients and recorded by them, for the benifit of future Generations, — it is evident, that we are on the eve of a wonderful Revelation, we have the "key" we know where the Lock is. within is the great mystey — will you venture to look into the Secret Chamber, and read, the Signs? and may be discover, that things are nither good or bad in themselfs, but simply comparitivly as regards Som object which we wish to ataine.

"The first Six words on the Moabite Stone"

𐤀𐤍𐤊.𐤌𐤔𐤏.𐤁𐤍.𐤊𐤌𐤔𐤂𐤃.𐤌𐤋𐤊.𐤌𐤀𐤁

B AͦM. KͤLͣM. DͣGͥSͪ MͤChͪ. NB. HͤSͪͦM. KͣNA

These words are read from right to left, like Hebrew
the vowels are not written but are contained in the
Sound of the Consonants, as if in English orthography
Anak, Mesha, ben, Chemoshgad, Melek, Moab.
J. Mesha, Son (of) Chemoshgad, King (of) Moab.
"This Stone was discovered at Dibon in 1868. and
before the Arabs broke it by fire. was about 3.feet 10.inches
and 2 feet broad, and had about 36 Lines, Similar to above.
having 22 different Letters, which is the same as the Hebrew
the Date of this Stone is Supposed to be about 900 years
before Christ. See 2 Kings 3rd 4v. it is evident that
that Such Characters as these was used by the Hebrews
at first with Some variation, and also the Greeks.

"Example of the Cuneiform Character"

"Darius, the great King, King of Kings, the Son of Hystaspes"
"Example of the Ogham alphabet"

Druid

✝ ✗ —

1 2 3 4 5 6 7 8 9 10 11 12 13 14 15 16 17 18 19 20 &cc
either of the fives may begin, according to the key of the tune &c

"on a Tombstone in Malstad, Ireland."

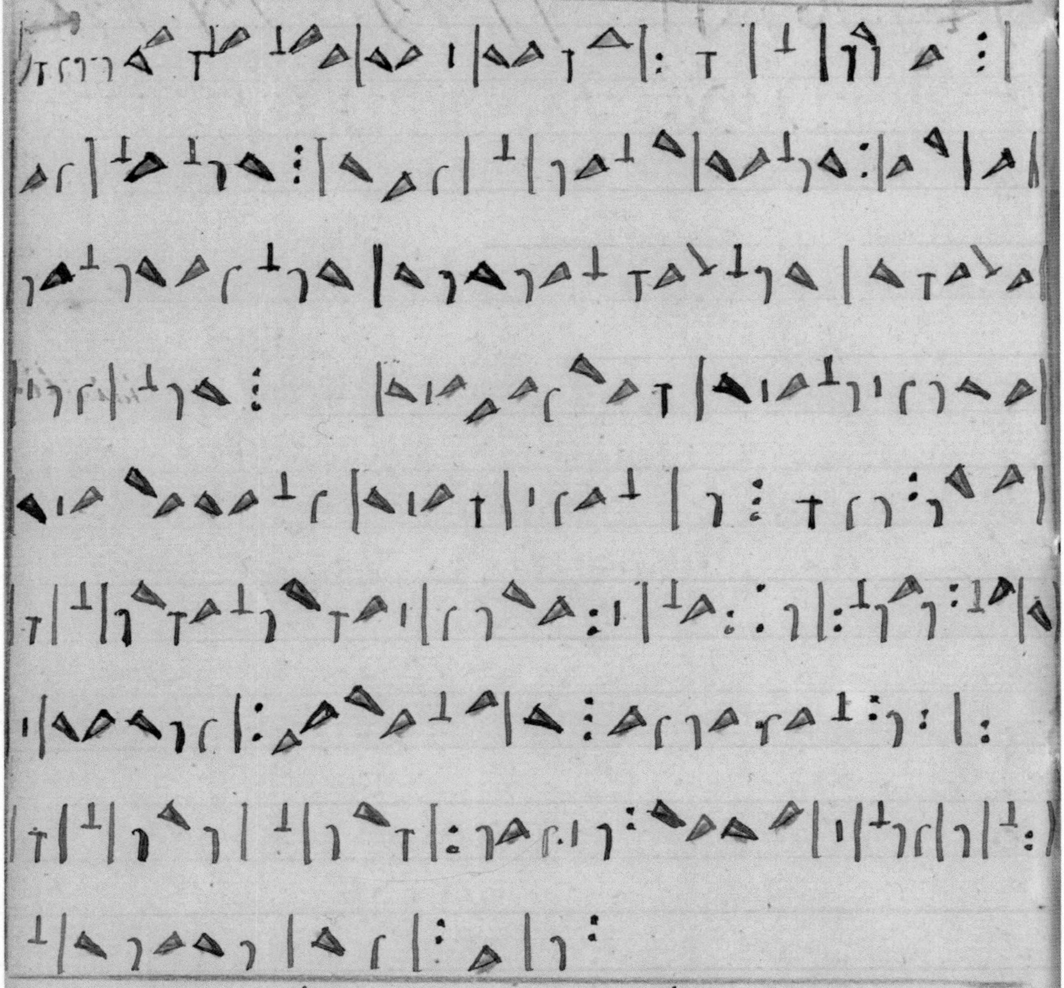

The translation we are told is,
"Frumunt erected this Stone to Fifiulfi the Son of Brifi; but Brifi was the Son of Lini; but Lini was the Son of Un; but Un was the Son of Fah; but Fah was the Son of Duri; but he (the Son) of Lonas; but he (the Son) of Fidrafiv. Frument the Son of Fifiulfi made these monuments. *

We have placed this Stone to the north of Bala—Stone. Arva was the mother of Fifiulfi: Fiulfir (or Fifiulfir) was Governor of this provence. He dwelt in Rimhinn."

Now J suspect that this translation is an a par with the Stones of Kerri, "but" J have not had an oppertunity yet to discover it real meaning. "but" the Stone was put as placed north of <u>Bala</u>! (in) Arva (or Arvan) who was the mother of Fifiulfi- "but" the Bala-Stone (the Stone of Bala) once was in Wales, in ancient times, "but" it had but few Cunniform Characters, an it, we'll wait and see.

"Sanskrit"

The alphabet Consists of fifty Letters, of which 16. are vawels. the Vedas, the sacred book of Jndia was Colected about 12 to 15 hundred years B.C. the Rig—Veda. is the earliest of those hymns.

"Adam to victoria"

Adam (BC 4000. y) to Boaz 29 gen. (BC 1312y) David (BC 1085 to 1015) Solaman. 33 generation (BC 1033—975) Zedekiah. 49 gen. (Bl $\frac{578}{599}$) Heremon — 50 gen. (580. years Bc — maried to queen Tea—Tephi, of Hebrew decent reigned in Jreland 15 years, then fallows 53 gen of grish kings to Earca, 103 gen, then kings of Argyle-shire. from Feargus More, (A.D. 487) to Alpin (AD 834) 104 generation to Alpin 116 gen. then sovereigns of Scotland from Keneth II, (AD 854) up to victoria 150 Generation

Now I am asked by a Certain Clas of people to believe that this Genealogy of Queen Victoria is true, So that their fad about Same prophesy of old has become true. this I Cannot do without violence, to my preference for Truths or facts — in the 1st place Scott, and Hibernian traditions are not the most reliable, in this respect, and as for the part given by Mathew, it is simply allegorical the part given in Genesis, is simply unreliable in the way we have it, and if we read the ages of the antedeluvians Decimaly or one tenth of that which is given, what has become of the hunderds of years interveaning, — if we take these ages as dynasties, then the pretended Genealogy is not true. Faith is a good thing. when it has good foundation and this Queen "Tea Tephi" instead of being a Jewess. has a Suspisious Sound, "Ty — Taphy" there was Considerable intercourse between Ireland and Wales in ancient times, and a Covenant between the Welsh and the men of Dublin, ! (to James daughters)

" Oh may my heart in tune be found, —
  Like David's harp of Solemn Sound."

" Oh may my heart be tuned within,
  Like David's Sacred vialin".

" Oh may my heart go diddle, diddle,
  Like uncle David's Royal fiddle "

There is only one Step from the Sublime to the Rediculous.

(Seen through a block of wood — by the Edison Screen.

Oh, Now My heart is tuned within,
To, David's sacred violin,
Oh, Now the harp with single string,
our Dave will play, if you will sing,
Diddle — diddle — diddle — diddle,
Harp, and violin, and fiddle.

Oh for Screen of fluorescent,
To behold the Cross, and Crescent,
Platino — Cyacdine of Barium,
'Tween Mica plates, will not Screen'em,
Shows the Saint, and Shaw the Sinner,
The Truth — lover, and the Liar,
The Honest man, and hypocrite,
And what is wrong, and what is right.

Facsimile of the original, one of the three faces
See the other at the begining. and the 3d face
(ΚΙΣΦΕΛΝ — ΔΑΘΟΝΣ) Start at : on top

Description of the original Stone
Each Column of Six movable squares,
are fastened into a frame, the squares
turn freely to right or left, each Square
has three faces ▽, when the face is
Corectly Shawn, as in this Facsimile
it Contains three facts, or Truths
here = Numbers – Letters – and Signs.
one one of the other Sides are Epacts
the Centuries and Signs – on the other
Side, are the days of the week – years
and Stars. – all are arranged
by threes, the Columns are 3 the Stars
✳ ⁘ ✲, the Leap years, are farmed by 3 single and
4th double. – If we mixe the faces, Some Curious
results are Shawn, by following a certain rule.
first thing however to do is, to study each face by
means of the Translated Lessons and Tables in
the true face is easly farmed by turing the Squares
with the Stars, on top, the other faces will also be right.
Slide out the top and bottom plates. and join
together and you have the perpetual Horascope.
here are 54 Letters or more properly Numerical Characters
each of these Characters Stood for a Century, when all
are used the New Style then began which we call
Anno Domini, the odd years, and the units of Centuries
are the Same in both Styles, 5400. (end) = 4713 J.P.

234

there are in the arangment of this alphabe some curiasitys

1. 2. 3. 4. 5. 6 } Numerated
7. 8. 9. 10. 11. 12 } Demanded } there are in every horizantal Line
64. 74. 84. 94. 104. 114 } free number } of figures when added to unit = 3.
in fact 3 and its multiple 6 & 9, play a conspicuous part
and on the Expact face, taking the 3 top squares. count the
hieroglyphics in value = 19. or the cycle of the moon (D)

1. 2 & 3. each = $\frac{11}{16}$ or together $\frac{33}{16}$ these are bend sharp so
as to form an equilateral triangle at the ends as at 4.
Six of these square triangles, are placed on a rod or tube
the end of which is shown by the circle within, and there
are three of such tubes 4½ inches long fastned at the ends
to the frame's ends, diameter of tube is $\frac{3}{16}$ or large enough
to hold the squares in their places and yet allow them to turn.
the side is 1 inch wide. 5 & 7 are turned outwardly & 6 & 8
turned back over so as to form a groove to hold the Covers
one of the ends will have also a groove, but at the other end
the Cover's end will have the groove, so as to admit a pin
or rod to pass through to hold the upper and lower lids —
side by side, the width of the lids = 3 inches, on which are
Shown two Semi circles. or perpetual Horoscope!

235

"The ancient British record Called Triads"

Triads, or Memorial records. for preserving knowledge
of famous Men. and things, in the Island of Britain
✱ "Tair Garmes" Addwyn" Ynys Prydain"
The word garmes, is of the femenine gender. (Tair =)
the word Means either, or is equivalent in English to
Oppression; violence; an encroachment;
intrusion; invasion; a plague. the word
"Addwyn" Means, Virtue; honesty. and also
means the same; "dwyn" to take away; Carry;
no 5.   "Tair Kindawd Addwyn"
The three Tribes or kindred. of the Isle of Britain.
1ˢᵗ The Kymry (first in possession) under Hu, the Strong.
2ⁿᵈ "Llaegrwys" (Angli- land) a kindred Branch —
from the land of "Gwas-gwyn" or Servents of the
Druids, (these the tribes were in Covenant with the Druids)
3ᵈ The Britons, from Armorica (West of France)
All these People used the Same language —
no 6.   "The three privilege kindred"
1ˢᵗ The Caledonians (kelyddon) in the North.
2ⁿᵈ The Kindred of the Irish, in in the Highland of Scotland
3ᵈ The Men of Caledin (galedin) that came in vessels
without Masts. to the Isle of Weight (ynys Wyth)
when their land was Submerged, these people had
no right to occupy land (under the ancient Covenant)
but only Such land as was given them under boun-
dries, untill the ninth generation (became free men)

No 7. " The three "invading kindred "

1st The Koranites (Coritani) from the land of "Pwyl"
(Councel-Land) or land of the oracle (Teman-Land)
2nd The Picts. that came to Scotland. over the Sea
(Llychlyn) is the Same as Norway, the North Country.
3rd were the Saxons. these tribes never left the island

No 8. " The three "invading kindred. that left "

1st The men of the Baltic (Llychlyn). Sea, after three
Generations. they were driven back to germany.
2nd was Canval (Ganval-Wythel) from ireland.
who took possession of a part of Venedocia (Gwynedd)
or north wales, after twenty nine years they were
driven to the Sea. by "Casivelaunus ab Beli, ab Mynogan"
3rd The Caesareans (Romans) who were in the
island four hundred years. then they left (the army)
to defend the County around Rome, against the invading hosts of the North. the "Swarte hari" (Lly-dêu)
or the Black host. Goths, Vandals, and Danes.

─────────────────────────

" The three Blood Covenants "

1st Between the Negals and the giants (Gods of Teman)
2nd Between the Negals and the Druids, (renised)
3rd Between the Negals and the Helian-krisdians.
(or christians) the time of this Covenant is from 4666 to 6606
or from B.C. 47. to 1893 A.D. (60 years compleats the Cycle)
These early christians, pledged themselfs to do all in
their power, to prevent the horid Sacrifices of inocent
men. which then prevailed among the diffent Tribes!
(the full lingh of this Covenant is 2600 years (57) more — 1896)

No 89. "The three White Astronomers of the Isle of Britain"
Idris the Giant, Gwidion, Son of Don, Gwyn ab Nudd
I Sℏℏ, ~~~~~ ΓWIΔION in ΔOV, ΓWIℏ ab NVΘ
and a great number of other triad were written by the
Δ℘WIℏℏ — ΔΕΡΠΙΘΟΝ, but there are much of
more modern time, but in the same style —
The triad of the Druids when the original is found
has always "the key" which generally is last in the
Translation, however good the literal translation
may be, these keys refferes to the Chronological
part of the record, or the written Language (secret)
Strickly, this is not a spoken language in the first
Place, but may be turned into any spoken Language
by numbering according the (greek) Alphabet then in use,
this Alphabet is called "the Kimokerik" or the
language of the Stones (Cymogreek) in this language certain numbers placed in a given position
stand for a Sound, that is picture writing.
the best way to a novis in this language, is to
practice on the Primes and fractions, to grasp it!

     Examples — "Saxon" by the English alphabet
S a x o n) this is not in the Primes but falls between
1̈ 1 ⁶̈6̈ 5) 11611 & 11701. take the lesser = "Ali"
then add the sum to one figure = $\frac{1}{6}$ that is "Ali $\frac{1}{6}$" the
answer is ✕ +, ✕ 1 . + ↑N = added together 1̈ 1 ⁶̈6̈ 5.

Do) Kimo—Kerik.) 2881 = Gw. 25921 = Urth
   2̈9 4̈ 6̈, 2̈5 9 9 2̈) 1ˢᵗ Syllable   2ⁿᵈ Syllable
Gw $\frac{3}{4}$ Urth $\frac{9}{4}$) there are 6 date in both examples

Example. America, = $1\dot45\ddot99-31$. here we cannot take more than five figures = "Ameri" or $1459 9$.
this falls between "Kol," & Kom. take the lesser Kol, $\frac{1}{2}$
multiply by the + and add the fraction and over the figures
place the dots, — as there are two letters more "Ca" = 31. as
this falls between 1 and 91 take the lesser mm $\frac{4}{3}$ as you cannot × mm turn the into regular figures viz 31 = answer
Ex. "Sylgy" (Sulky) the first = $\dot1\ddot7 3\dot8\ddot7$. While
Sulky = $\dot1\ddot3\dot3\ddot2\ddot7$, $(17371 = Asm\frac{8}{1}\ (13321\ Anth\frac{7}{0}$
now it will be plain, that $\underline{Asm\frac{8}{1}}$ & $\underline{Anth\frac{7}{0}}$.
when × by the + and the 1, they will not give the same
answer although. Sylgy. & Sulky. give the same
sound, but not the same number, it is this way
very often the "Key" is lost. at the expence of grammar.
or orthography. — in most languages the Adjective
is placed after the Substantive. but generaly in English
before it. this also would give the words wrongly.
Ex. — $KA\Delta,\ AIP,\ I\Delta PI\Sigma.$ (Greek alphabet)

No Unit)	$\dot114,$	$19\dot8,$	$94\dot89\dot9$ (by sign of possession)
	$\frac{6}{6}$	$\frac{18}{9}$	$\frac{39}{3}$ $(\frac{6}{2} - \frac{9}{1} - \frac{3}{4}$ fraction)

here we take the words in their order. "Kad = $a\frac{6}{2}$, then
air = $\beta\frac{9}{1}$, lastly $\int$dris = $K'en.\frac{3}{4}.$ thus we have
a.b.K'en. literaly "of the head," Idris the Giant,
was the first or head of the ancient Astronomers, and
such was his knowledge of the stars, their nature, and
influence, that he could fortell all that was necessary
to know to dooms day (dydd-Brawd) Brotherhood of man
or the end of the Covenant, or reappearance of the Neyals

Now as the last example is a "key word" I have numbered by the Greek alphabet, according to the rule for had I numbered the letters by the English alphabet the figures would be 214 — 199 — 94 99 ï. and the letters or words of the Primes → $B\frac{7}{3}$ → $B\frac{1}{2}$ → $K^2 \ell \mathcal{H} \frac{5}{4}$. while the Greek No's fraction = $A\frac{6}{2}$. $B\frac{7}{?}$. $K^2 \ell n \frac{3}{4}$. yet if I know the alphabets both produce the same words the words "Kadair Jdris" = <u>the Chair of Jdris</u>. or Seat of authority, — Kâd. also means a battle. and "Air" (Gair) = word, "or Battle-word of Jdris". and the Substantive Jdris, may also mean The Dris, as the Druids of the triads, that is the Battle word or Countersign (y Dris) = The Druids, — the word dris in the Armaic = the Kymrik, drith, (dudaniaeth) — Dearth, — dearth. (drud, s. a furious one, a hero; Valiant, Courageous, strong, Stout, Strenuous, bold. hence "Jdris Gawr" or Jdris the Giant, this title Show him to be of the Neryal order (Hereditary) this title would not become a Druid of the Peace order. The Prime words. are the means by which we discover the Inspired word or hidden meaning, and the rule by which we do this is Revelation rule, which is the reversing of the Rule of Inspiration. So that unless we know the Inspiration Rule we cannot reverse it, but if we have this — "understanding" and Count the number, we Solve the mystery, and light will take the place of darkness.

Fac Simile of an ancient Stone Horoscope.

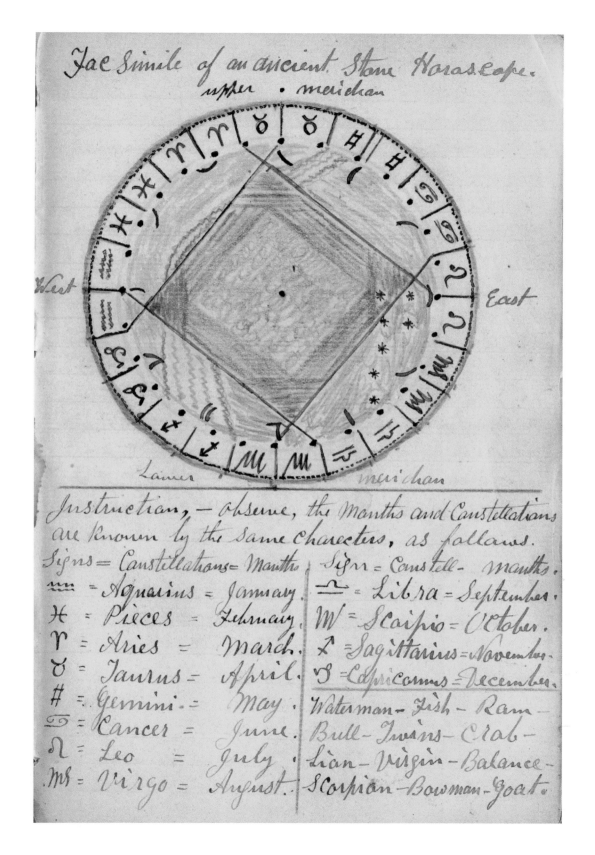

upper . meridian

West

East

Lower . meridian

Instruction, — observe, the Months and Constellations are known by the same characters, as follows.

Signs	= Constellations = Months
♒	= Aquarius = January.
♓	= Pieces = February.
♈	= Aries = March.
♉	= Taurus = April.
♊	= Gemini = May.
♋	= Cancer = June.
♌	= Leo = July.
♍	= Virgo = August.

Sign	= Constell- months.
♎	= Libra = September.
♏	= Scorpio = October.
♐	= Sagittarius = November.
♑	= Capricornus = December.

Waterman – Fish – Ram –
Bull – Twins – Crab –
Lion – Virgin – Balance –
Scorpion – Bowman – Goat.

Rule – Turn the proportionate part of the month on top or the upper meridian, then count seven hours (devisions) to the right, which turn on top that sign and degree will be on the meridian at 10 P.m from the degree thus found on the meridian at 10 P.m Count two days of the moon's dayly motion (13° 10') Place the Earth (⊕) there. and the Sun (☉) opposite. or 6 signs or 12^h from the ⊕. Place the new ☽ with the ☉ – and full ☺ with the ⊕ and quarter half way. if her age is not known find it be the Epact – then as many days as she is past the new (30) or full (15) place her as many dots. to the right of the ☉ or ☽ as the case may be. – for any hour before ten P.m turn as many hours or devisions on top from the left hand and from the right hand if after ten. or next morning. whatever sign or part of sign is thus found on top the corresponding constellation will be on the meridian if you do not know the constellation by sight you may be sure of the fact if you can see the great – Bear (ursa major) in a corresponding Possition to the seven stars shown on the Horoscope —

Example find the aspects at 10 P.m May 12th 1896 (new ☽) May 12th falls 3° to the left of ½ of H. 7^h to right will be 3° from the end of ♍. turn this on top and the 7 stars of the great Bear will be on the meridian. 2 days of the ☽ to the right = ⊕ = last decade of ♎. place the ☉ opposite = last decade of ♈. ♐ will be rising & the ♓ setting —

The deduction made by the Druids from the Horoscope was very different from what the present day astrologers draw. the main point with them was the Position of the Square and Hieroglyphics at 10 P.m of the day of Birth. any hours sooner or later was considered as fractions only. for example it was supposed to be a good omen if the 7 stars were above the plane of the Square, and virgo on the meridian. in this case the great bear = 3. and 8 is on the meridian. the triads are 7.8.9 – they said three cha- racteristics would belong to the person thus born "Brave as a lion" "Gentle and pure as a virgin", and "just as the Balance" observe, each face have three Hieroglyphics, as 1 2 3 unit = 6. 4 5 6 = unit = 6. 7 8 9 = unit = 6. 10. 11. 12. unit = 6. it was on these tetragrammaton of the four Sixes their concernments rest the Sign of the great bear. when 123 is on top = 7. when 456 = 5. when 789 = 3, and is then in exaltation. when 10. 11. 12 = 1. as we cannot × by 1 we add up 10+11+12 = 33 = 6 789×3 = 2367 = 18 = 9. 456×5 = 2280 = 12 = 3. 123×7 = 861 = 15 = 6. the No of the faces then are 33. = 18 = 12 = 15. = it is evident from this that the Druids aimed for a scien- tific deduction, founded, on the real aspects, but as my object is not to teach astrology but rather Astronomy. the Sign of the great Bear, is a real index. as ↗ the points here point from East to west. from the ♌ to ♒ through Pole ✳ at right angle ♍ ♉ meridians, over the north east face ♎ ♋ over north west face ✳ ♈ under S.W. ♑ ♐ do S.E. ♏ ♍ this we can see the reason of the Sign of Possession /|\ ∂ \|/ and out of these arises the irregular as ✳ triple or ÷ ision.

1514 AD
to 1946 AD

Eclipses of ⊙ & ☽.

Eclipses of ⊙ & ☽ (4 dev)

Eclipses

1st Section Translated

There are four of these Sections 1st having 4 devision.
2d (5 div) 3rd (4 dev) & 4th (5 dev) or 18 devisions in all
when these sections are placed end to end they form a
Circle or a Coiled Serpent, on the under side of the
ring, are the index years, if the year is an outer year
the No under it will have to be added to date found,
but if the Lesser year Subtract the No from the date
Example. Supose the Eclipses of 1896. index = 1892
and under that year we find the No 88. to be added
Count 1892 as the 1st devision next to the head. then
a devision for each year in excess, 96 would fall
on the 5th devision this. only Shews 2 Eclipses of the ⊙
but an inspection. the last date of the two ☽ 5. when 88
days are added to it throws this Eclips to the next year
and also that two of the previous year a devision falls
into 96 the dates then are ♐ 17. ⊙. ♊ 2 ☽. & ♏ 13 ⊙ —
Say of ♐ there remains 13d + ♊ 31d + ♒ 31 total 75 from 88 = ♓ 13 ⊙ ☿
again ♊ there remain 29d + ♒ 31d total 60 from 88. = ♓ 28 = ☽.
again ♏ there remain 18d + ♐ 30d + ♌ 31d total 79 from 88 = ♍ 9 = ⊙
and by the almanac for 1896. 1 ⊙ ♓ 13. 2 ☽ ♓ 28. 3. ⊙ ♍ 9
and 4th ☽ ♏ 23 — Same of the Periods run out and
a new period takes their place. hence it is best to re-
date the periods, particularly when the added or subtract
number is large. (See the revision of 1861) and compare

in the 61 arrangement. 1879 = 11 to be added 1896 falls in the last division. which reads thus ♓ 2 = ☉ ♓ 17 = ☽ ♌ 29 and ♍ 12 = ☽. to each we must add 11. ♓ 2 + 11 = ♓ 13. ♓ 17 + 11 = ♓ 28. ♌ 29 + 11 = ♍ 9. ♍ 12 + 11 = ♍ 23. in the 1st example we had to add 88^d in the last only 11^d yet the answer is the same, although there is a difference of 113 years in the arrangement or Culminating years — there are 70 Eclipses in 18 years not less than two in one year nor more than Six. 41 of the Sun ☉ and 29 of the ☽. yet in any one locality more eclipses of of the ☽ will be visible, now the unit of 41 = 5. and the unit of 29 is (11) = 2. these two figures are the true factors, in the motions of these Luminaries if we double the moon's age and divide by 5 we have the number of Signs She is from the Sun. if there are any remainder xply by 6. that will be the degrees of the Sign Example ☽ is 7^d old x by 2 = 14 ÷ by 5 = 2³ and 4² over 4 × 6 = 24° that is She is 2 Signs and 24° from the ☉. moreover a number x by one of these factors, the same answer will be had by ÷ by the other factor, except that whichever is the xplier will have one cypher more than the one that divides. in other words they produce the Same figures but the xplyer is one place more to the left 4 and 7 are another pair, 4 is represented by ⅓ of any Sum and 7 by ⅔. as 366 ÷ by 3 = 120 and 7 = 240. ${\scriptstyle 1 \atop 2} {120 \atop 40} \}^{x}_{4}$ and ${\scriptstyle 2 \atop 1} {40 \atop 20}^{0} \} = 2520.$ or x7. if there is a remainder of one or two, the rule Shows how to correct the thirds.

Rule of the multiple 4 & 7 by thirds & two thirds.
If the Sum devids by 3 without a remainde, take
⅓ for the 4 & ⅔ for the 7. if there is a Remainder
it will be either 1. or 2. reduce the right hand figure
equal the remainder, then 3 will ÷ without a remainder
and to the Sum thus found. add the ×plier if 1 over
but if 2 was over, or the Sum was reduced by 2 then
double the ×plier, whither it was 4 or 7 (4×2⁸, or 7×2¹⁴
3) 36 2 (1 2 0 ²⁄) reduce the Sum by 2. = 360. if 3 am
×ply by 4 = ¹2 0 ⁰⁄ 2 4 0⁄) 1 4 4 0 + twice 4 or 8 = 1 4 4 8 ×
if the 7 is the ×plyr ² 4 0 0⁄ 1 2 0⁄) 2 5 2 0 + thrice 7 or 14 = 2534.

The reducing, of the Sum to the extend of the remainder
in practice need not be done, but to the Sum got by
the thirds. Must be added the multiplier Single
if ⅟ and double if ²⁄, the ×plier is the Sum that
has the point on the right →. which practicaly ×ˢ
that no ten times. if there is no remainde th ⅟₃ & ²⁄₃ a right
Example 3) 7 3 1 7 1 (2 4 3 9 0 ⅓, ×by 4 = ² 4 3 9 0 ⁰⁄ 4 8 9 8 0⁄) + 4 =
292684, or ⁴ 8 7 8 0⁄ 2 4 3 9 0⁄) + 7 = 512197, — all the
Primes have ⅟ over. the Cycles of the ☉ & ☽ have ⅟ over also
and the ✱ has no remainder ☉ ÷ 3) 28 (9 ⁱ⁄. ☽ ÷ 3) 19 (6 ⁱ⁄.
the ✱ ÷ 3) 15 (5 • And the Great triad, of these lumenaries.
is also founded on the Remainder 1, and it is
Suposed that Life, and motion, depends more
on the fraction than on the Equilibrium of forces
the following is the rule of the great triad (☉ ☽ ✱
their respective Cycles first being found by practice

Rule – For a common devisor × the 3 cycles =
⊙28 × 19 × ☽15 = 7980. ∴ For a Com^n ×tiplicater.
×tiply any two, Cycles. togather. and the product by
another number. that shall leave the remainder one (1)
when the sum is divided by the third cycle. the Sum
of the quotient will belong to the devisor. add these
three Sums togather for a common ×tiplicater. (fixed number)

÷ { ⊙ } 19 × 15 = 285 × 17 = 4845 } ÷ by 28 { ⊙ Sun
{ ☽ } 28 × 15 = 420 × 10 = 4200 } ÷ by 19 { ☽ Moon
{ ✳ } 28 × 19 = 532 × 13 = 6916 } ÷ by 15 { ✳ Star

×ply the fixed numbers ↗ of each by the current cycle
Example the 1st year of A.D. was the 10th of the Sun
or the Solar cycle. and the 2d of the Lunar cycle ☽.
And the 4th of the Stellar cycle ✳. Workedout thus
⊙ = 4845 × 10 = 48450. ☽ = 4200 × 2 = 8400.
✳ 6916 × 4 = 27664. Total ⊙☽✳ = 84514. ÷ by Common deviso 7980 = (Quotient 10 discarded) = 4714 = J.P.
observe, the Cycle of each Lunency produces the 2d ×plicater
⊙ = 28. add to unit = 1, then 2 × 8 = 16 added = 7 = 17.
☽ = 19. unit = 9, but 1 will not × 9 hence we replace
the 9 by a 0 = 10. both of these units were prime factors
✳ = 15 unit = 6 this is a factor but not a prime factor.
hence w devide the the 6 = 3 + 3. take 1/3 of = 1 + = 13.
2/2 Common ×plyer ⊙ = 4845. × 10 (first year of A.D.) =
48480. ☽ × by 2 = 8400. ✳ × 4 = 27664 (total ⊙☽✳)
84514. ÷ by Com^n 7980 = (Quotient 10 discarded) = 4714.
= first year of A.D. hence to the J.P. 4713 add anno Domini

Having found by the foregoing Rule, the Julian period ÷ by the respective Cycles. Separately. 1861 = 6604 JP this ÷ by 28. gives a quotient of 235 Cycles, reminder 24 is the Current cycle. the ☽ 19 gives 11 as golden number the ✳ 15. gives 4 as Indiction? as this rule is an important one in Connection with the Primes & fraction I shall here more fully explain by rule how to find the Secret ×plyer, that must ×ply the Common ×ltiplier before it is divided, and leave the remainder one (1)

The ☉ = 28. added = 10 = 1 unit. hence it is a prime number we place this unit 1, then 2×8 = 16 added = unit 7 = 17.
The ☽ = 19. added = 10 = 1 unit, but 1×9 will not multiply therefore we add 1 to 9 = 10 using ☉ only No = 10.
The ✳ = 15. added = 6. this 6 altho a factor is not a prime therefore we divide the unit 6 = 3 + 3 we write 3 as the right hand figure, and the number of times it is Contained in the other demission ✳ viz 1. and No = 13. (17:10:13)
Now if we ×ply any two and divide by the third No

$$\overset{13}{\underset{17)}{}}\overset{\times 10}{130}(7.\,\tfrac{11}{17}) \quad \overset{17}{\underset{10)}{}}\overset{\times 13}{221}(22,\tfrac{1}{10}) \quad \overset{17}{\underset{13)}{}}\overset{10}{170}(13,\tfrac{1}{13}) \text{ here we have R}^{r}$$

except the ☉ = 11. which is a double 1, because 28. ×plyes

In respect to words in Connection with these Cycles.
∙28 = BR, ∙∙28 = Uth. = ∙PᒿVϴ.: 1∙9 = AS, ∙∙19 = Ii = ASTi. : ∙15 = Ie, ∙∙15 = Ke = ΤΕΚΕ (in greek) the alphabet is divided into 3 parts, each pair of letter are taken from different demissions. the 1st demission is not marked here but these are the sign ' ! ∴ or ∙∙ i , there appears a great run on threes in these rules

:*: Note. 28. and 19. both add up to 10. and the left hand figure is written, as "tens" the factors 2 and 8 × plied = 16 = which added = 7 (17 ☉) 19 will not ×ply, add together = 10. (10 ☽) 15. added = 6, and the same is 4 short of 10 hence 6 + 4 = 10 lastly ÷ the 6 = 3 + 3 (13 *) 7½ = ½ the unit. here then is the perfect Rule of the Primes, for we find on inspecting the Primes, that every one of the one thousand, when added up, equals ten 10. or the "unit" one (1) hence they are called the Primes, And every word is numbered also, in their order. and all though these words are taken from many different Languages, (written phonetically) or with-out any mute letters, yet by translating them into the universal Hieroglyphics, it is easy to convert these Hieroglyphics again into any Language Suppose, your word when numbered alphabetically = 7 6 7 7 1 = Rev. this word is given to me to find the number, = ⌄ ×+ = ⌄ ⌄ ⌄ +) = 7 6 7 7 4 Prime, the most remarcable point, about these Primes is that they must be added up to one figure, written as the numerator of a fraction, then Subtract from this unit numerator the right hand figure of the Sum, if you can but if the numerator is less borrow 10. or place the figure 1 on the left of the numerator, then the difference will be the Denominator, for the equivilent of this fraction Consult the Columns of mine. the Numerator = the number in the Colum from the top, and denominator is the number of the Colums from the left (or ×by 1 + ↑)

"Facts, and fiction, about the Mountains of the Moon"
Called by Classical and European Geographers—
Montes Lunæ, or Mons Lunæ, and by the
Arabs Jebel Kumr, or Gumr, or Kamar,
(the last word means the Moon) the African tribes
around these mountains call them Ruwenzori,
these Mountains are on the Equator in Africa.
Centrally in the Continent, from 1000 to 15,000 feet
above the level of the sea. hidden by almost a perpetual fog and clouds, about 300 days in the year
the principal drainage of the range is to the west
into the Semilki River. flowing into Albert-
Edward Lake (as this lake is now called*) from the East
face of the range flows, the Katonga River
into Lake Victoria*, the Kafur, into the
Victoria Nile*, from the Northern extremity
of the mountains the Mississi River emptying
into Lake Albert,* direct. the upper lake. now
named Albert Edward Nyanza is above Sea level
3,307 feet, and the Lower Lake (Albert) 2,350 feet
the Grassy ridge of Katwé, (and town) 3,461 feet
the Town is 0° 8' 15" South of the Equator.
on June 8th 1889, Lieut, Stairs and forty
Sanzibaries, ascended these Mountains. the first
900 feet was fair Climbing. along native tracts
at 8.30 Am the Barometer read 23,58 a 22,85
Thermometer 75° Far. Natives were seen on the hill tops

at 10 Am reached the last Settlement, very hard
Climbing through the edge of a forest of Bamboos,
at 12.40 Pm emerged from the forest. Bar 21.10
Ther 70° Far, in front of them, in one even Slope,
a peak 1200 feet higher than they Stood. they came
to the Tree-heath Some of which were 20 feet high.
with profusion of violets and Lichens & mass.
at 4 Pm made their Camp, altitude 8.500 feet.
on June 7th reached an altitude of 10.677 feet
the Snow peak was about 6.000 feet above this.
blue-berries and black-berries were found at 10,000 feet
the aneroid at top read 19.90 the party returned
from this elevation in 4½h arriving at 3 Pm June 7th
and now about the fiction or allegorical account
Ti- Tarshi, an arab traveller. and writer.
Says "that on the North of these mountains is the
grave of the great Hermes, and Hermes is the
Prophet Jdrisi (Enoch) who built Some
wonderful Copper Statutes, and a great Temple
beind these mountains is a Sea of blackness with
a wonderful Stream of light running through it!
and a great forest where the Pigmis dwell. &cc
Now in Wales there is a mountain called Cadair-
Idris, who is Called Idris the Giant, who was
a famous Astronomer, — the word Enoch is
found in the list of the ante deluvians, but the word
means (Enwok — or enwog) Renound. or Famous.
as you may discover on the Stones of Knowledge.

Example. the word "Gumr" = $3\overset{'}{\,2}\,\overset{`}{\,3}\,\overset{''}{\,8}$. nearest prime (less) is 3151. = Ge-$\frac{7}{9}$, the word Idris = $\overset{'}{9}\,4\,\overset{'}{8}\,\overset{'}{9}\,\overset{'}{9}$. the nearest prime = 94861 = K'en; $\frac{3}{4}$. again Ruwen-zari = $\overset{'}{8}\,\overset{`}{2}\,\overset{`}{6}\,\overset{'}{5}\,\overset{'}{4}$ – (82621 = Sath)$\frac{7}{3}$ Do $\overset{'}{6}\,\overset{`}{6}\,\overset{'}{8}\,\overset{'}{9}$ – (6661 = Hn $\frac{2}{3}$) or the words Sath-$\bar{E}$n. here we have translated Gumr into "Ge"-Earth, and Idris into "K'en" and Ruwen-zari, into "Sath-En" or Satan, K'en (Kenedl) nation or people, (the Earth of the people of Satan)!! Ken, also means Knowledge, also head, but we must not ignore the fractions. $\frac{7}{9}$ ($\overset{'}{8}\overset{`}{8}$) $\frac{3}{4}$ ($\overset{'}{3}\overset{`}{9}$) $\frac{7}{3}$ ($\overset{`}{3}\overset{'}{4}$) $\frac{2}{3}$ ($\overset{'}{2}\overset{`}{9}$) or $\underset{1}{Ge-thr}$, $\underset{2}{K'en-Vi}$, $\underset{3}{Sath-Mn}$, $\underset{4}{Hn-Li}$. 1 Arch Druid, 2 Discovered, 3 Satan's ancient flood. Now Hermes, in the greek language means interpreting or explaining. one of the names of Mercury – Son of Jupiter. born on "Mount Cyllene" He was the Messenger of the gods, He conducted the Souls of the dead into the infernal regions. He was the god of thieves, and all dishonest people. He was the inventor of letters, He first taught the art of buying and Selling. and trafficking, from whence he derived his name "Mercury" this happens to be a "keyword" $\underline{\{\overset{3}{M}\overset{`}{E}\overset{4}{R}\overset{1}{K}\overset{5}{U}\overset{'}{R}\overset{2}{I}\}}$ = "Er – Kimru (or Cymry) it will be seen that the letters are taken in regular order. middle last-first &c "Merchyr" or Mercury was the most in favour with the ancient Britons of all the gods! with perhaps one exception the god "Hesus"!

I Suspect. their present God is also the Same with a slight variation in the name (Jesu) and attribute. too Seems to agree wonderfully; as the first result of his Suffering was the Saving of a thiefe.! and it is quit undisputable that the Churches make much more ado about Saving a great Siner than an honest and truth loving man. — it is plain that Mercury is in the basom of the father (☉☿) and the virgin is not far ♀ which Naturaly reminds one of the Father, Son and Holy ghost, as all allegories must of necesity fall short of the fact on which it is founded, for example "the Primes and fractions" are founded on facts, and perfect rules, yet the words used are allegorical, because they are taken from many different Languages, whereas in the original there is but one Language, or one meaning, to each word and yet that word May take many forms, and therefore allegoricaly Mey represent Meany different things. Nevertheless the unit or root will always be the Same!

I Shall now describe one of the Stones of knowledge of the ancients, (Druids) which was once in my posession. and of which I have now a "Facsimile" or exact Coppy; — and of which I have also a translation, which was Made with great care, but yet it falls short of the original, in many things, this is owing to the fact that the original Characters (Hieroglyphics) have more than one Meaning, depending on the position hence the Sign of Possession, is indispensable —

"Description of the Astronomical Stone of Knowledge"
The inner Stone or frame is 6 inches long 3" broad 1½ thick
on the inside. with three Columns at equal distance lengthways
on these Rods. are 6 Stones each which Can be turned
around the rods, these smaller Stones have 3 faces
about ⅞ x ⅞ of an inch each, Carved with Hieroglyphics
in addition each face is distinguished by different characters
one face has the Capital greek Alphabet, which shews
how the Hieroglyphics are to be read, another face has
the twelve signs of the zodiac, which are read horizontally
in reading these Signs add the Denominator of the fraction
Standing over the Sign, to the Epact. famed, on the other face.
the third face has one, two, or three Stars on each Square
or 18 in all, So arranged that when the rods are upright
or towards you, the Stars will appear the same which
ever end is towards you. or in the horizontal position
but the Hieroglyphics have a different value in the
four different ways. Astronomicaly they must be read
thus ⌐¬ in which position they shew the Doc day
or the day of the week Corresponding to any date, whether
new or old Style. — and all the Leap years, also
if we turn the Stars to face the other side of the Stone
the hieroglyphics will be in a different position. yet
they are to be read horizontaly, as before. the Stars
are in a reverse position, but as regards their relation to each other they remain the Same (confused)
these Stars and hieroglyphics will discover any thing that
may be hidden, by the Setting of the Stars. (by rule)

254

The Rule, Let 3 persons be numbered 1. 2 and 3 to represent ☉. ☽², ♁³, and any 3 things belonging to the earth ⊕ also named and numbered 1. 2. & 3 the three persons will draw by lot, both their number, and articles are each, thus no one can tell what the others have, but all must follow the Rule, — He that ⚳ is Numbered 1. will turn one ⊞ Star down, No 2 turns ⊠ Stars down No 3 ⊠ Stars He that has article 1 turn down the same as for himself. article 2 thrice as many. and article 3 4 such times as many as the possessor of it turned down for himself, under No consideration can, by the rule, any more or less Stars be turned down, but it is optional as to which Stars are turned down, therefore there will always remain a certain number of Stars in Hieroglyphics. <u>and these are the witnesses</u> that point out to us where or in whose possession, each article are to be found 2ᵈ Rule — to find the Dominical day. — Turn all the balance of the Stars down. then turns the other face of the Square (Supposed to be the other side of the Earth,) the Hieroglyphics now form an arch, Start the Centuries 5400 (Century B C) = ☷, then 1ˢᵗ Century of A.D. = ♄, 2ᵈ C ♎ 3ᵈ C ☽. by the old or Julian Style all the Centuries ar Leapyears (366ᵈ) but by the New style only the 1ˢᵗ the others are Com" (365ᵈ) the 4ᵗʰ century = the first ∴ and every 400 year in same order. the last day thus shown as 1800 = ♎ the ~ is the Dom day there are certain years in each century that are = to the century which is found by the ✳ = 4 x 7 = 28 an its multiples 56 & 84.

The same ‿ also stands for the 4th & 7th month &c. the 1st day of which "is the Dominical day" — the days of the week begin at the left hand of the circle, ‿ Saturn appears as the foundation of both circle, but is counted as one day — it implies that Saturn is the Dominical day of every Leap year Century, that is ♄ is the 1st of April — and July, having found the Dom⁷ D⁷ of the Century, count 3 singly and the 4th Double (for the Leap year) for each year in excess, in the order of the days of the week → the Character on which the required year falls will be the D⁷ D⁷ of the year, that is the 1st of ♉ & ♌ for any other — month add as many days of the week as of stars shown thus ✳)² = ♒ ♏ §✳(= ♉ §⁺✳) = ♏♌ §⁺²⁄₅ = ♓ ♈ ||⁺✳✳ ⁄⁺✳ §⁺✳✳ |.♒✳✳
D.D.+   1   2   3   4   =♋5 =♒6 ♑

there is nothing added to ♉ ♌ nor to ♒ if it is a leap year for ♒ & ♓ are one day less in leap year. (♉ ♌ ♒ 0)(♏♌ ✳)

Rule of the Epacts.

Turn the face with the Greek alphabet on top — with the A at the upper left corner, the figures on the left of the letter is the Cycle of the Epact, and on the right the Corresponding Centuries, one • on the ᵈᵒᵗ left stands for 10. two ⋮ for 20. and three ⸫ = 30 which is always discarded or = 0, find the Century as (1800) =) φ × ⁙ , the left hand figure is the Epact of the Century. observe the square of A. is divided into two = parts. which in counting the place of the Century = 2 squares there are five equal years (see the reverse side under the month. 19. 38. 57. 76. & 95. Count 1 Epact for each year in excess downwards from the century or = year, the character in which the required year will fall will be the Epact of the last day of the previous year, or the age of the moon on the 1st of January (‿) for any other month, to the Epact add the Denominator of the fraction over that month.

$\Delta E = 1^C$, (of anno Domini) $M = \frac{2}{19}$, $B\Gamma = 3$, $K\Lambda = 4$, $P\Sigma = 5$, $I = \frac{6}{12}$, $\amalg = 7$, $\Omega = 8$, $\Xi = \frac{9}{15}$, $\Psi = \frac{10}{16}$, $N = 17$, $\Phi X = 18$, $T\Upsilon = 20$, Lower $+ = 21$, $Z = 22$, Middle $+ = 54$. or start with the Central Cross. then thrice 5 ↓ one 6 ↑ thrice then thrice 5 ↓ one 6 ↑ twice, one ↓ one ↑ thrice ↓ one ↑ (1 2 3 4 5 6 7 8 9 10 11 12 13 14 15 16 17 18 19 20 21 22 54 first last =

the order of the + & −, are 1st three Consecutive Crosses called "the omega" next + then □ above = $\frac{T}{\Omega}$, then the 3 □ above = $\frac{+}{\Xi}$, then 2nd above = $M\overline{+}$, Lastly 4th and 5th above, Z. & $\frac{\Delta}{E}$ −
the + makes the Epact of the Century, one more & − one less.

The Prime and fractions or Inspiration.

All words may be represented by figures by numbering each letter as it stands in the Alphabet, every Sum may be represented by a fraction, by adding the Sum to one figure, called the unit, or root, place this unit as the Numerator of Common fraction, then Subtract the right hand figure of the Sum from this numerator. and place as a denominator, Should the right hand figure of the Sum be greater, borrow 10, or place the figure 1. on the left of the unit then you can Subtract, but this borrowed figure is not to be left with the unit numerator. the 1st and last figures of the Column of nines are shown. the Numerator is the No in the Column. the Denominator = the Column

As all the Columns of Words Cannot be given in such a
Small space, I have extended the list = to 1000 words
Selected from Many different Languages, which is
practically the Same in principle as the universal language

Eclipses of the Sun and Moon.

The original is in the form of a coiled Serpent. I
have translated one of these cycles. ranging from 1514.
to 1946 A.D and also another of over a hundred years
later, So that the two may be Compared, Rule to read
on the back are the index years. and Corresponding No
to be added if the Sign is + or Subtracted if the sign is —
having discovered the index and its number Count that
year on the 1st division, then a division for each year
in excess, the division on which the required year
falls Shows the number of the Eclipses in that year.
Suppose for example the year 1800. the index = $\frac{1784+}{22\,\text{d.s}}$
1800 would fall on the 17th division Showing 4 Eclipses
2 of the ☉ & 2 of the ☽ the 1st is of the ☽ ♈ 17. + 22 = ♉ 8th
Again by the later table. for the Same year 1800
the index is 1789 — 44. this will fall on the 12th division
but the date here for 1st of the ☽ is ♒ 22. — 44, to do
this we add ♉ — 30 = 22 = 52 — 44 = ♉ 8th. both equal
The original must have the division turned on top
and read from left to right. but as there are directions
attached to these I shall pass on. to the Horoscope
and Show how we Can without any Calculation
discover the true aspects of the heavens at any time —

The Perpetual Horoscope

The path in which the Sun moon and planets move is called the Zodiac, it is devided into 12 signs. or Constellations, about 2200 years ago the 12 months of the year corresponded, but at present there is more than a sign of difference about 1° evy 72 years the ☉ falls back that is at Easter time the ☉ is found to be about 28° of ♒ having retrograded from the 1st point of ♈ through ♓. Now the 20th of March is the vernal Equinoxe (by the Christian Church) March is the third month |─|·| turn this on top. ─|☉|♃ two days of the ☽ to the right. Place the earth (⊕) as you may turn the 20 of ♈ on top, then count ♈ and 2d of the ☽ → (which will be the ♃♍) or more exact 9 hours to the right from the date required is the place of the ⊕. and exact opposite ♓|♒ is the place of the ☉, the new ☽ is with the ☉ and the full moon with the earth. and at the quarters ¼ way thus by simply turning the date of the month on the meridian then replacing this date by the 9th hour to the right that will be the part of the sign or Constellation that will be on the meridian at 10 Pm those on the right will be rising and those on the left Setting.— for any hour earlier than 10. turn on the meridian as many hour from the left ← or if later than 10. Pm as many hours from the right → and that you may be Sure that you are right. observe the position of the great Bear. on the Horoscope & also in the heavens, if alike you are right. if not alike then you have not followd the Rule as here given. and you had better reread the Rule, and try again

"The Tale is ferries, — Druidgs money.
or Token of Easter. Reveals the Easter Sunday
which Garlems the moveable feasts of the church.
this is in the form of money Gold. Silver or Copper.
"See also the Seals of the Covenant, and geographical Chart,
and the quarters with the Exeplaination of the Same.

Having ended my task of translating these relics
I have yet to arange them, in Systematical form
after that they shall be offered to the public —
for a certain Space of time, after that the original
Shall be Photographed. and issued in book form, for
the benifit of all who have learned to read the same.

These Lessons, have figures that never lie. !
facts that are Self evident truths requiring no
proof, and Allegories Containing Inspiration. !!
Which by reversing become Revelation. !!!
written in a language that all the nations may
read and understand. by Complying with rules
that are easy and Simple, — By the ancient Covenants
of the Nergals, — Druids — and Krisdian (Christians)
These ancient Stores of Knowledge were to be Sealed
and kept Secred during a Stipulated time, with
the Sacret relics and Spoils of war, and offerings,
but in the last day of the Covenant from C-C to CCCC.
these relics were to be distributed, to those Claiming
under the Covenant, Heirs of the Nergals (Lords of Tennan)

and the three order of the Druids, and the Kristion,
(Christians) who can read the ancient Stanes (records)
and are living in peace and under the tinngue of good
report, and whose names must be on the records
before the same shall be made public. Therfore,
Know ye all men, that HAN. ФAN. ΣTPEBOP.
has the qualification, and anthoraty, and hereditary —
right to open the Seals, and enter on the records. Such
as shall be found worthy, and qualified by the ancient,—
right of the Covenant, — and all such as are registed,
shall receive the proportian due to their Station!

. The Station is determined by merit or qualification
by conforming with certain rights, and custom. and
by Hereditary-right or Claim, as by law shall be decreed.
Such as claim Hereditary right, but can show no proof
of the same, have the right to prove, by trial-test.
to do this the consent, of the Claimant must be freely given
and afterwards must never be divulged, to any person
outside of the order or covenant, untill the record
shall be made public. and the distribution take place.

The Recorder may apoint others to act in his name
Male, or female, that posess the qualification
necessary. for the work, and shall bind themselfs
not to enter into discusion, or controversy. either
Political. Theoretical. Religious, or Social.
with any Person or persons. but shall confine themselfs to the teaching the Stanes of Knowledge &c
More particularly the jnspired portians!

"To the Students, and those who wish to Learn"
what is written on these ancient Stones of Knowledge
very naturaly you would like to be told how I
became aquainted with them, More particularly
Since our teacher tell us the Druids left No record of any kind, as far as they _know_, this may be
quite true, but it is not in good taste, to proclaim
this _No-Knowledge_ of theirs as a mater of fact.
I am one of the witnesses, "That Came, and Saw,
and Conquered, (ΦΕΥΧ ΦΕΣΙ ΦΙΥΙ) $3549. 3549. 3999$
the one at the bejining and the other at the end
and the one that came between was also of the same
order — called the Hereditary Druids (Lords of Tennan)
we inherit a certain right or privelege under the Covenant; provided we can form to certain ordinances
among these rights, are the privleges of reading
these wonderful record of nearly 73 hundred years!
as a part of these Stones is written in what is comm-
monly called the Greek alphabet, this alphabet was
the first I learned, and as soon as I was able to read
my guardian took me to see these "Wise Stones"
there were meny written in these greek letters,
and others in uniform hieroglyphics, and others
with pictures, and emblems and Scrolls —
So that I became familior with them by sight,
but was ignorant of their contents. and when
by accident I discovered a Similar Stone in a

in another part of the country, and not wishing to take the Stone away at the time, I made a facsimile of the Characters. and noted the dementions of the several parts of the stone,—this was in the year 1842 A.D. Six years after this in 1848, I discovered another Stone in the ruins of an old church undermined by the sea. of which I also took a coppy, which I have since discovered to be the "Ogham a" once common enough in the British Isles. Again in the year 1887, I made a third discovery. in the heart of a very large fir tree, which was at Least 7 or 8 hundred years old, this time the Characters were in a sheet of the gum at the 180th ring! It so happened that in the year 1846 I joined two gentlemen, for the purpose of exploring in North America more particularly in Mexico, before starting my Guardian, presented me with a small Charm. under a promish not to Look into it, while the Giver Lived. unless under certain circumstances and if I did see the contents, I must destroy the original, as soon as I translated the secret in this I readly promished from regard to the giver. rather than any benifit that I expected from it. —

It turned out however that there was enclosed in the charm, "a Key" to these hieroglyphics !!! and for the last nine years, I devoted all my time to the study and Translation, of these ancient Secret Inspiration, and Revelation. ✱✱✱

And having devided these into   Lessons, which
may be had Singly, that is the translations, or if
all the Lessons are taken the Facsimile go with them.
The following is the List and the Price of each Lesson

1st A table of the Dominical day, and Leap years.
or the day of the week Corespanding to any date. in
the Past — Present — or Future, Price
also written instruction, or verbal Price

2nd Table of the Epacts of Centuries, & odd years.
or the age of the Moon on the 1st of any Month from 5400
to 2200 A.D. Price   Instruction. Price.

3d Table of the Eclipses of Sun & Moon. for any
year, (for 500 years — including the present Century) two
Examples of 113 years difference in dates Price
Printed instruction, or verbal explanation Price

4th The perpetual Horascope, gives the true place of
the ☉ ☽ ✳ & the ⊕ on any hour of the day in any year.
also the hour of the day and Month & year Price
the printed instruction are the same as verbal, Price

if the four Lessons are taken, the Facsimile will be
included, without instruction, Instruction may
be had on certain Condition. (by Inspiration. &c)

                    Rules of Inspiration and Revelation
1st Unit of multiplication, of the five genders ✳
2nd the Select Gender, Masculine and Feminine to be xplyd
to be xplyd by any Single figure, Neuter to add 1 figure
3d The perpetual triad, of Generations, forward or backward
and the Great Key of the Fathers (Saturn)

th The Tetra-grammaton words of many meanings.
th the Migrating tribe, and place (Decimal System)
th The figurative man — (Picture and scroll writing)
th The Secret Alphabet, and Caman alphabet (Greek)
th The Seals of the covenant of the Der-Krisdian)
Each Rule, with printed instruction Price   Each
if all the rules are taken the Book of Primes and
Fractions will be included in the Set,
These are the most important, — and if any of these rules
are allready known to the Student. one of the auxillary Lessons may be chosen in place of Such rule.

Auxiliary Lessons

1st The Taleisferies (Druid's Easter money)
2nd The Ogham, writing (maen hir)
3rd The Scandinavian Runes (Futhark)
4th The original Alphabet (the Bardic harmony) (5th greek) roots)
5th Ancient Geological Maps, and pictorial writing.
6th Poetical translation — the Book of Job of usy.
or any of the other interesting Subject. Such as the
First Christian Sermon on record. — Julius —
Caesar's account of the Druids. — Address of the last
Arch Druid (in Britain) and many Scientific treaties

Rule for proving Table of Dom. Day.

$1600 = 7 (h^d)$ $1700 = 5 (4)$ $1800 = 3 (8)$ $1900 = 1 (0)$ to every 400 years
the years 28. 56 & 84. = the Century preceding; Subtract the
equal years from the odd years, if more than 28 but
if odd years are less count. as remainder. the Months =
$8 = 6$ ins $m = 1$. # 2. M? 3. $x^v = 4$, $= 5$, $= 6$. More

Rule — Subtract 28, as many times as it contains in the odd years, — for every 4 contained in remainder add one for each full four. Also No of the Century and the Month. — Subtract or divide by Seven (7). The remainder will be the day of the week.

Find 22 April 1828.   Find 2 January 1831.

$$\frac{00 | 28}{28} = \Bigg\{$$ if the total is more than 7. $$\frac{00 | 31}{28} \Bigg\}$$

Centy $= \div \begin{array}{c} 00 \\ 3 \end{array}$ ÷ by 7. remainder is the day $\overline{}\ 3$

$\emptyset\quad = + 0$ Find 15 Feb 1855.   Cent $+\ 3$

$= \vec{\sigma}\quad 3$ in this the quatient (is discarded) $\cancel{m}\ +\ 1$
$\hbar^d = 7$

$$\frac{00 | 55}{28} \Bigg\{$$ and the remainder 5 or Thursday is the day

4 in $= \Big\} \ 27$ and you may prove this rule by the
6 times $+\ 6$
Cent $+\ 3$ Table. (1800) angle of 28 $= \vec{\sigma} (+ \emptyset\ 0 + 22\ 0)$
$\Eta \quad +\ 4$ for (1831) nearest Leap year 28 $= \vec{\sigma} \cdot +$

$\div 7) \ \dfrac{40}{35} (5$ 3 days ($\emptyset, 4, \varphi$) Friday is Day day $\cancel{m} + 1$

$4 = 5 \Big|$ $= \hbar^d = 1^{st}$ and $\odot^d$ must have been the 2nd.

we have thus a proof of either the Rule or Table —

"The Charm"   Fac simile.

which
proved   an allegorical
to be a   Day of the week
key to the   corresponding to
Hieroglyphics   any date forever.

there are 12 rays of the $\odot$

the upper 4 rays point to the Cycle of 4 Centuries.
the lower 8 rays divide the 12 months into 7 groups
the 7 days of the week around the $\oplus$. outside $=$ years
the top or Key-stone. $= 24^h \times 15 = 360^c$ or 1 Cycle

Question – how many men and women are shown here
Answer – ↑ one man and two women, Man on the right
Do ↓ two men and one woman, the woman on the left
which is the middle one? ↑ Female, Do ↓ a man !!!
Since you cannot agree in such simple mater, there
must be some cause for it, either you do not know
masculine gender from the feminine gender, or els
it is your (social) position is at fault. change places

These three heads were copied from the Stones of Knowledge
the two top ones are the first pair created, Gen 1. 27.
the middle one is Cêd (Keridwen) & Avagthū.
her Son, (the hidden. Avag – or avog in the dark
or lame child, = ( ) for Cêd = 5511. (( ) for Son = 5511
by pairing 5 & 1 we have 6 twice for both that is 66 + 66.

"The Wizards' Cabalistic Secrets.

Let A, & B, write any sum, then add up as. A = 254 = 11. B = 150 = 6. the Wizards writes A = 11 = 1. B = 6 = 1, if the sums are added, unit of the Product = 1 + 1 = 1. but if the lesser sum is subtracted, it will be the difference, and this difference is of three kind, 1st when the unit of the lesser sum is the least = Difference of the units, but when the lesser sum has the greatest unit then add 1, to the lesser unit, as A = 1 + 1 = 11 — the 1 (of the lesser sum) = 1. lastly if the two units of the sums are equal, the unit of product will = 1, the sums are not shown to the Wizard unless in case of a dispute, and so challenged the Wizard will write his answer for both + & — and an umpire may be appointed to add or subtract the sums, in case of a dispute — the umpire will examine and compare the two sides. as this is a scientific secret, accuracy is indispensable, Gabriel, nor Belzibub, are not in this secret, but the Reader may be! this game may be made a moral exercise, and entertainment to the mind. the stakes belongs to the Wizard if he Calculates Correctly, but if he fails through his own mistake he pays double stakes, provided the figures that was given, were correctly given by the Arithmetical Rule Governing the case, to be a Good Wizard of this kind, is Something to be wished for !

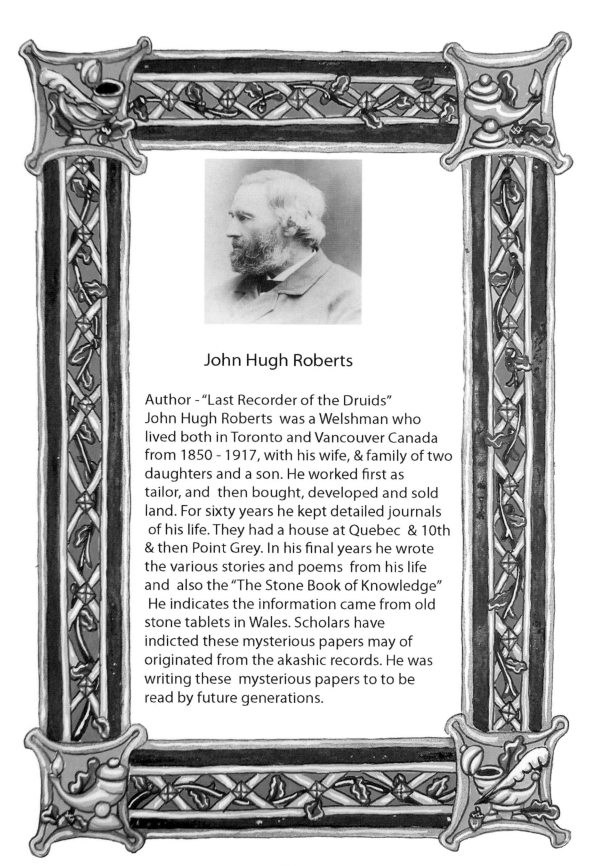

John Hugh Roberts

Author - "Last Recorder of the Druids"
John Hugh Roberts was a Welshman who
lived both in Toronto and Vancouver Canada
from 1850 - 1917, with his wife, & family of two
daughters and a son. He worked first as
tailor, and then bought, developed and sold
land. For sixty years he kept detailed journals
of his life. They had a house at Quebec & 10th
& then Point Grey. In his final years he wrote
the various stories and poems from his life
and also the "The Stone Book of Knowledge"
He indicates the information came from old
stone tablets in Wales. Scholars have
indicted these mysterious papers may of
originated from the akashic records. He was
writing these mysterious papers to to be
read by future generations.

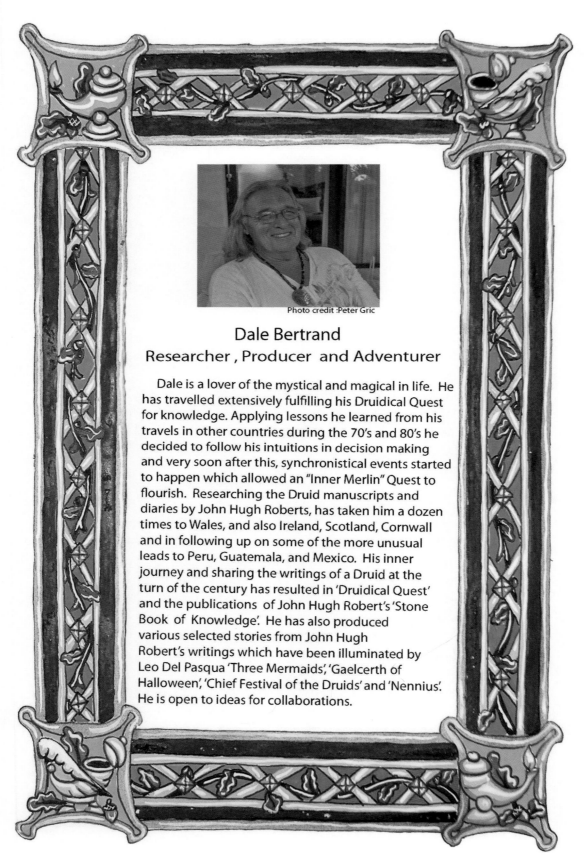

Dale Bertrand
Researcher , Producer and Adventurer

Dale is a lover of the mystical and magical in life. He has travelled extensively fulfilling his Druidical Quest for knowledge. Applying lessons he learned from his travels in other countries during the 70's and 80's he decided to follow his intuitions in decision making and very soon after this, synchronistical events started to happen which allowed an "Inner Merlin" Quest to flourish. Researching the Druid manuscripts and diaries by John Hugh Roberts, has taken him a dozen times to Wales, and also Ireland, Scotland, Cornwall and in following up on some of the more unusual leads to Peru, Guatemala, and Mexico. His inner journey and sharing the writings of a Druid at the turn of the century has resulted in 'Druidical Quest' and the publications of John Hugh Robert's 'Stone Book of Knowledge'. He has also produced various selected stories from John Hugh Robert's writings which have been illuminated by Leo Del Pasqua 'Three Mermaids', 'Gaelcerth of Halloween', 'Chief Festival of the Druids' and 'Nennius'. He is open to ideas for collaborations.

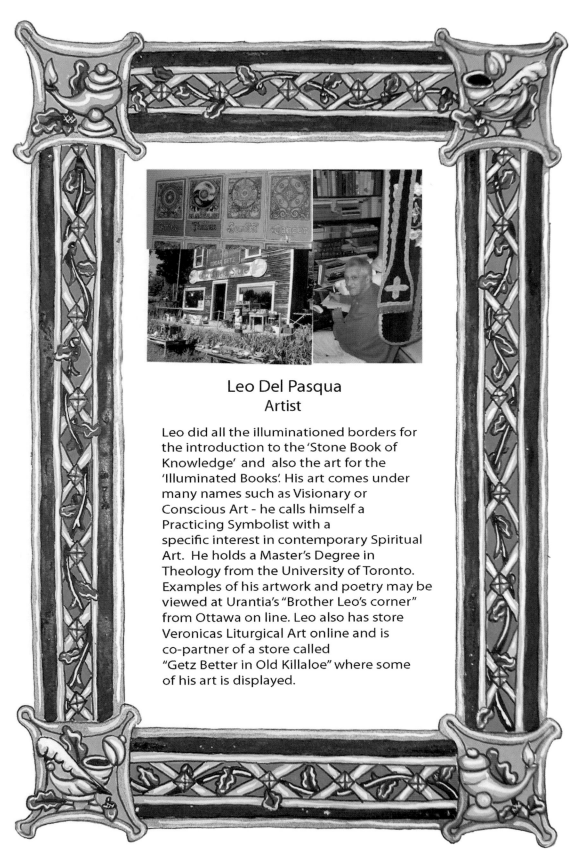

Leo Del Pasqua
Artist

Leo did all the illuminationed borders for the introduction to the 'Stone Book of Knowledge' and also the art for the 'Illuminated Books'. His art comes under many names such as Visionary or Conscious Art - he calls himself a Practicing Symbolist with a specific interest in contemporary Spiritual Art. He holds a Master's Degree in Theology from the University of Toronto. Examples of his artwork and poetry may be viewed at Urantia's "Brother Leo's corner" from Ottawa on line. Leo also has store Veronicas Liturgical Art online and is co-partner of a store called "Getz Better in Old Killaloe" where some of his art is displayed.

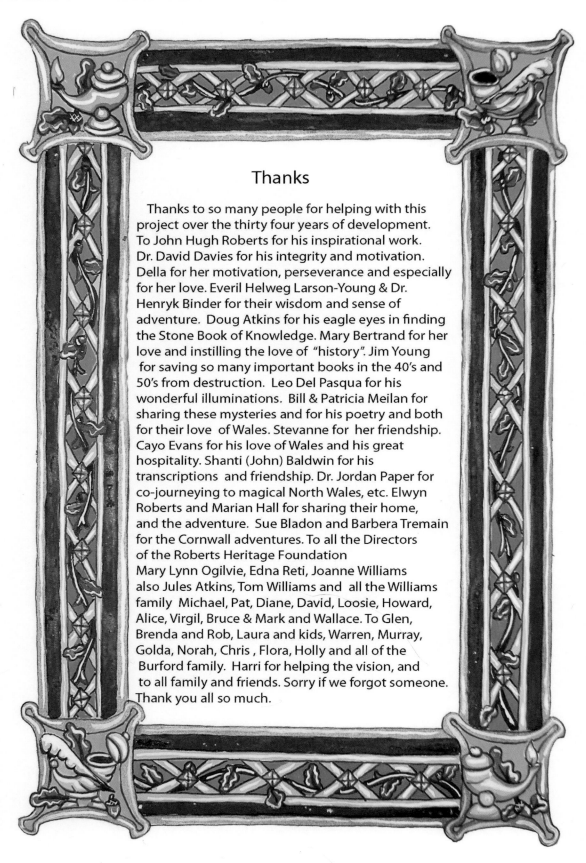

Thanks

Thanks to so many people for helping with this project over the thirty four years of development. To John Hugh Roberts for his inspirational work. Dr. David Davies for his integrity and motivation. Della for her motivation, perseverance and especially for her love. Everil Helweg Larson-Young & Dr. Henryk Binder for their wisdom and sense of adventure. Doug Atkins for his eagle eyes in finding the Stone Book of Knowledge. Mary Bertrand for her love and instilling the love of "history". Jim Young for saving so many important books in the 40's and 50's from destruction. Leo Del Pasqua for his wonderful illuminations. Bill & Patricia Meilan for sharing these mysteries and for his poetry and both for their love of Wales. Stevanne for her friendship. Cayo Evans for his love of Wales and his great hospitality. Shanti (John) Baldwin for his transcriptions and friendship. Dr. Jordan Paper for co-journeying to magical North Wales, etc. Elwyn Roberts and Marian Hall for sharing their home, and the adventure. Sue Bladon and Barbera Tremain for the Cornwall adventures. To all the Directors of the Roberts Heritage Foundation Mary Lynn Ogilvie, Edna Reti, Joanne Williams also Jules Atkins, Tom Williams and all the Williams family Michael, Pat, Diane, David, Loosie, Howard, Alice, Virgil, Bruce & Mark and Wallace. To Glen, Brenda and Rob, Laura and kids, Warren, Murray, Golda, Norah, Chris , Flora, Holly and all of the Burford family. Harri for helping the vision, and to all family and friends. Sorry if we forgot someone. Thank you all so much.